THE MAN IN SONG

THE MAN

A Discographic Biography of Johnny Cash

IN SONG

JOHN M. ALEXANDER

THE UNIVERSITY OF ARKANSAS PRESS • FAYETTEVILLE • 2018

ISBN: 978-1-68226-051-7

eISBN: 978-1-61075-628-0

22 21 20 19 18   5 4 3 2 1

Designer: April Leidig

∞ The paper used in this publication meets the minimum
requirements of the American National Standard for
Permanence of Paper for Printed

Library Materials Z39.48-1984.

FRONTIS: October 1959 in recording studio.
Photo: Don Hunstein © Sony Music Entertainment.

Library of Congress Control Number: 2017956139

To my mother, Raymonde Alexander,

who spent endless hours listening to Johnny Cash

records with me. She was my best friend and inspiration.

I miss her every day and take comfort knowing

that we will meet again one day on the

"Far Side Banks of Jordan."

Contents

Acknowledgments

THIS BOOK IS the fruition of a lifelong dream, and there are many people to thank for making it a reality. I would like to thank Lou and Karen Robin for arranging my first meeting with Johnny and June; John Carter Cash for his approval of this book; Rosanne Cash for her generous comments, and especially Larry Gatlin for always being an inspiration and friend to me.

To my daughters, Amanda and Samantha, and my son Johnny, who was named after the Man in Black, and most importantly my wife Denise, for her love, guidance, and invaluable help in putting this book together.

To my father Alex and my uncle Albert Alexander for passing down their love of music; to my cousin Laila Khoury for her faith in me as an author; Paul Khoury for all his insightful ideas and observations; Lloyd LaRousse, my friend and fellow Cashologist, for his remarkable eye for photos; Robert Rich and Vincent Rohan for their encouragement and sound advice; John Lamberton, Richie Merhige, Mark Hamwi, Robert Shaouy, and Thomas Mayrose for patiently listening to me talk about Johnny Cash for so many years; Father Paul Schneirla and Father Michael Ellias for their friendship and spiritual guidance.

Also: J. Dozier Hasty, Jim Bessman, Peter Lewry, Matt Lindsey, Allen Reynolds, Shelby Singleton and John Singleton at Sun Records, Earl Thomas Conley, Fred Conley, Mitchell Sirls, Michael Sirls, Rick Peoples, John L. Smith, Michael Streissguth, Don Murry Grubbs, Randy Howard, Tracy Parker, Steve Cooper, Karen Cunningham, Lisa Grauso, Toby Silver and Tom Tierney at Sony Music, and David Scott Cunningham at the University of Arkansas Press.

And finally, to Johnny Cash whose songs and stories inspired a chubby little boy from Brooklyn to develop a lifetime love of music and literature.

1959 on the Arkansas farm. *Photo: Don Hunstein © Sony Music Entertainment.*

A Foreword from Larry Gatlin

Dear Folks,

J. R. was my big brother. "WE" called him J. R. It's "J. R." on the birth certificate, so "WE" called him J. R. Of all the things in my life that I am thankful for, being one of the "WEs" in J. R.'s life is in the top 10.

So when my old and good friend, J. A., asked me to write the foreword for his new book about J. R., "Johnny Cash, The Man in Song," I said, YESSIR!! I must admit that I whispered under my breath something like, "What the world really needs right now is yet another book about Johnny Cash." And if it hadn't been my old friend J. A. doing the asking, I would have probably said, NOSIR!!

I was sitting up in bed watching ESPN and Fox News when Janis walked into our bedroom and pitched "yet another book about Johnny Cash" in my lap. I dutifully picked it up and began to thumb through it. Before long, the thumbing turned to browsing. Not long after that, the browsing turned to reading, then to laughing, crying and devouring, then to joy, enlightenment, and gratitude — gratitude to God for making J. R. my big brother, for allowing me to be one of the "WEs" in his inner circle, and grateful for J. A., who has focused a totally different light on J. R. than I have ever seen before. J. A.'s "yet another book about Johnny Cash" is a masterpiece, written by a learned historian and renowned musicologist — and an expert on Johnny Cash and his music. I give *The Man in Song* ★ ★ ★ ★ ★. You have in your hands a wonderful book, written by a true craftsman, about an American legend — J. R. Cash, forever my big brother.

Keep the Faith,

Introduction

WHO WOULD HAVE DREAMED that a humble sharecropper's son would go on to become one of the most honored and beloved figures in popular music? J. R. Cash was born on February 26, 1932, in the town of Kingsland in Cleveland County, Arkansas, which is southwest of Pine Bluff. Kingsland is actually located between Pine Bluff and Little Rock. He was the fourth of seven children born to Ray Cash, a farmer, and his wife, Carrie Rivers Cash. The Cash children were older brothers Roy and Jack, older sister Margaret Louise, and younger sisters Reba Ann and Joanne and baby brother Tommy. In 1935, when Cash was three years old, the family moved to Dyess, Arkansas. It was here that he started accruing material for the songs he would later write that were steeped in the cold, hard realities of the Great Depression.

J. R. would ultimately be known as Johnny Cash and would go on to sell more than fifty million albums in forty years and one day receive the prestigious Kennedy Center Honors. He was, and is, an American treasure who holds the distinction of being the only performer inducted into the Rock and Roll Hall of Fame, the Country Music Hall of Fame, the Songwriters Hall of Fame, and the Gospel Music Hall of Fame. He'd certainly come a long way from those hot and stifling fields where he picked and chopped cotton during the Great Depression. And the road was often a weary one. His mother always believed that God had anointed her son and that he was destined for greatness.

The one saving grace during those early, tumultuous years was the music that came flowing out of the family radio. Johnny loved to listen to the songs that carried him away from the burdens of daily life in the cotton fields. As he would later recall, he listened to the radio by the coal-oil light until he fell asleep with what little contentment he could find from the songs of the day. Of course years later his mother's faith in him would be rewarded with an amazing career built on his love of music. And, in as much as the man defined the songs he wrote and selected, the songs also helped define the man.

« October 1959 in recording studio.
Photo: Don Hunstein © Sony Music Entertainment.

October 1959 in recording studio. *Photo: Don Hunstein © Sony Music Entertainment.*

Many books have been written about the life of Johnny Cash. His trials and tribulations, his bouts with drugs and painkillers, his marriage to his first sweetheart Vivian Liberto, the birth of their four daughters Rosanne, Kathleen, Cindy, and Tara, his romance with and marriage to the love of his life, June Carter, and the birth of their son John Carter Cash. But through it all, it's the incredible catalog of songs that ultimately defines the true artistry of the man.

Along the way Johnny enjoyed many exhilarating career highs of gold and platinum records, an acclaimed television series, starring roles in motion pictures and worldwide fame that were oftentimes overshadowed by numbing tragedies, including the loss of his dearly beloved brother Jack in a terrifying sawmill accident and the death of his friend and colleague Luther Perkins in a house fire. But Johnny Cash endured it all and emerged scarred but still standing tall, thanks to his unwavering faith in God and the support and devotion of his wife June Carter.

It was the songs that gave him the strength to persevere. Cash wrote his first songs and poems when he was around twelve years old, mostly sad songs, after the death of his brother Jack. Fresh out of the service in 1954, Cash worked as an appliance salesman in Memphis, Tennessee. That's where he and Vivian lived, and at night he would play music with Marshall Grant on bass and Luther Perkins on guitar. They called themselves Johnny Cash

October 1959 in recording studio. *Photo: Don Hunstein © Sony Music Entertainment.*

and the Tennessee Two, and later that year they were granted an audition before Sam Phillips, who owned and ran the legendary Sun Records. Sam liked what he heard, and in 1955 he added Cash to his talented stable of stars, which included Carl

Perkins, Jerry Lee Lewis, Roy Orbison, Charlie Rich, and Elvis Presley. Cash's output during those formative years, 1955–58 was mighty impressive indeed. He charted fourteen top-ten records, including four number-one hits while on the Sun label.

When Johnny and the Tennessee Two auditioned for Sam Phillips, they played him their finest gospel songs. Phillips was less impressed with Cash's inspirational lyrics than he was with his unique sound and style. He came back to Phillips with two country songs he had written, and thus began a career built on songs and albums that would help redefine the perception of popular music. Johnny Cash was able to write and choose the finest country, folk, western, rockabilly, gospel and pop songs throughout his dynamic career.

It was those inspirational songs that formed my first personal encounter with Johnny Cash. In 1997, I began work on *Johnny Cash: Timeless Inspiration*, a three-CD box set that would compile Cash's greatest gospel recordings all in one place for the first time. Having been aware of the song "Man in White," which Cash had recorded as a cassette-only gift for his fan club, I called his manager, Lou Robin, and asked for Cash's permission to include it in the album. Cash not only granted permission, but had his long-time associate David Ferguson take the song back into the studio and remaster it from the original tapes. The end result was an album we were all very proud of. Cash even sent me the following letter:

Dear John:

This is an album that has always been my dream project. I always tried and I always prayed to do justice to the gospel in my music. I don't have a shelf of Dove Awards but a monumental release like "Johnny Cash: Timeless Inspiration" works much better for me.

And I am eternally thankful someone like yourself could share this love with me, and put it out there for the people to hear.

I would love to have at least half a dozen additional copies, if I can get them. I know of many others I would love to share this with.

Gratefully,
Johnny Cash

That letter still means the world to me and, needless to say, Johnny received all the copies he needed and a relationship began that ultimately saw the release of four additional Cash box sets.

In 1998, while I was working on the *Reader's Digest* box set, *The Legendary Johnny Cash*, I asked Johnny to list his favorite songs for inclusion on a CD entitled "Johnny's Personal Favorites." Cash sent me the list of songs he selected, but asked that we change the title to "Among Johnny's Personal Favorites," because he did not want to offend any songwriters whose songs he did not select. This simple act spoke volumes about the artist and the man.

On June 29, 1999, my wife and I were invited to join Lou Robin and his wife Karen for lunch at the

1960 portrait. *Photo: Don Hunstein © Sony Music Entertainment.*

Plaza Athénée hotel on East Sixty-Fourth Street in New York City. My wife was home taking care of our two pre-school daughters and could not make it. I asked a friend and colleague of mine, Lloyd LaRousse, to join me, being that he was as devoted a Cash fan as I was. Upon arriving for the luncheon we were greeted by Lou and Karen. As I turned to walk into the restaurant dining room, Lou said, "I don't know what's keeping them, they're usually very prompt." Lloyd and I looked at each other as if we'd won the lottery, for when the elevator doors opened, to our great surprise and delight, there stood Johnny and June. We spent the entire day together listening to Cash entertain us with stories and observations from his incredible life.

What struck me the most was Cash's amazing sense of humor, something you don't always associate with the Man in Black. When I mentioned that I was working on a new box set called *Memories Are Made of This*, he reminded me that he had just recently recorded that song and would like his version to be included. I nervously tried to explain that we were using the original Dean Martin recording, but he continued to insist that his version should be used. Seeing me become flustered, he let out a large laugh and said, "I'm only kidding with you, I like the Dean Martin recording, too."

I distinctly remember Cash eating butter patties as if they were peanuts while we were waiting for our order to be taken. When we were handed the menus, to my surprise, it was all in French. I tried hard recalling my high school and college French so that I could decipher some of it. When the waiter came to Cash, and asked what he would like, Cash said, "I would like a BLT, you know, a bacon, lettuce and tomato sandwich. Could I please get a BLT?" I watched the look of horror on the waiter's face, knowing he could not say no to Johnny Cash. My mind raced as I imagined someone from the wait staff running furiously down the street to the nearest deli and bringing back the BLT that Cash was ultimately served.

Johnny Cash's smile and presence lit up the room. And though visibly weakened from his health issues, he appeared to be enjoying himself enough to spend the entire day with us. Lloyd and I left that day with a lifetime's worth of memories. Meeting someone you greatly admire and whose music has helped shape and define your entire life is not always easy, but in this case Johnny Cash certainly lived up to every expectation I had and more. To this day I say that the three greatest milestones in my life are the day I married my wife, the birth of my three children, and the first time I met Johnny Cash . . . in no particular order. People do get married and have kids, but not everyone gets to spend a day with Johnny Cash.

This book examines Cash's incredible life through all the songs he wrote and recorded. In the process, we discover exactly why he wrote a given song or chose to record it. In his book *Corn Flakes with John Lennon*, rock journalist Robert Hilburn,

1960 at home with family in Encino, California — Kathy, Vivian, Rosanne, Johnny and Cindy.
Photo: Don Hunstein © Sony Music Entertainment.

who accompanied Cash to Folsom Prison, quotes Hugh Cherry, a California disc jockey and emcee of the Folsom Prison concert, saying that Johnny "is one person who doesn't think about hit singles, he thinks about songs that make a difference in people's lives." In 1990, Cash wrote and recorded a song called "Songs That Make a Difference" for his *Highwayman 2* album with Waylon Jennings, Willie Nelson, and Kris Kristofferson.

That was precisely what Johnny Cash was all about: writing and recording songs that made people think, feel, and react, with joy, sorrow, anger, or with a newfound understanding of what life, love, and the human condition are all about. His songs could be brutally honest and revealing or touchingly tender in their execution, but the one common trait they all possess is that they mattered greatly to Cash, and ultimately to the listener. The goal of Cash and these songs is to enrage, enrapture, enlighten, and entertain us as no one has done before.

THE MAN IN SONG

Chapter 1

FIVE FEET HIGH AND RISING

AUTOBIOGRAPHICAL, GEOGRAPHICAL, AND SOCIETAL SONGS

The songs that were shaped and influenced by Johnny Cash's childhood years growing up in Arkansas

Johnny Cash, or J. R. Cash, as was listed on his birth certificate (because his parents couldn't decide on a name), grew up loving music and searching for it throughout his early childhood. The Cash family made the two-day, 250-mile trip to Dyess Colony, in Mississippi County, northeast Arkansas in March 1935. They settled in Homestead No. 266 on Road No. 3, to work on twenty acres of rich flatland delta dirt. The family had moved from Kingsland, Arkansas, in Cleveland County, in a truck with everything they owned. It was just Ray Cash, Johnny's father, his mother Carrie Cloveree Rivers Cash, older brothers Roy and Jack, and sisters Margaret Louise and

Reba. J. R. was three, and Joanne and Tommy were not born yet. The family had a battery-operated radio that young J. R. would listen to after coming home from work in the cotton fields. He loved the country and gospel music that was broadcast from radio stations in places as far away as New Orleans, Oklahoma, Chicago, and Texas. And it was those songs that carried J. R. away from the suffocating cotton fields and filled him with dreams of a better life somewhere far away.

In an interview with Sylvie Simmons in 2003 Cash said, "I picked cotton by hand from the age of five until I was eighteen years old, every day, after school right until dark. I would sing to myself

<< Songs of Our Soil. *Courtesy of Sony Music Entertainment.*

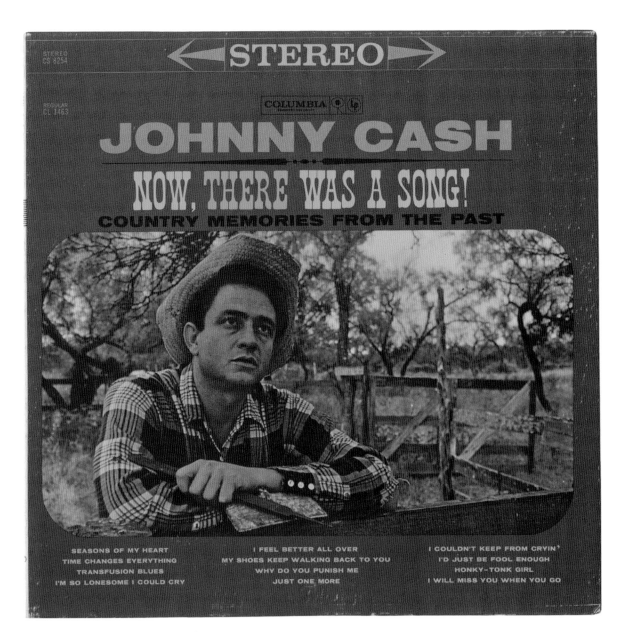

Now, There Was A Song! *Courtesy of Sony Music Entertainment.*

when I walked home from the fields at night. Songs were my magic to take me through the dark places." Cash's gift for exaggeration is revealed here because he certainly did not pick cotton every day, since it could only be picked during harvest time. Cash stored up all his childhood memories, the good — recalling the love of his mother, who always believed that God had His hand on J. R. to become something more than the son of a black-land farmer — and the bad — the tragic death of his beloved older brother Jack. J. R. especially loved the music of the Carter Family, which he listened to at night on a radio station broadcasting out of Del Rio, Texas. He also enjoyed listening to the Louvin Brothers, whom he had met when they played a show in Dyess in 1947. That's when Johnny realized that his calling in life was to be a singer.

But it was those early, formative years that helped shape J. R. into the man he would become. He would never forget the hard times and hardships of working the unforgiving cotton land. And it was in 1959 that Cash captured that life experience in his song "Five Feet High and Rising" from his perfectly titled album *Songs of Our Soil*, in a memory-filled recollection that he would perform nightly for the better part of his life. Those waters and this frightening episode in young Cash's life would be the musical baptism that would permeate his creativity and imbue his catalog of songs. "How high's the water, mama?" With those words Johnny Cash captured the impending terror of the rising river waters attempting to engulf his childhood home. The song "Five Feet High and Rising," clocking in at only one minute and forty-six seconds, begins with the young Cash curiously questioning the height and depth of the muddy water as it begins to invade his home. As with any child, the fear is not apparent as the boy attempts to remain brave in the face of sheer adversity. His mother's response, "Two feet high and rising," is of little comfort to the boy who measures his fear with the rising of the river water.

President Franklin Delano Roosevelt responded to the economic catastrophe of the Great Depression by enacting the New Deal, a series of programs to help find some semblance of relief for unemployed and poor laborers. Cash's father signed on for Colonization Project Number 1, one of the first planned communities. The farmers were granted a house, a barn and twenty acres of land for no money down. They were also given a cow and mule, so that they could work the land successfully, and eventually pay the government back for the cost of the property, the house, and the small stipend they received. Once this was accomplished, the farmer would receive the deed to the property. Ray Cash, the son of a Baptist pastor, had served in the army during World War I. But times were hard, and following his discharge Ray worked many jobs, including cutting wood at a sawmill, and riding the rails as a hobo in order to find work anywhere he could. Ray and his oldest son, Roy, worked the land hard from dusk till dawn, so when the devastating flood of 1937 hit, the family stood to lose everything they had worked so hard to secure.

"Five Feet High and Rising" is an epic, true-to-life account of the devastating flood of 1937 that the Cash family endured, forcing them to flee from their land. In *Cash: The Autobiography*, Cash writes, "this song came from my own experience — not some storybook" (Cash, *Autobiography*, 27). We feel the surging waters rising as Cash recounts the horror of seeing all the devastation around him, and a young boy calling out to his mother "How high's the water, mama?" both in fear and anticipation. We are along for the journey as they prepare to leave their home in a homemade boat in order to make it safely to the road. The imagery is honest and frightening as we see the the cows in water past their knees and chickens huddled for safety in the trees. The song depicts the sheer terror of knowing your livelihood is gone and your life and the lives of your family are in jeopardy, make this recounting one of Cash's most enduring tales of his early childhood in Dyess, Arkansas. Ultimately, the family desperately flees to higher ground, facing an uncertain future knowing that they can't return home until the floodwaters recede.

Well, the water did recede, and the Cash family was ultimately able to return home safely, but not before leaving an indelible impression on young J. R. Though he was too young to personally recall the episode, it only helped to sharpen his inherent abilities as a storyteller, relating the flood as a family adventure that brought the family closer together. Cash recalled years later that the only good thing that came from the flood was the rich, black dirt that washed over their land, which brought them the best cotton crop they ever had the following year. It also brought Cash a bona fide classic recording that reached number 14 on the country chart, and 76 on the pop chart as the B-side of "I Got Stripes." This was a genuine "song of the soil." During his introduction to "Five Feet High And Rising," Cash would often tell about the devastating rain that had been falling for two weeks, leading to the great flood that broke the levee and washed black water and river dirt all over their land.

The Water Boy

In "Pickin' Time," another song drawn from Cash's experiences on the cotton farm, he revisits his childhood and those early years spent picking cotton. He recalled, "The time we all looked forward to the whole year was picking time. We were paid for picking the cotton, and pickin' time was the only time we'd have any income from the crops" (Cash, *Man in Black*, 26). Cash's first job, at age four, was as a "water boy," carrying water out to the thirsty adults laboring out in the field. By the time he was twelve, he was working hard out in the fields himself, alongside his older siblings. Had he stayed

1959 on the Arkansas farm. *Photo: Don Hunstein © Sony Music Entertainment.*

behind and made a career out of cotton farming, this might have been his own story. Instead, the lyrics of "Pickin' Time" embody the persona of his father, or any other cotton farmer with a family. It's an honest appraisal of the hard times, and the hard life of a cotton picker. It's also a first-rate folk song with some sharp lines and vivid remembrances. The poor farmer is unable to contribute when they pass the collection hat, "But the Preacher smiled and said 'that's fine, the Lord'll wait till pickin' time.'"

Cash wrote many songs reflecting back on his younger days. These ballads became some of his sharpest and most insightful musings on a way of life that helped shape him into the first-rate songwriter he would become. Cash also had an incredible knack for finding and revitalizing songs that spoke on subject matter he could understand and relate to. In 1962 Cash took the song "In Them Old Cotton Fields Back Home," which was originally recorded by Lead Belly in 1940, and turned it into a country classic. This just might be one of the finest renditions of this song ever recorded. A year earlier, in 1961, the folk group the Highwaymen (not to be confused with the 1985 super group consisting of Cash, Willie Nelson, Waylon Jennings, and Kris Kristofferson) scored a number 13 hit on the pop chart with the song. Cash was always a fan of folk music and decided to record his own version. Many great stars have recorded this song, from Harry Belafonte to the Beach Boys to Creedence Clearwater Revival, but Cash truly owns it and his sounds like an original, firsthand account of those brutally hot cotton fields he had grown up working in and loathing.

Other songs that reflect back on Cash's time in the cotton fields are "Cotton Pickin' Hands," which was written by Cash and June Carter, and would ultimately be issued as the B-side of his future single, "The One on the Right Is on the Left." However, it was recorded during the *Blood, Sweat and Tears* recording sessions and would have fit nicely into the fabric of the album. It's a song about a cotton picker with "fair to middlin' hands," referring to the various grades of cotton quality. Cash relies on his vast knowledge of cotton picking to paint a vivid picture of a hardworking man and the woman who loves him. Another song that further explains the intricacies of the cotton-farming life is "The Frozen Four-Hundred Pound Fair-to-Middlin' Cotton Picker." In this song Cash uses his cotton farming experience and literary invention to tell the story of the narrator's friend, Jim McCann, who is determined to pick four hundred pounds of cotton in one day. Despite the freezing temperature, Jim refused to give up. The narrator finds his friend's frozen body the next morning with his cotton sack containing the four hundred pounds of cotton he promised to harvest. It is highly unlikely that anyone ever froze to death picking cotton, especially since cotton is harvested in the fall when the weather is not so cold. The song may be exaggerated, but the story is engaging, and that's what matters to Cash. "Fair-to-middlin'," Cash explains in his liner notes to *From Sea to Shining Sea,* is a term used by cotton buyers to describe a certain grade of cotton. "The length of the fibers as well as their condition determines the grade of cotton as well as the price it will bring."

"Pick a Bale O'Cotton" is a simple, repetitious song that Cash wrote on the subject of cotton. The carefree lyric "Jump down, turn around, pick a bale o' cotton," tries to put a positive spin on the grueling, merciless work of the cotton farmer. It might have been sung out in the fields as the cotton was being gathered to help alleviate the backbreaking boredom that would set in daily. The song was not released at the time. As a songwriter himself, Cash was drawn to songs by other writers he admired that reflected his own memories and experiences. Cash turned to one of country music's greatest songwriters, Harlan Howard, for the song "Busted," about the devastating effects of poverty on a man and his family. Cash had first heard the song on a Burl Ives album. Harlan recalled, "When I first wrote 'Busted,' it was about coal miners, but it wound up being about a cotton farmer. I took the coal mining song to Johnny Cash. He liked it, except he said, 'Would you mind if we switched the story around to cotton farmers, because I've picked cotton, but I've never been a coal miner and I'd feel more comfortable doing it about cotton

farmers'" (Horstman, 300). From the opening line, "My bills are all due and the babies needs shoes, but I'm busted," we are drawn into the sad plight of a working man who's fallen on hard times and can no longer feed his family. Johnny's version of this now-classic song reached number 13 on the country chart in 1963. Later that year, Ray Charles would release his own version of the song and take it to number 4 on the pop chart. The song could not have fallen into the hands of two more worthy artists. Almost twenty years later, singer John Conlee's version would make it into the country Top Ten.

Cash devoted an entire side of his album *The Johnny Cash Show,* to reminiscences about his boyhood. The second "Come Along and Ride This Train" medley on the album takes us down to the Mississippi Delta, where cotton was king, not unlike Johnny's own childhood back home in the cotton fields of Arkansas. It opens with Harlan Howard's poignant "Mississippi Delta Land," which tells how the cotton fields robbed the sharecropper of his youth and gave him back so little in return, declaring, "All you gave back was a one room shack, and a mind that learned the truth." Next, Cash delivers a superb version of the country classic "Detroit City," cowritten by Danny Dill, who previously was a cowriter on "The Long Black Veil," and 1976 Country Music Association (CMA) Country Entertainer of the Year Mel Tillis. The song was originally recorded by Bobby Bare and made it to number 6 on the country chart and number 16 on the pop chart. It tells of a poor cotton farmer who migrates north to Detroit in hopes of finding work in the car factories there, as Cash did after graduating from Dyess High School in 1950, and going to work at the Fisher auto-body plant in Pontiac, Michigan. But the singer's southern roots run deep as he longs for his loved ones, and ultimately decides to leave Detroit and head back home, just as Cash did, leaving Pontiac less than a month after moving there and returning home to Dyess.

Two inspirational songs follow in the medley, as the train takes Cash back to the cotton fields of Dyess, where he would pick cotton all day with his family. He recalls singing "Uncloudy Day" with his sister Louise while they worked the cotton. Anita Carter takes on his sister's role as she performs a gorgeous rendition of the gospel standard, also known as "The Unclouded Day." That song segues into "No Setting Sun" (also known as "A Beautiful Life"), in which Anita duets with Cash on a song that he describes as one that he and his sister would sing at the end of a hard workday. It is a standout recording, and Anita's voice beautifully complements Cash's own tender performance.

Each evening, after the sun sets, the sharecropper family would move inside for their evening meal. "Supper-Time," from Cash's 1959 album *The Fabulous Johnny Cash,* tells a simple story of a family gathered around the table to dine together. Gospel songwriter Ira Stanphill, who also penned "Mansion Over the Hilltop" for Elvis Presley, wrote it. Cash couldn't have found a more perfect song to fit his sound and style. It truly evokes the nostalgic recollections of his childhood, as the sun sets and the shadows lengthen, the narrator anxiously waits for his mother to call him home for suppertime. The narrator realizes that these precious memories need to suffice him throughout his entire life until he and his family meet again in heaven "for the greatest supper-time of them all with our Lord."

Cash juxtaposed those backbreaking, sweltering days in the cotton field with songs about the joys and pleasures of his childhood, like "Country Boy," a perfect example of Cash embracing and celebrating his rural roots in song. "Country boy, ain't got no shoes, country boy, ain't got no blues . . ." Not a care in the world, this country boy just loves fishing and playing. One can almost imagine Cash longing for the simplicity of his childhood days, hard work and all, once he had tasted success and fame. After its original release on Sun, the song rested for many years until Cash revived it and recorded it for his second American Recordings album *Unchained.* Cash first wrote and recorded "Country Boy" in the summer of 1957. To hear him cover it anew nearly forty years later is quite interesting. The later arrangement is much more contemporary with a country-rock flavor. It's a grittier rendition of a song that has held up surprisingly well over the years.

A song with a similar theme is "Country Trash," a vivid, imagery-laden song about the virtues of living by the land and proudly being considered "country trash." The song first appeared on the 1973 album *Any Old Wind That Blows*, and it is an honest paean to Cash's rural roots. The singer lists all the things he has to do to keep his farm going and happily acknowledges that he's doing okay for country trash, quipping, "we'll all be equal when we're under the grass, and God's got a heaven for Country trash." And that is, according to Cash, the great equalizer. It's interesting to note that Cash would revisit the song nearly three decades later for his album *American III: Solitary Man*.

Even if Cash didn't write a given song himself, he could easily make one believe that he had. Cash turned to Larry Gatlin, an esteemed protégé, for "The Good Earth," another song from the *Any Old Wind That Blows* album. The song returns to the theme of equality of the poorest that Cash had addressed in "Country Trash." Gatlin was discovered by Dottie West, and had just released his first album, *The Pilgrim*, which Johnny wrote the liner notes for. Cash had also given Gatlin the nickname "The Pilgrim." Gatlin would go on to enjoy an incredible career in country music alongside his brothers, Steve and Rudy.[1] "The Good Earth"

is an inspirational song about realizing the value of where you come from and that sometimes it's better not to forget, or leave behind, the people and the places that really matter. The singer eventually returns back home and realizes that he is a product of the land and soil he grew up on, and ultimately "the good earth over Jordan by the Sea of Galilee."

Another song that sounds as if Cash had written it himself is "Pick the Wildwood Flower," which he recorded with Mother Maybelle Carter. Cash loved and revered June's mother, Maybelle Carter, and they often enjoyed going fishing together. This duet finds them both doing what they do best — Johnny singing and Mother Maybelle picking the "Wildwood Flower." Actually the song is about a boy's mother calling him to come home from the hot cotton fields, to get his guitar and pick the "wildwood flower." The song's writer, Joe Allen, has written hits for artists including Loretta Lynn, Don Williams, and Gene Watson. While Cash and Mother Maybelle only made it to number 34 on the country chart in 1973, Gene Watson's version of "Pick the Wildwood Flower" reached number 5 in 1979.

"Jesus Was Our Savior (Cotton Was Our King)" was the first Billy Joe Shaver song Cash recorded. Cash would take great interest in Shaver in the years to come. The legendary singer-songwriter had already caught the attention of Cash friends

Waylon Jennings and Tom T. Hall. Jennings had recorded an entire album of Shaver's songs with his classic *Honky Tonk Heroes*. Cash joined the party with this classic tale about growing up picking cotton. Cash personalizes the words of the opening line, "Wagon wheels were turning, with a cobble colored sound / When me and little Tommy rode the first load in to town." Both Cash and Shaver shared this history and Cash turns in a fine performance of this first-rate reminiscence.

Losing Jack

The most earth-shattering event in young J. R. Cash's life was the death of his beloved brother Jack at the age of fourteen. Jack was the older, more grounded brother who always walked the path of righteousness, dreaming of becoming a minister one day. J. R. looked up to Jack as a role model and inspiration. He was a kindhearted, generous, thoughtful young man who had the ability to draw people around him. J. R. was the moody, brooding sibling who wanted badly to follow in his brother's footsteps but stumbled doing so. On May 13, 1944, twelve-year-old J. R.'s world would be altered forever. Despite his pleas, J. R. could not convince Jack to spend the day fishing with him. Cash recalls in his autobiography that although Jack had a premonition, he turned J. R. down because he needed the money. When their mother said, "Jack, you seem like you don't feel you should go," Jack answered, "I don't. I feel like something's going to happen"

(Cash, *Autobiography*, 32). J. R. went fishing alone that day, only to have his father frantically come and get him, telling him that Jack was hurt badly in an accident while cutting oak trees into fence posts on a table saw. Jack was somehow pulled into the saw blade and his body was sliced from his ribs down through his belly, all the way to his groin. Jack was rushed to the hospital, but his injuries were too severe, and he died a little over a week later. Cash recalled, "Losing Jack was terrible. It was awful at the time and it's still a big, cold sad place in my heart and soul," (Cash, *Autobiography*, 36). When J. R. lost Jack, he lost a part of himself, and that horrific loss would permeate many of his songs through the years.

"Just as I Am," included on Cash's 1976 *Sings Precious Memories* album, is a heartfelt plea to God to accept us just as we are, "tossed about with many a conflict and many a doubt." Charlotte Elliott wrote this well-known hymn in 1835. Johnny recalled the importance of this song in his life, and gave a chapter in his autobiography *Man in Black* the title "Just as I Am." This was the song Johnny's beloved brother Jack sang to him on the day Cash was born again and accepted Christ as his Savior. He writes, "Jack was up on the front row holding his Bible, his eyes closed, singing, 'Just as I am, without one plea, But that Thy blood was shed for me, And that Thou bidd'st me come to Thee, O Lamb of God, I come, I come.' I finally got up the courage to step out of that pew, walk down the aisle, and take the preacher's hand. There was not any big burst of shouting or fireworks, but a beautiful peace came over me that night" (Cash, *Man in Black*, 34).

"Christmas as I Knew It" is another personal recollection about the singer's childhood Christmases in Dyess, Arkansas, that's credited to June Carter and Jan Howard. Jan Howard was a friend of the Carter sisters and scored a number 1 country hit in 1967 with the song "For Loving You," a duet with Bill Anderson. "Christmas as I Knew It" was written specifically for Cash as it recalls his memories of his family in the cotton fields, and his mother reassuring them that even though they had little money that year, they had each other's love. The song names all of Johnny's siblings, and has Johnny gifting his beloved brother Jack with a whistle he whittled for him, remembering "when I gave Jack that whistle he knew I thought the world of him." It's a truly stirring narration, and it's hard to believe that Cash did not have a hand in writing it.

Rhythm and blues legend Joe Tex wrote "Look at Them Beans" and recorded it under its original title "Papa's Dream." Cash tweaked the lyrics a bit and made it a semi-autobiographical story about his father's dream to always grow a good bean crop. Don Davis, who found "One Piece at a Time" for Cash, recalls that Cash reached out to him to find him another hit. Davis found "Look at Them Beans" and pitched it to Cash. Cash gives the song a highly animated and energetic performance as he excitedly narrates the story of his deceased papa's dream finally coming true. This was the first single from the album *Look at Them Beans,* and it made it to number 17 on the country chart.

Searching for Uncle Moses

Cash wrote and recorded many songs that revolved around his childhood days in Arkansas. "Cisco Clifton's Fillin' Station" is one of the best songs from Cash's album *From Sea to Shining Sea,* and one of Cash's finest reminiscences. It tells the tale of the smalltown gas station owner who is being squeezed out by the coming of the highways. Cisco Clifton's fillin' station was a meeting place for friends to gather for a "howdy and a checker game." We are told that Cisco would give anyone anything he had, and that once a big black Cadillac spent seven dollars there. Eventually, the interstate comes in and he loses most of his business, though he manages to keep his fillin' station open by taking odd jobs at night. Ultimately, we know that Cisco's days are numbered and at some point a piece of pure Americana will be lost forever. This could be Cash's ultimate metaphor for his lost youth and remembrances of things past.

Sometimes Cash would find ways to personalize a song's story by introducing it with a preamble relating it to his own life experience. "Boss Jack," from the *Ride This Train* album, was written by country legend Tex Ritter, who was a singer, songwriter, movie star, and a member of the Country

Music Hall of Fame. He was the father of the late actor John Ritter and the grandfather of Jason Ritter. He was also an artist who Johnny greatly admired. Tex's biggest hits include "Green Grow the Lilacs" and "High Noon (Do Not Forsake Me)." The narration that precedes "Boss Jack" takes us to Dyess, Arkansas, and Johnny's childhood home. The time is 1855 and the narrator, Boss Jack, owns a six-hundred-acre cotton plantation with slaves working the land. When one of the slaves fails to come home at the end of the day, Boss Jack goes out searching for Uncle Moses. When he finds him, Uncle Moses sings a song for, and about, Boss Jack. The slaves love Boss Jack so much that they believe he will free them someday. This is mythmaking of the highest order. The song might give us some insight into Cash's racial views, but the idea that slaves and plantation owners got along just fine during slavery is rejected by historians. Cash is simply shooting for nostalgia here.

Johnny delivers a stellar rendition of the Porter Wagoner hit "Green, Green Grass of Home," from the album *Johnny Cash at Folsom Prison*. Songwriter Curly Putman, who cowrote such classic country songs as "He Stopped Loving Her Today," for George Jones and "D-I-V-O-R-C-E," for Tammy Wynette, wrote the song. Putman was inspired to write it after watching the movie *The Asphalt Jungle*, "about a criminal in a big city who, despite being a robber, longed to go back home" (Eng, 169). Cash turns in one of his finest vocals on this song, sung in the first person, as the narrator has returned home to see his family and stroll down the lane with his sweet Mary. It's only toward the end of the song that we learn that the narrator is in prison and only dreaming about his loved ones, knowing that he will only see them again when they carry his body back to be buried beneath the green, green grass of home. One can attribute the believability of Cash's performance to his own desperate longing to somehow turn back time and return, even temporarily, to the comforts of his childhood home and family.

The Family Circle

Over the years Cash recorded many songs about his parents and visiting the old homestead. The most popular of these might be "Daddy Sang Bass." Carl Perkins wrote "Daddy Sang Bass" while in a dressing room in Kansas. He recalled, "I was messing around with my guitar before a show, thinking about my family and growing up in Jackson, Tennessee. . . . Johnny Cash passed by in the hall while I was singing the song and stopped in and asked if I wrote it. He recorded it soon after, and it became a hit" (Horstman, 41). It's a powerful song about family, hope, unity, and faith in the life ever after. Carl Perkins was a masterful songwriter, and this song was truly a gift to his friend Johnny. Cash recalled in *Man in Black* that, "with his coming back to God in 1967 Carl wrote a song which I recorded the following year, as did dozens of gospel singers and groups afterwards. The song was

The Johnny Cash Show with Tex Ritter. *Courtesy of Sony Music Entertainment.*

about our lives as boys — mine and Carl's — and the love in our families and the family circle that would not be broken, for someday we'd sing around God's throne. There was even a line in the song about my brother Jack: 'Me and little brother will join right in there'" (137). Cash delivers one of his finest performances on this biographical song that incorporates a chorus borrowed from the gospel standard "Will the Circle Be Unbroken." The Statlers and the Carters add angelic harmonies to a classic Cash recording. "Daddy Sang Bass" remained on top of the country chart for six weeks,

and made it to number 42 on the pop chart. It also won Johnny the Country Music Association Song of the Year Award in 1969.

Cash's relationship with his father was quite complicated. He was constantly drawn to songs about the relationship between father and son. Ray Cash was not a warm, demonstrative man, and he could be downright cruel at times. His drinking sometimes led him to do the unthinkable. One time Cash came home from school to find his dog lying dead in the woods near the house. He was devastated to learn that his father had shot him because the dog had broken into the chicken coop and killed six chickens. Cash even believed that his father somehow even blamed him for Jack's death. But he kept his feelings toward his father hidden, and preferred to remember him as the hardworking, stoic, Depression-era father that helped his family weather the hard times.

Sometimes Cash did attempt to address his father's bouts with drinking and depression in song. "Papa Was a Good Man" is an inspirational ballad written by songwriter Hal Bynum, who would go on to cowrite the giant Kenny Rogers hit "Lucille," as well as the Cash–Waylon Jennings duet "There Ain't No Good Chain Gang." The song tells of a family's faith in, and frustration with, their father, who is fighting a battle with the bottle. It's a story-song with a potent message, as the family is headed to Cincinnati with their mattress on top of the car, searching for a better life and hoping Papa has finally stopped drinking. It's the faith of his family and the support of his wife that helps him get through it. Cash could certainly relate to this subject, as he and his family had moved many times while living in Kingsland during the Great Depression, hoping to find some measure of prosperity in the next place they settled in. This was the first single released from *A Thing Called Love*, and maybe because of its preachy tone, it only made it to number 16 on the country chart.

More in keeping with Cash's idealized notion of his father is the song "Daddy," written by Don and Harold Reid of the Statler Brothers. It also appears on the album *A Thing Called Love*, and offers a heartfelt eulogy to a father "whose deeds were never published for the public, the things he did were never done for show." In a few short verses we learn everything about an unassuming man who left an incredible legacy of love behind. Don and Harold Reid are two of America's finest songwriters. The Statler Brothers originally performed gospel and started out as the Four Star Quartet, and later the Kingsmen. When they decided to go secular, they became the Statler Brothers, despite the fact that only Harold and Don Reid were brothers. They took the name "Statler" from a box of facial tissues they found in a hotel room. What separates the Statler Brothers from many other groups in country music is that they wrote the majority of their songs, and "Daddy" is a prime example.

Cash wrote "Ridin' on the Cotton Belt" specifically to pay tribute to his father, who actually did spend time working on the Cotton Belt train line. He explains it all in his intro, as he talks of recently having attended a family homecoming in Cleveland County, Arkansas, where he was born. Cash writes from his father's perspective. It's a panoramic travelogue through the places where his father had spent time working in Arkansas, and it recounts the struggles Ray Cash had to endure as a hobo travelling from town to town trying to find work to support his family. The lyric celebrates his father's happiness upon returning home with fourteen dollars for his wife and family. This is a very good train song that benefits from being a personal narrative about Cash's father, and one of the standout tracks on Cash's 1977 album *The Last Gunfighter Ballad.* Another song on the album Cash dedicates to his father is "That Silver Haired Daddy of Mine." Cash had performed the song in 1974 on the *På Österåker* album, recorded live in Sweden. What makes the 1977 version so special is that it's a duet performance with his brother Tommy Cash. And it's the perfect duet for the two siblings, as they recall their love for their aging father.

Take Me Home Again

"Abner Brown" is Cash's strongest self-penned song on the album *I Would Like to See You Again*. It's a story-song about an old drunk the singer knew named Abner Brown. It's a simple arrangement that opens with a guitar-strummed, spoken intro and proceeds to sing the praises of a good man who had many friends and was beloved by towns-folk and children alike who loved to hear his stories. The singer says, "the truest friend that I ever found was a good old drunk named Abner Brown." Cash puts Abner Brown on the same plane as all the great men he's known. Near the end of the song Cash sings what might be the most sincere lines he ever sang: "Lord take me back to the cotton land, to Arkansas, take me home again, let me be the boy that I once have been, let me walk that road to the

cotton gin." Cash's epitaph for Abner Brown is also a fond remembrance of things past that Cash has lost along the way. And in the end, Cash thanks the "Lord for making Abner Brown." We know that this is his connection to his lost innocence and the only way he can reclaim his childhood past.

Jo-El Sonnier cowrote "Lay Me Down in Dixie," a tender duet between Johnny and daughter Cindy Cash, from the album *A Believer Sings the Truth*. This is the least religious song on the album, but certainly one of the most spiritual. It's a fervent plea to be taken back home when the time comes to be buried in Dixie. It is truly one of the most beautiful songs on this, or any other, Cash album, and makes one wonder why Cindy Cash did not record more songs solo or with her father. Cindy is Johnny's third daughter, born July 29, 1959. She was married to singer Marty Stuart from 1979 to 1986. Cindy is also an actress who appeared in the 1983 television movie *The Cradle Will Fall* and is the author of *The Cash Family Scrapbook*, which was published in 1998.

Cash takes "John's," a Joe Allen composition featured on Cash's 1982 album *The Adventures of Johnny Cash*, and imbues it with so much believability you would think he wrote it himself. Cash had earlier enjoyed a hit with songwriter and bass player Allen's "Pick the Wildwood Flower," and turns in a credible performance of this song about his boyhood memories in Arkansas of a place called John's. The song is quite reminiscent of Cash's earlier salute to "Cisco Clifton's Fillin' Station." The lyric warmly relates all the fond memories of how John taught him about country music and, ultimately, life in general.

"Arkansas Lovin' Man," was written by songwriter Red Lane, who had his songs recorded by a wide array of country artists, including Merle Haggard, George Strait, and Kathy Mattea. This lighthearted story-song sounds as if it was written especially for Cash, and Cash delivers it with a wink and a nod that finds the singer proclaiming that he's "a natural, actual, real authentical Arkansas lovin' man."

"Kneeling Drunkard's Plea," from Cash's 1996 album *Unchained,* was written by the second generation of the Carter Family, Mother Maybelle and daughters June, Helen, and Anita Carter. And it could just as easily fit into the original Carter Family's incredible song canon. It was first recorded by the Louvin Brothers in 1960, for their classic album *Satan Is Real.* In the liner notes, Cash explains that as a boy he was a huge fan of the Louvin Brothers, and that he listened to them every day on the radio when they performed on the *Eddie Hill Show.* In the liner notes to *Unchained,* Cash recalls, "The biggest thrill of my life was when, in 1947, I made a trip to Memphis, hitch-hiking, and saw the show live. . . . I was thrilled beyond words. It was my first time to see a country show. I sent a request backstage to dedicate a song to my mother, and they did it! On the show, Eddie Hill said, 'Here's a song for Carrie Cash of Dyess, Arkansas,' and the Louvin Brothers sang their new record, 'Kneeling Drunkard's Plea.'" The song opens with a church organ before picking up the tempo and relating the drunkard's prayer for the Lord to have mercy upon him. The song takes a tragic turn when the drunkard's dying mother asks to see him, but he arrives one day too late. And finally, he dies three years later and is laid to rest beside her. And the singer explains that he knows that God will heed the drunkard's plea and he will see his mother in heaven. Tom Petty adds a beautiful harmony vocal to this outstanding album track. And Petty's own "Southern Accents," also included on *Unchained,* is a song that always sounded like it was written for Johnny Cash. When Cash sings, "I got my own way of talking but everything is done with a southern accent where I come from," we know he's speaking from his own experience, and his southern pride shines through.

Nowhere is Cash's southern pride more evident than in his own "The Ballad of Barbara." The song first appeared as the B-side to the 1973 single "Praise the Lord and Pass the Soup." The singer recounts the story of a girl he loved, who loved him enough to marry him and follow him away from his country home to live in the city. The song's opening lines, "In a southern town, where I was born, that's where I got my education. I worked in the fields, and I walked in the woods, and I wondered at creation," introduce us to the narrator, who wants more out of life than what a small town can provide him. Cash borrowed the melody from the traditional folk ballad "Barbara Allen," and created his own paradigm of the ambitious young boy who longs for greener pastures, only to learn through experience that there's just no place like home. Barbara entices him with her hazel eyes and carries him away before she turns into "concrete and steel," choosing the exciting city life over her devoted country boy. Ultimately, the values and life he left behind become his holy grail, as he leaves the "breathtaking, lofty steeples," and returns home "where I belong, much wiser now and older." It's easy to see how much Cash mirrored his own life story in this stirring saga that juxtaposes his songs of innocence with a lifetime's worth of experience. Those stifling Arkansas cotton fields would constantly tug at Cash's heartstrings, reminding him of all he's gained . . . and all he's lost through the years.

Chapter 2

I WALK THE LINE

THE SUN YEARS

Where it all began for Johnny Cash and the Tennessee Two
at Sam Phillips's Sun Studios in Memphis, Tennessee

By 1950, the Cash family farm was so run-down that Ray Cash had to take a job in a margarine factory. J. R. also worked there briefly, but quickly left to join the United States Air Force on July 7, 1950. He enlisted just one week before the start of the Korean War, and was stationed at Brooks Air Force Base in San Antonio, Texas. The Air Force would not accept initials on the enlistment papers, so Cash signed John R. Cash for the first time. It was while stationed in San Antonio that Cash met his future wife, Vivian. Later that year he was assigned to the Twelfth Radio Squadron Mobile of the U.S. Air Force Security Service at Landsberg, Germany. Cash's job was to intercept Soviet radio communications. He was the first person in the U.S. military to learn of Joseph Stalin's death (Cash, *Autobiography,* 79). While stationed in Germany, Cash visited Spain and Great Britain and attended the coronation of Queen Elizabeth II in 1953. It was in Germany that Cash bought his first guitar and taught himself to play. During this period Cash would play music with his friends in the service. They played the country hits of the day, which included songs by the Carter Family, the Louvin Brothers and Hank Williams. J. R., now known as

« Johnny Cash With His Hot and Blue Guitar.
Courtesy of Sun Entertainment Corporation.

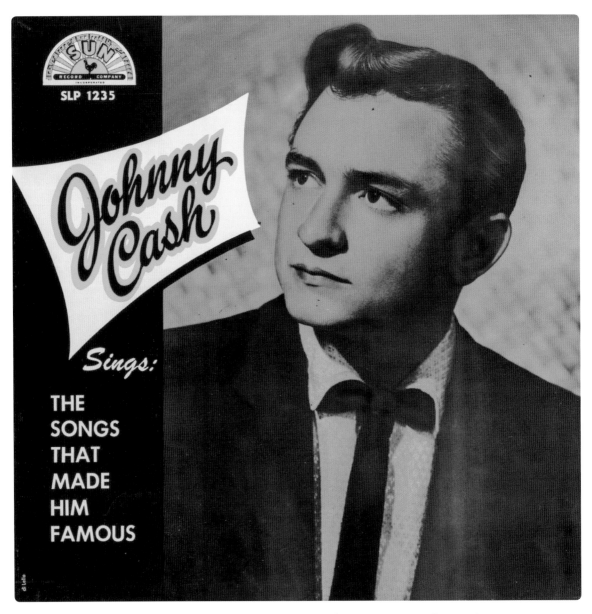

Johnny Cash Sings: The Songs That Made Him Famous. *Courtesy of Sun Entertainment Corporation.*

John, also began writing his own songs during this time, many of which would form the bedrock for his future recording career at Sun Records. There was an innocence about those early songs that one can hear in his Sun catalog. He wrote fast and furiously back then and everything around him served to influence his writing. He formed a group with his Air Force buddies called the Landsberg Barbarians, and he purchased a cheap reel-to-reel tape recorder so that he could record the songs he was writing.

Cash was honorably discharged from the Air Force in 1954 with the rank of Staff Sergeant. He went to Texas, and later that same year he married his sweetheart Vivian. He was raised a Baptist and Vivian a devout Catholic. They were married at St. Ann's Catholic Church and they settled down in Memphis, Tennessee. Cash immediately enrolled at the Keegan School of Broadcasting for a career in radio. But with a baby on the way (Rosanne, born May 24, 1955) he opted to study part-time and take a job selling electrical appliances for the Home Equipment Company. In late 1954 his brother Roy, who had himself started a band called the Delta Rhythm Ramblers, was working at Automotive Sales Garage on Union Avenue, and, knowing how much John loved music, introduced him to Luther Perkins and Marshall Grant, two mechanics working at the garage. The three hit it off and began to play together. They would meet up daily and rehearse at Luther's house. Initially all three played acoustic guitars, but John suggested that they try different instruments. Luther learned to play electric guitar while Marshall took up the upright bass. Thanks to the sponsorship of John's boss at the Home Equipment Company, they got the opportunity to play a fifteen-minute show on country station KWEM on Saturdays.

John, Marshall, and Luther, along with a steel guitar player named A. W. "Red" Kernodle eventually managed to get an audition with Sam Phillips at Sun Records. Cash's heart was in gospel music, and for their first audition they performed three songs, two gospel and one country. They played "I Was There When It Happened," Cash's own "Belshazzar," or "Belshazah," as it was originally spelled, and the Hank Snow hit "I Don't Hurt Anymore," which was number 1 on the country chart at the time.

Kernodle was too nervous to perform so he dropped out of the group. Phillips liked what he heard but was still not totally convinced that their sound was unique enough. This was where Cash saw his opportunity to present his own compositions for consideration. He went home after that first audition and delved into the songs he had written while in the service. He presented "Hey Porter," and this time Phillips was impressed enough to suggest that John go home and write another song for the B-side. That would ultimately be "Cry! Cry! Cry!" and, while these were not the first songs they recorded for Sun, they were the songs that began

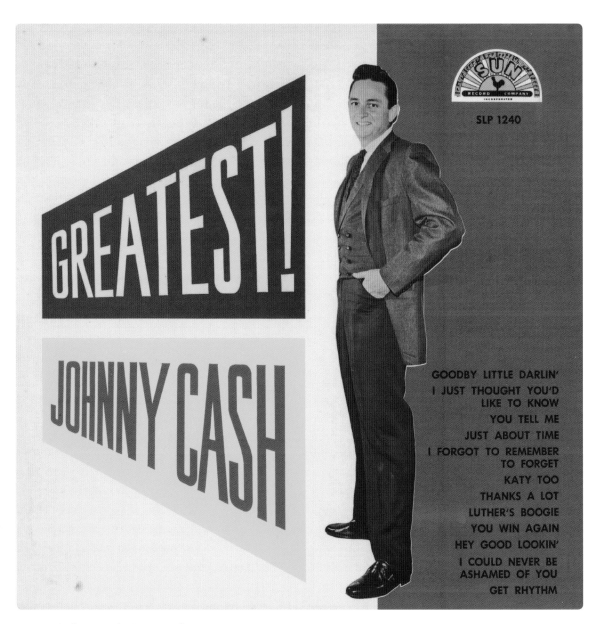

Greatest! Johnny Cash. *Courtesy of Sun Entertainment Corporation.*

his recording career. Sam Phillips renamed him "Johnny," and between 1955 and 1957 Johnny Cash and the Tennessee Two would go on to play shows with country stars Webb Pierce, George Jones, Johnny Horton, and Sun labelmate Elvis Presley on *Louisiana Hayride.*

Many artists and critics regard the songs from the Sun years as the most significant of Cash's recorded output. Once he had established himself with a hit single, Phillips let Cash have more freedom to record his own songs in the studio. And Cash certainly took advantage of the opportunity he had been afforded. He wrote at breakneck speed: love songs to Vivian, heartbreak songs, story-songs, and even a few spiritual songs he was able to slip into the sessions. The songs from the Sun years tell the story of an immensely talented young man who was carving out his own unique niche in popular music. His songs were not quite rock or even rockabilly in the true sense of the latter genre, nor were they standard country songs. They contained a little bit of blues, a little bit of folk, and a whole lot of Johnny Cash.

Cash's songwriting output at Sun was his greatest from any phase of his career because he had so much passion and hope inside him that he could not write the songs fast enough. There was a genuine simplicity to the songs he was writing, yet they were imbued with a poetry that was profound. It was honest music coming from a man who had not yet been tainted by the rules of the record industry

or the trials of life on the road. He was young and wild, with the ability to write and record songs that would make young girls swoon and their parents tap their feet along to his patented *boom-chicka-boom* beat. While Elvis's music was perceived as overtly sexual and dangerous, Cash's songs were more constrained and simply, slyly mischievous at worst. Cash's songwriting would develop and mature over the years, and he would continue to present songs that would have a major impact on his audience. But he would also struggle to recapture the magic and simplicity of those early Sun recordings. In fact, after Johnny left Sun in 1958, his writing became more sporadic. In 1974, when he released his album *Ragged Old Flag*, he reflected that he hadn't written so many songs since his Sun days. And without a doubt most of those songs from the Sun days have held up quite well over the years.

The First Recording Session

Johnny Cash and the Tennessee Two recorded their first session for Sun Records in 1954, with Sam Phillips as producer. That initial session resulted in two songs that were both written by Cash. "Wide Open Road" was a breezy kiss-off to a girl who says she's had enough, and the singer's response is to tell her to just leave and head down that wide open road. Right away Cash invokes a carefree persona who refuses to be a victim. However, he does eventually regret the decision and tries to win her back by searching for her in order to tell her that things have gone crazy for him since she left. The road then becomes a means for her to find her way back home. The theme of second thoughts and regrets due to rash judgment would reemerge in many Cash songs through the years. Cash recalled in his autobiography how he wrote the song on a "cold, rainy morning when I sat in the barracks in Germany with my five-dollar guitar and conjured that song up out of the air" (Cash, *Autobiography,* 110).

The second song they recorded was "You're My Baby." This was Cash's attempt to write a more pop-oriented, up-tempo love song with country roots. Even though the singer owes money on bills that are due, he would prefer to spend his money on his baby. It's really a sliver of a song but it does reveal Cash's willingness to go in a different musical direction. Though initially intended for immediate release, the song at the time was not released.

Cash's second recording session at Sun, in early 1955, included two more takes on "Wide Open Road," along with six other tracks. While Johnny was serving in the Air Force and stationed in Germany, his commanding officer had the men watch the film *Inside the Walls of Folsom Prison.* This inspired him to write "Folsom Prison Blues," one of the most defining songs of his career. He was also influenced to write it after hearing "Crescent City Blues," written by Gordon Jenkins and sung by Beverly Mahr, Jenkins's wife. The song appeared on Jenkins's 1953 album entitled *Seven Dreams.* Cash may have heard the album while he was stationed in Germany. Jenkins's song was itself inspired by a 1930s instrumental titled "Crescent City Blues," by Little Brother Montgomery. Cash would ultimately become the voice of the incarcerated man and his live-album performances at Folsom and San Quentin Prisons became landmark recordings.

"Folsom Prison Blues" is an aching saga of life gone wrong and the price one pays for committing a crime. It includes the classic lyric "I shot a man in Reno just to watch him die." As Cash later explained in *Cash: The Autobiography,* "I sat down with my pen in my hand, trying to think of the worst reason a person would have for killing another person, and that's what came to mind. It did come to mind quite easily, though" (Cash, 76–77). Sam Phillips was initially hesitant about Cash releasing this song and suggested he might pitch it to Tennessee Ernie Ford, a major recording artist at that time. Cash kept working on the song and finally convinced Phillips to release his version. He would play it many times through the years and it would chart as a single for him twice — it was his second Sun single and reached number 4 on the country chart in 1956. Cash recorded the song live for his *Johnny Cash at Folsom Prison* album, and that version made it to number 1 on the country chart for four weeks in 1968. The latter version also made it to number 32 on the pop chart.

"Hey Porter" was Johnny's first of many train songs. This was the song that impressed Sam Phillips enough to invite Johnny and the Tennessee Two back to his studio for their first official recording session. Cash explains in *Cash: The Autobiography* that even though he (Cash) didn't think the song was any good, Sam liked it enough to release it as Cash's first single. However, once it was released, the record's B-side, "Cry! Cry! Cry!" would go on to chart. But, "Hey Porter" has become a deserved Cash classic. Cash said that he wrote this song on the way home from Germany. He had been honorably discharged from the Air Force and was daydreaming while counting the miles it would take for him to get back home to his family. It was Dyess he was dreaming about, though he changed the destination in the song to Tennessee. "Hey Porter" is a mid-tempo tale of a train rider anxiously waiting to cross the Mason–Dixon line, and return to the comforting warmth of the South and home in Tennessee. There's a sense of innocence, much like a child constantly asking "are we there yet?" and a strong feeling of motion as the song chugs along like the train the rider is aboard. He yearns to smell frost on cotton leaves and once again feel that soothing southern breeze.

"Goodnight Irene" was the first song Cash recorded that he did not write. Huddie Ledbetter, aka Lead Belly, and folklorist John A. Lomax are credited with writing this ballad. Lead Belly was the first to popularize the song about a spurned lover who loves his Irene so much that he's contemplating jumping in the river and drowning. There's an all-encompassing sense of sadness and tragedy set against a soft and lovely lullaby melody. Lead Belly had been performing his version of the song since 1908. In 1950 the Weavers reached number 1 on the pop chart with their rendition of the song. Everyone from Frank Sinatra to Ernest Tubb and Red Foley, whose duet version was a number 1 country hit, took a turn performing it. Cash's version ranks right up there with the best of them.

The song "Two Timin' Woman" is an out-and-out cheating song about a spurned lover dealing with a woman who has another "daddy" waiting down at the end of the hall —"a two timin' woman with a heart of solid stone." The singer hopes, however, that she will return to him so he can tame her by chaining her to the floor until she's eating from his hand. The song was written by Hank Snow, and might have been too stark for country radio at the time, yet it does reveal Cash's honest, descriptive way of interpreting a song lyric.

The B-Side

After recording "Hey Porter," Sam Phillips told Cash to go home and write a love song, a real weeper, for the B-side of the single. Johnny was inspired to write "Cry! Cry! Cry!" after hearing country disc jockey Eddie Hill tell his radio listeners to "Stay tuned, we're gonna squall and bawl and climb the walls." Cash originally wrote the lyric as, "You're gonna bawl, bawl, bawl." He wrote the song the same night that Phillips made his suggestion, and a couple of weeks later he brought Phillips "Cry! Cry! Cry!" The record was released with "Hey Porter" as the A-side, but radio deejays preferred "Cry! Cry! Cry!" The song was Johnny's first Top 20 single, reaching number 14 on the country chart. When Johnny tried to update his sound on songs like "You're My Baby," the results were mixed. Here he was able to naturally imbue a stone-country lyric with a fresh rockabilly feel. The lyric depicts a quintessential yearning of a spurned lover who hopes his straying woman will feel the pain he's enduring and eventually regret her actions. He warns her that she will "cry, cry, cry, and cry alone" when she realizes what a fool she's been. Even though she's shamed him with her wandering ways, he still takes the time to warn her of the loneliness that she will endure if she leaves him. This was an interesting take on the situation. Cash refuses to play the part of the victim in the song. The lyric foreshadows the time when the singer will be the one to walk away from the woman after she comes crawling back to him. Cash revered Hank Williams, and here he had written a song that embodies the finest attributes of a Hank Williams classic.

On July 30, 1955, Cash returned to Sun Studios to work on some previously recorded tracks and three brand-new songs that he had written. "So Doggone Lonesome" was Cash's second Sun single, and it reached number 4 on the country chart (as did its B-side "Folsom Prison Blues"). Cash wrote the song with country legend Ernest Tubb in mind. Tubb liked the song, recorded it, and tried to rush-release his version to radio, but Cash's record had already charted. In the song, Cash once again inhabits the role of the rejected lover aching for his darling. He puts on a happy face for friends as his heart breaks for the one he loves. He's okay during the day "until that moon comes shining through" and he gets "so doggone lonesome." Cash uses time as a motif throughout the song, as the obsessed lover rationalizes even though he could have a dozen others, he prefers to keep on missing her. This is Cash taking the notion of the victim and transforming him into an enigmatic figure who prefers to choose his own destiny and not listen to anyone else, despite the pain. He's strong enough to take it, and this song certainly resonated with radio listeners.

"Luther Played the Boogie" or "Luther's Boogie," is a striking rockabilly ode to Cash's Tennessee Two guitarist Luther Perkins. Perkins was the silent, stoic figure who stood behind Cash on stage and who was crucial in helping to define Cash's sound and style. This sincere song of friendship remains one of Cash's most honest attempts to acknowledge someone he loved like a brother. Luther Monroe Perkins was born in Memphis, Tennessee, in 1928.

He, along with bass player Marshall Grant, created the signature *boom-chicka-boom* sound that Cash became known for. Tragically, on August 3, 1968, Luther fell asleep holding a lit cigarette. His house caught fire and Luther barely made it to the door before succumbing to smoke inhalation. Luther was rushed to the hospital and died two days later. Though his guitar playing was stark and simple, even for the times, it has been imitated and emulated by musicians for decades. As the song lyric states, Luther certainly "played the boogie strange" and brilliantly. The song was released as a single in 1959, after Cash had left Sun, and it reached number 8 on the country chart.

"Mean Eyed Cat" is an all-out rockabilly rave-up about a fellow who gives his woman money to shop at the general store, just so she can go and spend it on "store-bought cat food for her mean eyed cat." The cat conceit is stretched a bit, since that's the only time it's used in the song. She ultimately leaves him with a "Dear John" note on her pillow as he heads to town to bring her back. Again, the train becomes a symbol of escape and freedom, as the hard-pressed woman catches an eastbound train.

"I Couldn't Keep From Crying" is a pure country heartbreaker from the pen of future country legend Marty Robbins. Cash sings it sad and mournful, as the song's narrator watches the woman he loves slip away from him and into the arms of another man. Haunting lyrics permeate the ballad as he "stood and watched him steal a kiss, from two lips I knew I'd miss."

"New Mexico" is credited to songwriters Lambson and Johnson and is the first of many story-songs Cash would record over the years. Although he did not write it, he conveys the lyrics with true conviction. The story tells of a cowboy in 1883 who undertakes a journey to the uncharted badlands of New Mexico. It's like a John Wayne movie set to music, as the travelers endure heat, hunger, and Indian attacks along the way. The moral of the story is "go back to your friends and loved ones; tell others not to go to the God-forsaken country they call New Mexico." This was Cash's first song to mention the American Indian, albeit briefly, as the Indians posed a danger to the travellers on their journey.

In late 1955, Cash would write and record "Rock 'n' Roll Ruby," his first attempt at an all-out rock and roll song. Working at Sun, in the shadow of Elvis, Cash must have been tempted to try to cross over and top the pop charts. What we learn from all this is that Cash had his own distinct place among the Sun recording artists. He didn't need to follow in anyone's footsteps. And, years later, so many rock icons would embrace him as their own because he was such a musical maverick. "Rock 'n' Roll Ruby" is an important song because it proved that Cash could do anything he wanted to musically, and he was never afraid to try his hand at any genre of music. This demo was first released in the

United States in 2006 on the Reader's Digest box set *Johnny Cash: The Complete Early Hits Collection.*

Because You're Mine

In April 1956 Cash went back into the studio to record one of the most important sessions of his career. The first song they worked on was Cash's self-penned "Get Rhythm." He wrote the song near College Station, Texas, in the back of the Plymouth he shared with Grant and Perkins while traveling from show to show. Charting as the B-side of the "I Walk the Line" single, this breezy, animated, up-tempo favorite was re-released in 1969 at the height of Cash's popularity and made it to number 23 on the country chart. Cash also contributed vocals to a cover of this song recorded by singer Martin Delray that reached number 27 in 1991. Cash would include the song in his live performances through the years, and feature it on the *Survivors Live* album he made with Jerry Lee Lewis and Carl Perkins in 1982. Cash has said that he wrote the song for Elvis but decided to keep it for himself (Streissguth, *Johnny Cash: The Biography,* 83). The song is a positive reaffirmation of the benefits of a sunny outlook on life, as the singer converses with "a little shoeshine boy who never gets lowdown, but he's got the dirtiest job in town . . ." The metronomic pop of the shoeshine rag mirrors the infectious beat of the song, much like the "windshield wipers slapping time" in Kris Kristofferson's "Me and Bobby McGee" years later. One doesn't usually think of Cash asking us to dance and get rhythm when we get the blues, but that's exactly what makes this song so special. There always was a sunny side to the typically dark, brooding Man in Black.

Who would have thought that a simple declaration of fidelity and devotion to the woman he loved would become Cash's signature song. Cash wrote "I Walk the Line" in 1956 for his bride of two years, Vivian. He wrote the song on the first night he had been away from home since he'd gotten married. In *Johnny Cash: The Autobiography,* Cash recalls, "I wrote 'I Walk the Line' when I was on the road in Texas in 1956, having a hard time resisting the temptation to be unfaithful to my wife back in Memphis. I put those feelings into the beginning of a song and sang the first two verses for Carl Perkins backstage before a show. 'What do you think?' I asked. 'I'm calling it "Because You're Mine."' 'Hmm,' Carl said, '"I Walk the Line" would be a better title.' Then he went on stage, and I finished the song while he did his set. It came fast and easy, almost without conscious thought" (78).

In its sheer simplicity, the song evokes more power and passion in a few short lines than many books on the subject. The song was Cash's first number 1 country hit, and it remained at the top of the charts for six weeks. It was also his first song to make the pop chart, climbing to number 17. Cash would rerecord the song many times over the years — in 1964, as the title track for a Columbia Records album; in 1969, as part of his legendary

San Quentin concert; in 1970, in a slowed down version for the movie *I Walk the Line*; and in 1988, for his *Classic Cash* album on Mercury records. The song would also become the title of the 2005 Cash biopic *Walk the Line*, starring Joaquin Phoenix as Cash, and Reese Witherspoon in her Academy Award–winning performance as June. Ironically, the movie depicted the torrid love affair between Johnny and June, not his first wife, Vivian, for whom it was originally written. As Cash's voice mellowed and matured, his rerecordings of the song find the lyric becoming even more emphatic as a treatise of true devotion. If Cash had never recorded another song, this one would have cemented his place in music history.

Cash followed up his smash hit "I Walk the Line" with "There You Go," a song he had written about a jilted lover. The singer is dejected, but not surprised, to learn that his love has left him again. From the haunting opening lines —"You're gonna break another heart, you're gonna tell another lie"— we are immediately drawn into the singer's narrative and anxious to find out what has transpired. There's a masochistic streak in the singer who's been through this before with his lover, but continues to put up with her lies because he loves her so much. The song reached number 1 on the country chart in December 1956, and stayed there for five weeks. Whereas everyone knows "I Walk the Line," "There You Go" has been somewhat forgotten; that's a shame, because in its own way it was a solid record, which its success on radio at the time proved.

"Train of Love" was Cash's second charting train song. It differs from "Hey Porter" in that the train in question is a metaphor for love. In stark contrast to "Hey Porter," the narrator in this song asks the trainman when his baby's coming home. It seems that everyone's baby is returning, except his. The train as a symbol of escape and freedom also serves as the force that has stolen away the one he loves. As the B-side to "There You Go" the song managed to reach number 7 on the country chart. In a 1973 *Rolling Stone* interview with Robert Hilburn, Cash recalled writing the song in 1955 when he was on the *Louisiana Hayride* show in Shreveport, Louisiana. Sam Phillips was in the audience, and he liked the song so much that they recorded it at their next session. In 2002, Bob Dylan chose to record this song for the album *Kindred Spirits: A Tribute to the Songs of Johnny Cash*.

On April 16, 1956, Cash's second daughter, Kathleen, was born in Memphis, Tennessee. In December 1956, Phillips turned the production of Cash's records over to his right-hand man, steel guitarist and studio engineer Jack Clement. Cash and Clement had become friends, and their mutual respect for one another would keep them working together on various projects throughout Cash's career. "Goodbye Little Darlin'," which was written by cowboy legend Gene Autry and songwriter Johnny Marvin, was the first Cash song Jack

Clement produced. Its haunting beauty reveals a side of Cash not yet realized. His final farewell to a lover who is leaving him is truly heartbreaking. While the song was never released as a single, Cash had faith in it and would rerecord it in 1964 for his *I Walk the Line* album on Columbia Records. Both versions are impeccable, and either one would have made a worthy single for either label.

Songwriter Leon Payne wrote "I Love You Because." Cash always loved country music and one of his favorite artists was Ernest Tubb. Both Tubb and Payne topped the country chart with this ballad in 1950. Cash imbued the song with his distinctive sound and style. Like "I Walk the Line," it's a sincere affirmation of true love. While Sun didn't initially issue the track as a single, it did release it in 1960, after Cash had left the label. Interestingly, in 1969 country singer Carl Smith also reached the country Top 20 with this song. Smith was June Carter's first husband and the father of their daughter, singer Carlene Carter.

Million Dollar Quartet

On December 4, 1956, Carl Perkins was at Sun Studios recording his new single, with Jerry Lee Lewis playing the piano. Elvis, who had already left Sun Records and was newly signed to RCA Records, happened to come by his old studio. And then Cash stopped by, resulting in what has come to be known as the "Million Dollar Quartet" session. Jack Clement was working the session and left the microphones on as they all joined together in a rollicking, impromptu performance of hits, old favorites, and gospel standards. Cash's participation in the session has always been questioned. He was there but is not clearly heard on the tapes. One theory was that Cash had left the session to go and buy a pack of cigarettes; another was that he left to go shopping with Vivian. But Cash has explained that he was simply down at the far end of the studio and standing far away from the microphone. The historic session lasted nearly two hours, and the musicians did not know that they were being recorded.

On April 4, 1957, Cash reentered the studio with Clement to record two new songs he had written. "Next in Line" reached number 9 on the country chart. In this song the singer boldly tells the object of his affection that he is the next in line to love her. He warns her that it's her time to love him. He's patiently waited for her, explaining that, "the next in line will want your love forever." The song also scratched the bottom of the pop charts, reaching number 99.

"Don't Make Me Go" was the B-side of "Next in Line," and in this song Cash is the victim who pleads with a lover to give him one more chance before she leaves him. It is that rare Cash song that presents the singer in a very weak light. But there are great lines in the song such as, "two hearts in love must give and take, when one heart fails the other breaks."

In July, Cash returned to the studio to record five new songs he had written, cowritten or adapted and arranged. "Home of the Blues" was Cash's first bona fide cowrite with songwriters Glenn Douglas Tubb and Lillie McAlpin. The song made it up to number 3 on the country chart and number 88 on the pop chart. It's about a broken man who dwells in an unhappy home. He clings to the memories of better times, but those happy memories leave him feeling so sad in the present that he just wants to give up and die. It's a sad lament in which the singer invites listeners who've just lost a sweetheart to come along and join him "down the street that losers use" at the home of the blues. Cash was inspired to write the song after visiting a record shop called Home of the Blues, that was located on Beale Street.

"Give My Love to Rose" is arguably one of Johnny's finest compositions. It has held up remarkably well over the years and established Cash as a master of the story-song. Cash might have found the inspiration for this song after meeting a former San Quentin inmate who asked him to pass on a message to his wife the next time he was in Shreveport (Turner, 74). Cash wrote the song while sitting backstage in Brisbane, California, in 1956, within sight of San Quentin Prison. Cash says he "started thinking about the men in there," and the result was "Give My Love to Rose" (Dawidoff, 185). Cash may have been influenced by an old folk song called "Give My Love to Nell." However, that song's story differs greatly from Cash's. In "Give My Love to Rose," Cash takes on the persona of a man who happens upon a convict who has just escaped from prison but now lays dying. The convict implores the narrator, "Tell my boy his daddy's so proud of him, and don't forget to give my love to Rose."

"Rock Island Line" was a song that Cash arranged and adapted. It was an Arkansas prison song dating back to the 1930s. Lead Belly had originally performed it, and English skiffle artist Lonnie Donegan released it in 1956 when it reached number 8 on the pop chart. The song seemed tailor-made for Cash, who managed to turn it into a rockabilly classic. It's a story-song that tells of the Rock Island Line running down into New Orleans. When the train driver is asked what he has on board, he lies and says he has livestock so as not to pay any toll. Just as he passes he picks up steam and screams, "Well, I fooled you, I fooled you, I got pig iron, I got all pig iron." Cash shows his mischievous, rebellious side in this chugging favorite that he would perform in his live shows and on television for years to come. Sun records released the track as a single in 1970, which reached number 35 on the country chart.

"Wreck of the Old 97" is yet another great train story-song arranged and adapted by Cash. The Old 97 was a Southern Railway train officially known as the Fast Mail. It ran from Washington, DC, to Atlanta. On September 27, 1903 while en route to

Monroe, Virginia, the train derailed near Danville, Virginia. "Eleven men died in the crash; five railroad workers (including the engineer Joseph Andrew "Steve" Brody) and six postal workers" (Wilentz and Marcus, 160). This inspired Cash to write his own version of the song about the wreck and what might have caused it. Though the song suggests the wreck was unavoidable and even goes as far as to romanticize the heroics of the "brave engineer," facts indicate that Brody was driving the train recklessly, and much too fast. The song is credited to G. B. Grayson and Henry Whitter. Vernon Dalhart released his version of the song in 1927, and it is recognized as the first million-selling country song. Many artists have performed and recorded the song over the years, but none more successfully than Cash, who included it in almost all his live shows during his popular train-medley segment, before a backdrop of two trains colliding together.

The First Gospel Song

"Belshazzar" was Cash's first recording of an original inspirational song. Cash was at odds with Sam Phillips because Phillips preferred he not record any gospel songs and stick to secular recordings. In 1958 this became a major issue when Cash opted to leave Sun for Columbia Records. Columbia enticed Cash with the promise that he could record a gospel album immediately. And they delivered on the promise. His second album for the label was a hymn collection. Cash says in *The Autobiography* that this was his favorite song at the time among his own compositions. "Belshazzar" tells of the Biblical king who ruled Babylon and all its land, and ultimately was "weighed in the balance and found wanting . . . his houses were built upon the sand" (Cash, *Autobiography*, 99). It is a morality tale that Cash delivers with conviction. Cash always said his love of gospel music preceded his love of country music. Throughout his career he would write and record many inspirational songs. And he always set aside a gospel segment as part of his live show.

In August 1957, Cash, Perkins and Grant went into the studio to record seven new songs with only two original Cash compositions. "Leave That Junk Alone" was a minor Sun track in which Cash implores a friend to leave that junk (liquor) alone and drink water. He's willing to make any concessions needed for her to change her ways. The song was recorded as a demo and not released at the time. The second song Cash wrote for the session was the much stronger (and previously discussed) "Country Boy."

"Doin' My Time" is a prison song Cash recorded from the pen of Jimmie Skinner. Cash's empathy for prisoners has become the stuff of legend, and, like "Folsom Prison Blues," this early recording relates the hard life of a convict working on "that old rock pile." The difference is that in this song the prisoner is ultimately freed and able to reunite with his gal. The lyric also mentions by name the legendary steel driver John Henry, and, as such, foreshadows Cash's classic recording of "The Legend of John Henry's Hammer" in 1962.

In "If the Good Lord's Willing," the singer explains that "if the creeks don't rise," he'll be in his darling's arms again. This simple courting song is another celebration of the country lifestyle. Renowned country music producer and publisher Bill Lowery signed an eighteen-year-old Jerry Reed to his publishing company. Lowry was able to get Reed's song placed with Johnny Cash, earning Reed his first major songwriting credit. Reed would go on to enjoy a successful career as a country singer, songwriter and guitarist, charting songs such as "Amos Moses" and "When You're Hot, You're Hot." He also appeared in the *Smokey and the Bandit* movie series with Burt Reynolds. Nearly fifteen years later, Cash would record Reed's "A Thing Called Love" as the title track of his 1971 studio album.

Johnny Cash was greatly influenced by the songs of Hank Williams. "I Heard That Lonesome Whistle Blow" was the first of many of Hank's songs that Johnny would record. This mournful train song fit perfectly in Cash's repertoire. The narrator gets in trouble and has to leave his home and in the process breaks his darling's heart. He ends up in prison working on a Georgia chain gang and listening for that lonesome whistle to blow. It combines all of Cash's great themes: prison, trains,

disappointing loved ones, and paying the price. Hank Williams's own version had reached number 9 on the country chart in 1951 under the title "Lonesome Whistle." Country singer-songwriter Don Gibson would also take it into the Top 30 in 1971. Cash never released it as a single, but his version is one of the best.

Cash turns in a fine rendition of the Stuart Hamblen hit "Remember Me (I'm the One Who Loves You)." Hamblen reached number 2 on the country chart with the song in 1950, while Ernest Tubb made it to number 5 that same year. Cash's version stands right up there with the best of them. The theme of the singer offering his love to someone in need of love and friendship is an interesting twist for Cash, who more often takes on the role of the jilted lover.

"I Was There When It Happened" was Cash's second gospel recording at Sun. This one was a cover of a Jimmie Davis song and featured Marshall Grant on the chorus. It became a fixture in Cash's early performances with the Tennessee Two and remained a favorite he would return to time and again during concerts. It's a devotional testament to Cash's strong faith and the moment he was saved by Jesus.

On August 31, 1957, Cash appeared on the popular *Town Hall Party* broadcast. It was backstage at this program that Cash and Carl Perkins met Columbia Records producer Don Law, who asked if they would be interested in signing with Columbia when their Sun contracts expired. Both were interested, and Cash signed on the dotted line with Columbia one year later on August 1, 1958.

In October 1957 Cash recorded his composition "Come In Stranger." It's an interesting song about the singer coming home to the one he loves after being away awhile. She welcomes him home, saying, "Come in, stranger, oh how I miss you when you're gone." She implores him to "stay long enough so that the one I love is not a stranger to me." Cash was away from home touring a great deal, and this song's lyric might be the response he hoped he would receive from his wife when he would come in off the road. Its clever wordplay and familiar country accompaniment helped the song reach number 6 in 1958 as the B-side of "Guess Things Happen That Way." It also made it to number 66 on the pop chart.

One month later, Cash went back into the studio to close out the year with two classic recordings. "Ballad of a Teenage Queen" is a country-pop-infused story about a young man who works at the candy store, while pining for the girl he loves who's gone off to seek fame and fortune in Hollywood. Written by producer Jack Clement, this song holds the distinction of being Cash's longest-charting number 1 hit, according to *Billboard* magazine. It stayed atop the country chart for ten weeks in 1958, reached number 14 on the pop chart, and helped make Johnny Cash into a teen idol. Interestingly,

Sam Phillips did not like the song and initially refused to release it. No doubt the happy ending of the girl who leaves Hollywood after becoming a star, and ultimately gives up all her fame and fortune to come back to the boy next door, "who worked at the candy store" helped make it the smash hit it became. Clement wrote the song about a beautiful young brunette named Barbara Pittman, a friend and neighbor of Elvis Presley. Elvis introduced her to Sam Phillips, and Pittman became one of the few female artists signed to Sun. Clement was in love with her: they dated, he produced her session, and she became the inspiration for his song. Clement had recorded the song himself and planned on releasing it until Cash expressed interest in it. Cash was the label's big star at the time, and Clement figured it would be in his best interest to let Cash have it. Cash would revive the song for his Mercury records album *Water from the Wells of Home*, in 1988 as a collaboration with the Everly Brothers and his daughter Rosanne Cash. That version made it to number 45, thirty-two years after the original first charted.

"Big River," the B-side of "The Ballad of a Teenage Queen," reached number 4 on the country chart in 1958. Cash wrote this song in the backseat of a car in White Plains, New York, after reading an article about himself titled, "Johnny Cash Has the Big River Blues in His Voice" (Turner, 74). According to Waylon Jennings in his autobiography, Cash was influenced to write the song after listening to delta blues singers like Robert Johnson and Pink Anderson (Jennings, *Waylon*, 345). "Big River" was originally conceived as a slow, twelve-bar blues. Sam Phillips preferred to pick up the song's tempo and asked Jack Clement to rearrange it. The result is undoubtedly one of Cash's finest compositions. The poetic lyric tells the story of a rambler who "taught the weeping willow how to cry, and showed the clouds how to cover up a clear blue sky." He goes off in search of his dream girl, whom he met accidentally in St. Paul, Minnesota. The woman in question has rambling in her blood, and the narrator follows her to Davenport, Iowa, St. Louis, Memphis, and Baton Rouge where he gives up and realizes that, "she loves you, Big River, more than me." Johnny would perform this song throughout his entire career, rerecording it many times. Most notably, he revisited it with the Highwaymen (himself, Willie Nelson, Waylon Jennings, and Kris Kristofferson) on their debut album in 1985, wherein he reinstated a fourth verse that Waylon sang about searching for her in Natchez, Mississippi, but not finding her there. Cash also recorded a duet version with Bob Dylan for the legendary (and unreleased) Nashville sessions. The Grateful Dead covered it, as did the Band.

The Shortest Song

On April 9, 1958, Cash entered the studio with Jack Clement and crew to work on "Come In Stranger" and record two brand-new tracks. "Guess Things Happen That Way" is a song of resignation and realization from the pen of Clement. This was Cash's second longest-reigning number 1 single, remaining in the top spot for eight weeks in 1958. It also brought him his highest charting hit on the pop chart thus far, reaching number 11 nationwide. It's a simple song about a man coming to terms with the loss of his lady, admitting "I don't like it but I guess things happen that way." It was the perfect country-pop crossover for Cash with its doo-wop intro and catchy lyric. Clocking in at one minute forty-eight seconds, this song also holds the distinction of being one of the shortest songs ever to top the country chart and reach the pop Top 20. In 1997, on the *VH1 Storytellers: Johnny Cash & Willie Nelson* album Cash explained that Jack Clement had told Cash he had stolen the melody for the song from the 1926 hit "When the Red, Red Robin (Comes Bob, Bob, Bobbin' Along)." Cash admitted that he never realized it when he recorded the song.

The second new song they tackled was "Oh, Lonesome Me," which was written by Don Gibson. Cash imbues it with his own brand of heartache when he admits "Everybody's going out and having fun, I'm just a fool for staying home and having none." It was a great song for Cash, and Sun released it as a single in 1961, three years after he had left the label. It's testament to the power of this performance that the song made it to number 13 on the country chart and number 93 on the pop chart, higher than he was charting with some of his newer Columbia singles. Songwriter Don Gibson reached number 1 country with the song in 1958, and number 7 pop. This was Cash's last charting Sun single for eight years, until Sun reissued "Get Rhythm" in 1969.

One month later, Cash returned to the studio to record three sessions during May 1958. The first track he laid down was "Sugartime," which was written by Charlie Phillips and Odis Echols. Johnny recorded this timely track a year after the McGuire Sisters took it to the top of the pop chart. With a full backing band and chorus, he turned it into a good-time country sing-along. With his now-signature *boom-chicka-boom* rhythm, the song is a standout for its infectious beat and feel-good flavor.

"You're the Nearest Thing to Heaven" has a hauntingly beautiful lyric with distinct poetic overtones and was written by Cash, Hoyt Johnson, and Jimmy Atkins. The singer relates all the wondrous things he's seen in God's creation, but his sweetheart is the "nearest thing to heaven on this earth." While Cash had arranged and adapted songs at Sun, this was a rare cowrite, and only one of four he would cowrite while at Sun. Through the years Johnny would collaborate on songs with other writers, but this was, arguably, one of his fin-

est. It was issued as the B-side of "The Ways of a Woman in Love" in 1958 and reached number 5 on the country chart.

After the ethereal "Heaven," Cash chose to cover Frankie Brown's "Born to Lose." This song was undoubtedly the saddest song Cash had recorded thus far. Its sparse, mournful lyrics are about a man who has lost everything, and cries, "Born to lose, I've lived my life in vain, every dream has only brought me pain, all my life I've always been so blue, born to lose and now I'm losing you." Cash brilliantly conveys the narrator's sense of extreme pain and misery. Cash's performance of this song emotes pure sorrow, and was one of his most compelling vocals to date. The song was originally a number 3 country hit for Texas singer-songwriter Ted Daffan in 1944. Ray Charles's version would make it to number 41 on the pop chart in 1962. While many have recorded this heartbreaking ballad, Cash's rendition is among the finest.

"Always Alone" is another lonely lament about a hopeless man who is left alone by the one he loves. Written by Daffan, this obscure ballad fits Cash nicely, but it pales in comparison to "Born to Lose." It's one of the lesser-known of Cash's Sun recordings, although among a lesser body of work it would have stood out.

"Story of a Broken Heart" proved to be yet another first-rate Cash performance on a lovelorn lament with a rare writer's credit by Sam Phillips.

The song tells of the singer's dreading the coming of spring, when wedding bells will be ringing for his loved one. He's left with only his memories of when they were together. The ultimate heartache comes when his former love asks him to give her away in marriage.

It was during this session that Cash recorded "You Tell Me," his first Roy Orbison penned ballad. Along with Elvis, Jerry Lee Lewis, and Carl Perkins, legendary singer-songwriter Roy Orbison also started his career at Sun. He enjoyed his first charting single, "Ooby Dooby," in 1956 while working at Sun. Cash and Orbison formed a lifelong friendship, and this song by Orbison started it all. It almost feels incomplete, however, and while Cash tries to inhabit it, it does remain simply a noble attempt in his canon of songs.

"Life Goes On" is a songwriting collaboration between Cash and Clement. These two talented individuals would become great friends and continue to work together throughout their lives. "Life Goes On" features a strong vocal performance by Cash on a well-written ballad of losing love, rationalizing that "time goes by and life goes on." In fact, this would have been a worthy single had Phillips opted to release it.

The Hank Williams Recordings

In May 1958 Cash devoted two recording sessions to Hank Williams's songs. This might have been Cash's way to easily fulfill his contractual obligation to Sun, while at the same time recording songs he knew well and had already been performing. The first song selected was "You Win Again." Hank's own version of "You Win Again" made the country Top 10 in 1952, as did the B-side of "Settin' the Woods on Fire." In April 1958 Jerry Lee Lewis took "You Win Again" to number 4 on the country chart as the B-side of "Great Balls of Fire." In 1980, country hit-maker Charley Pride finally took it to number 1. The theme and lyric was a natural fit for Cash, as the heartbroken lover pines for the woman who has left him for someone else. Hank's lyrics, infused with passion, and sharp lines like "just trusting you was my great sin, what can I do, you win again" make this song a standout.

Next, Cash covered "I Could Never Be Ashamed of You," and he delivers a formidable performance of this lesser-known Hank Williams composition. No matter what other people have to say about the singer's loved one, and even though she's proved to be untrue, his love for her is so strong that he can forgive her all her indiscretions and never be ashamed of anything she did or does. This might have been a good choice of single for Cash since Hank never charted with it himself.

Cash's recording of "Cold, Cold Heart" is a noteworthy cover of an oft-recorded Williams standard. This was one of Hank's great signature songs that the songwriter took to number 1 on the country chart in 1951. Tony Bennett took it to number 1 on the pop chart that same year. Labelmate Jerry Lee Lewis charted twice with it, in 1961 and 1979. It is a true testament to Cash's talent as an interpreter of song that he is able to embody such a scathing lyric of heartbreak and insecurity. In 1958, when "Cold, Cold Heart" was recorded, Cash's home life was relatively stable, yet he could easily convey the persona of the wounded, hurt, or dejected lover in song. When he sings "Another love before my time made your heart sad and blue / and so my heart is paying now for things I didn't do," we feel his frustration and inability to convince his lover that he will not hurt her. While Hank was living these songs as he wrote them, Cash had the luxury of not having to have gone through the pain at the time. But one would never know it by the way he performs these songs.

"Hey, Good Lookin'" shows off both Williams's and Cash's ease and charm with a classic come-on to a beautiful woman. Hank topped the charts with his version in 1951. It's a fresh, frisky change of pace for Cash as he sets his sights on one girl and gets ready to "throw my date-book over the fence." There's sparseness in Williams's lyrics that Cash easily tapped into and, as a result, was able to embody in the song.

For the final Williams song, Cash and Clement chose "I Can't Help It (if I'm Still in Love with You)," one of Hank Williams's harshest lyrics. The pain seems to bleed through every line and Cash gives the song everything he's got. The spurned lover sees his loved one walking down the street with somebody new and is terrified by the sight. We feel the hurt and pain as he sings "it's hard to know another's lips will kiss you / and hold you just the way I used to do." Hank reached number 2 on the country chart with it in 1951, and almost twenty-five years later Linda Ronstadt reached the same position. Cash's version was never released as a single.

After covering the Hank Williams songbook, Cash recorded songwriter Billy Smith's "Blue Train." This was another train metaphor that equated losing a love with riding on a blue train. The singer will ride the blue train until he learns to smile again. By now, Sun writers knew precisely how to write for Cash, and this song is a perfect example. Although Cash did not write it, you would think he had written it.

"Katy Too," cowritten by Cash and Clement, would be the last song Cash wrote or cowrote for Sun. The prevailing thought was that Cash was saving his new compositions for Columbia, where he would begin recording a few months later. "Katy Too" is a light, clever play on words, in which the singer lists all his girlfriends and what each does best. Although he can't make up his mind, and would like to marry all of them, he still misses "ol' Katy," too. It was released as a single by Sun in 1959, and reached number 11 on the country chart and number 66 pop.

Final Sun Sessions

In July 1958, Cash returned to the studio for his final sessions at Sun. There were no original Cash compositions in the mix. The first song recorded was songwriter Danny Wolfe's "Fools Hall of Fame." Cash sings convincingly about a man who has his name hung in the fools' hall of fame over his love for a woman. He's sorry for doing her wrong and begs her forgiveness, singing "don't leave me here in shame, in the fools' hall of fame." It's a clever conceit, and the song works well for Cash.

Cash scored his last big Sun hit with "The Ways of a Woman in Love," a Charlie Rich and Bill Justis cowrite about a man who senses his woman is falling in love with another man. She's changing her ways, and it's killing the singer. He can't stop thinking about her and wishing he was the other guy. This fine ballad made it to number 2 on the country chart and number 24 pop. Just over two months later Johnny would issue his first single for Columbia. In *Johnny Cash: The Autobiography* the singer writes, regarding Charlie Rich, "To my mind, he was the best thing to hit Sun since Elvis" (114).

"Thanks A Lot" was another strong Charlie Rich composition about a guy who sarcastically thanks his lover for all the pain she's putting him through. We feel the singer's hurt as he watches his lover leave him for somebody new. The song was the B-side of "Luther Played the Boogie," which was officially released as a single in 1959 after Cash had left Sun for Columbia.

"It's Just About Time" is a solid Jack Clement ballad with a honky-tonk flavor. Just about the time the singer thinks it's over for him and his careless love, he starts missing her. Sun rush-released this song as a single, hot on the heels of Johnny's second Columbia single, "Don't Take Your Guns to Town." Despite all the attention surrounding that Columbia single, "It's Just About Time" made it to number 30 on the country chart and number 47 pop.

Charlie Rich was having great success writing songs for Cash. "I Just Thought You'd Like to Know" was a fine example of how the future country star had tapped into the Cash persona and was writing songs tailor-made for his unique style. It's another honky-tonk-infused tale of a woman getting ready to leave her lover and the pain it's causing the singer. Charlie Rich would struggle to find his place in country music for the next fifteen years before hitting it big in 1973 with "Behind Closed Doors."

It's interesting to note that Johnny recorded his version of "I Forgot to Remember to Forget," Elvis's first number 1 country hit from 1955, during his last session for Sun Records. The song was cowritten by Stan Kesler and Charlie Feathers. Kesler was a steel-guitar player who worked at Sun, and Feathers was a recording artist at the label. Cash must have always felt an affinity for

February 1959 performance.

Photo: Don Hunstein © Sony Music Entertainment

the song, and he certainly succeeds in imbuing it with his own inimitable style. It's a great song about still pining for a loved one, and had Elvis not had such success with it, Cash might have enjoyed another smash single of his own with it.

"Down the Street to 301" was the last track Cash recorded at Sun Studios, courtesy of Charlie Rich. It's a story about a boy who is dating the girl who lives at 301. It appears that they were aiming for a song, and a sound, similar to Cash's giant hit "Ballad of a Teenage Queen." It almost feels like a follow-up to that song, with its doo-wop harmonies and pop production. It was never released as a single, but certainly stands as a fitting finale to Cash's incredible Sun recording career. On July 17, Cash completed his final recording session for Sun Records in Memphis. On July 29, Cash and Vivian welcomed their third daughter, Cindy, as they made plans to leave Memphis and move to California. On July 24, 1958, Johnny began work on his debut album for Columbia Records in Nashville, before officially signing his contract with the label on August 1, 1958. Because Sun Records was a singles oriented company, only one Cash LP was released during his tenure there: *Johnny Cash with His Hot and Blue Guitar*, released on September 10, 1957. A little over a year later, on November 17, 1958, Sun issued the album *Johnny Cash Sings the Songs That Made Him Famous*. He had already signed with Columbia Records at that time, and would release his first Columbia album that same month.

In October of 1959, Sun released *Greatest! Johnny Cash*, which despite the title was not a greatest hits collection, but rather a compilation of more recent singles including "Goodbye Little Darlin'," "It's Just About Time," "Katy Too," "Thanks A Lot" and "Luther Played the Boogie," the highest charting track from the album that reached No. 8 in March of 1959.

Columbia
Stereo
C 30550

Johnny Cash

Man In Black

The Preacher Said, "Jesus Said" (with Billy Graham)

Orphan Of The Road
You've Got A New Light
Shining In Your Eyes
If Not For Love
Man In Black

Singin' In Viet Nam Talkin' Blues

Ned Kelly
Look For Me
   (with June Carter Cash)
Dear Mrs.
I Talk To Jesus Every Day
   (with June Carter Cash)

Chapter 3

WHAT IS TRUTH

SONGS OF PERSONAL CONVICTION

Johnny Cash's brave attempt to record
songs that made a difference

Johnny Cash never shied away from expressing his heartfelt beliefs in song. In this regard, he was the consummate folk singer who believed that his true calling in life was to entertain and educate his audience, using a variety of different musical styles. Like Woody Guthrie and Pete Seeger before him, Cash was not afraid to record songs that took a hard stand. These were the songs that mattered most to him. Cash's catalog of recorded songs is vital because he always attempted to sing songs that made a difference. Through the years Cash had proudly hosted what he called "guitar pulls" where friends, fellow artists, and songwriters would join

together at Cash's house, pass around a guitar and play their songs for each other all night long. One such memorable evening occurred in 1969 and included artists like Joni Mitchell, Graham Nash, Bob Dylan, Shel Silverstein, and Kris Kristofferson. In "Songs That Make a Difference," we learn that this was the night Kristofferson sang "Me and Bobby McGee" for the first time and Joni Mitchell performed "Both Sides Now." Cash captures this momentous event in detail, and recalls in the song's lyrics that, "we sang songs that made a difference, and we can again somehow." It's a plea from Cash to "keep it from the heart and down to earth, sing the songs that make a difference, give

« Man In Black. *Courtesy of Sony Music Entertainment.*

us all our money's worth." Those are the kind of songs that we carry with us throughout our lives, and Cash wrote and recorded many of them.

In 1970, at the height of his popularity, Cash wrote and released the single "What Is Truth." In the Bible, Pontius Pilate posed the question "What is truth?" before he went out to tell the Jews that he found no basis for their charges against Jesus. Johnny chose to follow up his hit duet "If I Were a Carpenter" with this daring song of empathy with the young people of the day. It would have been easy for him to release another love song or ballad, but that never was his motivation. Instead he used his celebrity to defend the youth, who he felt were being judged and persecuted for their appearance and their beliefs. In his introduction to his performance of the song at the White House on April 17, 1970, Cash explains that "What Is Truth" was originally written as a twelve-verse poem to the youth of America from which he pulled four verses for the recorded version. He further explains in the presence of President Richard M. Nixon, that he wrote it on the side of the youth, which is the way he was feeling at the time.

This song ranks with the most important songs in Cash's catalog. For a nearing elder statesman of country music to point the finger at his own generation, and defy popular opinion and stand up with the longhaired younger generation, was unheard of. He openly supported their right to wear the clothes they wanted, grow their hair as long as they liked it, and speak out about the things that mattered to them. He bravely reprimanded the elders, proclaiming, "Yeah, the ones that you're calling wild / are gonna be the leaders in a little while. . . . This whole world's waking to a newborn day / and I solemnly swear that it'll be their way." This song was never included on an album at the time despite its success as a single. It was a number 3 country hit and made the pop Top 20. "What Is Truth" epitomized what Johnny Cash stood for then and what his artistic legacy stands for now.

Musical Preacher

Cash embraced the role of musical preacher, and even dressed the part by always appearing in black. As people wondered why Cash always wore black, Cash found the opportunity to address their curiosity in song. Cash explained on *The Mike Douglas Show* in 1981 why he wore black. He said, "The first concert I ever did in public I think was in a church in North Memphis, and the band and I were trying to find shirts alike, and the only thing we had alike was black. So, it'd be better for church anyway. So, it kinda felt good that day and we stuck with it." Cash may have conveniently forgotten that he wore red suits at his early shows, as well as white linen sportjackets, before adopting the all-black look years later.

Over the years the color of Cash's garments would take on added significance. More than a performer in a church, he became the preacher who preached his message to the world through his songs. Cash wrote "Man in Black" to perform for the student body of Vanderbilt University in Nashville. He always perceived himself to be the voice of the people, and this protest song allowed him to express his deepest views on various subjects. As he had done earlier with songs like "The Ballad of Ira Hayes" and "What Is Truth," "Man in Black" finds Cash wholeheartedly taking on the cause of the poor and the beaten down, the prisoners, the illiterates, the drug addicts, the soldiers who were dying for our freedom overseas, the sick and lonely elderly, all the ones who've been held back by societal constraints: "But 'til we start to make a move to make a few things right / You'll never see me wear a suit of white." The song was a powerful commentary on contemporary society and a plea for understanding, change, and the end of injustice. It was released as the first single from the album of the same name and made it to number 3 on the country chart, and number 58 pop.

Not even the president of the United States could persuade Cash to shed his values when Cash performed at the White House in Washington, DC, in 1970. Cash, the Tennessee Three, Carl Perkins, the Carter Family, and the Statler Brothers were invited to perform for President Richard M. Nixon at the White House. Nixon requested Cash perform the songs "Okie from Muskogee," and "Welfare Cadillac." Both songs were hits at the time for Merle Haggard and Guy Drake, respectively. And both songs were satirical but could be viewed as right-wing expressions of disdain for the youth and counterculture. "Welfare Cadillac" in particular was a slap at the welfare system, wherein a fellow collects welfare money only to buy a Cadillac and laugh at those who paid their taxes. According to Antonino D'Ambrosio, in his essay "The Bitter Tears Of Johnny Cash," Cash's response to Nixon upon his song request was, "I don't know those songs, but I got a few of my own I can play for you." Nixon and the White House audience were treated to songs like "What Is Truth," Cash's defense of youth and freedom of expression, followed by Cash expressing his antiwar sentiments.

Cash also voiced his personal views regarding the Civil War. He reached number 24 on the country chart in 1962 with "The Big Battle," an intriguing story-song set against the backdrop of the Civil War. It tells of the aftermath of the battle when all that's left are the dead and the dying with the "blue lying alongside the gray." It's a harsh recounting of the tragic toll that war takes on everyone on either side. There's an ominous feel to the song, as Cash successfully paints a devastating portrait of the high cost of war. This is one of Cash's most thought-out and fully developed compositions. The song drives home the message that the repercussions of war never cease and the battle goes on long after the fighting is over.

Cash's southern birthright is further explored in the song "God Bless Robert E. Lee," from the

1983 album *Johnny 99*. Cash seems to be truly immersed in his performance of this compelling Civil War saga that celebrates the Confederate general, penned by songwriters Bobby Borchers and Mack Vickery. The song salutes Robert E. Lee for choosing to surrender to Grant at Appomattox, rather than risk the loss of more lives in battle. The premise of the song is of a young man going off to fight with the general in order to preserve his beloved Dixie. In the introduction to the song, Cash claims that this is not about the North or the South, but we can sense his allegiance in the sneering way he pronounces the name, "Ulysses S. Grant."

Texas folksinger and songwriter Jane Bowers wrote "Remember the Alamo." It recounts the harrowing last days before the Alamo fell and the last stand of Mexican general Santa Anna at the hands of freedom fighters, including Jim Bowie and Davy Crockett, so that Texas could become sovereign and free. Tex Ritter was the first to record it in 1955, along with the Kingston Trio and pop-folk singer Donovan. Cash was immersing himself in the then-growing folk movement, and he may have discovered this song on the Kingston Trio's 1959 album, *The Kingston Trio at Large*. As usual, Cash put everything he had into the song and made it even more memorable. It was originally released as part of the four-song 1959 EP, *Johnny Cash Sings the Rebel-Johnny Yuma*.

The Vietnam War

Cash was not afraid to voice his opinion on the issues of the day. The war in Vietnam was an unpopular war and, while many country entertainers preferred to stay out of the debate, Cash had no such desire. While he opposed American involvement in Vietnam, he supported our troops and took his show to Vietnam to play for them. What resulted was the song "Singin' in Vietnam Talkin' Blues," a dramatic account of that experience and a plea to bring U.S. troops back home. He passionately sings "we did our best to let them know that we care," before declaring, "I hope that war is over with and they all come back home to stay in peace." It would have been one thing to leave the song as simply an album track, but Cash insisted that it be released as a single, which would gain it wide exposure. Despite its controversial subject matter, the single did make it to number 18 on the country chart. The country audience at the time was very conservative, but that didn't stop Cash from insisting the song be released.

Cash continued to express his views on the global situation at the time. When he performed a concert at New York's Madison Square Garden on December 5, 1969, he included a moving rendition of folksinger-songwriter Ed McCurdy's anti-war classic "Last Night I Had the Strangest Dream." Performers such as Pete Seeger, Joan Baez, and

Simon and Garfunkel had previously recorded the song. Garth Brooks would also release a respectable cover of the song in 2005. This was the only new song included on the 2002 release (of the 1969 performance) *Johnny Cash at Madison Square Garden,* and it's impressive. The song's opening lines are, "Last night I had the strangest dream I've ever known before / I dreamed that all the world agreed to put an end to war." Cash explains his views regarding the Vietnam War in the song's spoken introduction. He explains that he took his show to perform for the service men stationed in Vietnam and offers a one-liner about a reporter asking him if that makes him a "hawk," a term used to describe someone who supported the war effort. Cash explains that, no, he's not a hawk, but after seeing what went on there and all the wounded, he might be described as a "dove with claws."

"Route #1, Box 144," from Cash's 1970 album *Hello, I'm Johnny Cash,* tells the story of a soldier who was killed in action fighting for our country. He grew up on a small farm, married his high-school sweetheart, though even in town only a few people knew him. It's a song that celebrates the sacrifice of a common man who "never did great things to be remembered . . . but you'd have thought that he was president or something, at Route one, Box 144." Johnny's empathy and dedication to these unsung heroes permeates many of his finest ballads, and this heart-wrenching narrative is no exception.

Cash wrote the song "Drive On," which finds the narrator recounting the story of his time spent in Vietnam along with his friend, Tex. Listeners are taken for a trip back in time, full of vivid imagery of the old soldier's struggles while serving in Vietnam. In this song Cash embodies the persona of an old soldier who is still trying to come to terms with what he witnessed and experienced during that cruel war. The narrator knows his family loves him, but still they don't understand what he has had to endure. The final verse finds the narrator having to deal with the death of his friend and the guilt associated with being a survivor. Originally included on Cash's 1994 album, *American Recordings,* he also performed the song on the 1998 release *VH1 Storytellers: Johnny Cash & Willie Nelson.* Cash explains that he and June had read "all the books about Vietnam" and how the title refers to language used by soldiers as a way to deal with a tough situation. For example, he explains, "If a guy would lose his leg they would say, 'drive on, it don't mean nothin',' when it really meant everything."

"Like a Soldier," from Cash's 1994 *American Recordings* album, while not specifically a war song, is rather a personal treatise on aging and looking back on one's life in the twilight years. The singer informs us that he's like a soldier getting over the war, which becomes a metaphor for his life. He's thankful for his life's journey and glad that he survived the battles. The singer is coming to terms with his life and offering us a deeper understanding of what we have to look forward to.

Possibly Cash's most devastating antiwar song is his cover of John Prine's "Sam Stone." "Sam Stone" was recorded in 1987 for a concert for the show *Austin City Limits*. The live album of this show was released in 2005. Cash had been working on this song in the studio for a while, but it was never released. He explains in the song's introduction that Kris Kristofferson introduced him to the music of John Prine, and this tune in particular. "Sam Stone" is one of John Prine's finest compositions. It tells the harrowing tale of a returning veteran who comes back from war a broken, drug addicted man. The tragic saga includes such stark lines as "There's a hole in daddy's arm where all the money goes." Interestingly, Cash changes the next line of the song from Prine's original, "And Jesus Christ died for nothing I suppose," to "Daddy must have suffered a lot back then, I suppose." As a Christian, Cash may have had difficulty singing Prine's original line. It's still a great song, and a worthy performance by Cash, but changing the line also diminishes the impact of Prine's song, as the original lyrics convey the ravages of war and a godless world. Sam Stone ultimately goes to work to make enough money to feed his drug habit, where "the gold rolled through his veins like a thousand railroad trains," and ultimately the song's tragic ending leaves us shaken and reeling from Sam Stone's final act of desperation. He trades the house that he bought on the G.I. Bill for "a flag-draped casket on a local hero's hill."

Injustice and Inequality

Cash wrote "All God's Children Ain't Free" about injustice and inequality. It was included on his 1965 album *Orange Blossom Special*. Cash would regularly take on the plight of the downtrodden, and this song is a perfect example of Cash standing up for the rights of certain individuals. This song is a precursor to later Cash songs like "What Is Truth" and "Man in Black," as he explains, "I'm gonna sing the blues for the man they done wrong, 'cause all God's children ain't free." The poor, the beaten down, and the prisoner are all mentioned in this song, wherein Cash begins moving further into his role as a reformer who would use his fame for the betterment of society.

"All God's Children" follows in the footsteps of folk songs written by Guthrie and Seeger. Cash paid homage to Guthrie in his recording of Bob Dylan's "Song to Woody," along with Earl Scruggs. Cash also joined forces with Willie Nelson and Johnny Rodriguez on a cover of the Guthrie classic, "Deportee (Plane Wreck at Los Gatos)." It tells the true story of a plane crash that occurred on January 29, 1948, during the deportation of a group of Mexican farmworkers from California. It's a well-written protest song that tells a harrowing story of mistreatment and cruelty and the ultimate price paid by innocent people. Cash opens the song explaining the sad scenario of how they're flying the poor Mexican migrant workers back to Mexico just so they can wade back across the river to find refuge in America. Johnny Rodriguez, himself a Mexican, sings the second verse about the family's history of trying to cross the river, with some dying in the hills and others in the valleys, as they were chased down. Cash sings the third verse with Willie, explaining how the deportees are chased like outlaws and rustlers and thieves. And finally, Cash and Willie describe the horrific plane crash with the nameless individuals who will only be known as deportees. Thirty-two people died in that crash, and Woody Guthrie wrote a song worthy of their tragic legacy. Many artists have recorded this song, including Pete Seeger, Joan Baez, Peter, Paul and Mary, and, of course, Woody Guthrie.

Cash and Waylon Jennings recorded Kristofferson's moving ballad "Love Is the Way" for their 1986 duet album *Heroes*. It's a spiritual song, conveying the message that our world may be doomed if we do not change our ways and realize that love is the only way left for us to survive this turmoil. The brave lyrics explain, "The warriors are waving their old rusty sabers and preachers are preaching a gospel of hate / by their behavior determined to teach us a lesson we're soon to be learning too late." It's a true antiwar protest song and a warning for us to stop before it's too late. The song is

not about politics, but rather about humanity and what we all must do to remedy the situation while we can. Kris included his version of the song on his 1986 album *Repossessed*.

In 1985, Cash released the Kristofferson-penned "They Killed Him." It was one of Johnny's last singles for Columbia Records. And, in truth, it's as potent and powerful a song as Cash had ever recorded. It tells of the tragic fate of historical visionaries who endured great suffering and ultimately death in order to hold onto their beliefs and convictions. Cash sings about Mahatma Gandhi, Martin Luther King, John and Robert Kennedy, and Jesus Christ, all heroic figures who bravely died for peace. Whereas Dion more quietly reflected on the plight of good men who died for their cause in "Abraham, Martin and John," in this song Cash boldly states the fact that these holy men were brutally killed for their ideology. Unfortunately, the song did not chart for Cash. Kristofferson recorded it himself for his *Repossessed* album in 1986, and Bob Dylan covered it on his *Knocked Out Loaded* album the same year.

Interestingly, Cash recorded a laid-back guitar and vocal demo of Larry Murray's "Six White Horses," that names our fallen leaders as their achievements are celebrated and they are carried through history on six white horses. John F. Kennedy, Martin Luther King, and Robert Kennedy are remembered and eulogized and mourned because they were taken away before they could sing their song. Much like Dion's classic "Abraham, Martin and John," this song addresses these tragedies head on. Johnny's brother Tommy recorded it and took it to number 4 on the country chart in 1969. Waylon Jennings also covered it on his album *The Taker/Tulsa* in 1971.

American Patriot

Johnny Cash was an American patriot in the truest sense of the word. He loved his country and proved his love for it by entertaining soldiers the world over throughout his career. Cash is often regarded as a type of mythical figure whose political views are sometimes thought to mirror those of right-wing American icons like John Wayne. The truth of the matter is that Cash was a political anomaly. He was not right or left, but stood squarely on the side of the common man, the misunderstood, the disenfranchised, all the individuals he embraced in songs like "What Is Truth." If anything, Cash stood for the politics of inclusion, and at heart he was more a Democrat than the conservative he was sometimes mistakenly thought to be.[1]

In December 1996 Cash received the Kennedy Center Lifetime Achievement Award, honoring his incredible body of work. Kris Kristofferson, Emmylou Harris, and Lyle Lovett were there to salute him by performing a selection of his hits. Longtime friend of the family, Vice President Al Gore had nominated him for the honor. Gore's father had known June since she was a little girl performing with her family on Nashville's WSM radio. When Gore was elected to Congress, his district included Hendersonville, where Cash lived. In a letter Gore wrote while visiting Branson, Missouri, he recalled, "As I got to know Johnny Cash the man, I loved his music much more — not for the normal reason that you appreciate the work of your friends, but because it was just obvious at close range that what made his songs so great was that the man himself was deep, deep, deep."

April 1974 saw the release of the album *Ragged Old Flag*. After relying for the most part on songs by other writers, Johnny decided to record an album comprised of twelve songs that he had written himself. *Ragged Old Flag* allowed Cash to creatively return to his songwriting roots. His liner notes for the album reflect his enthusiasm for this project, as he writes, "I got so excited writing songs for this album that you'd think I just started in the music business. It's something I always wanted to do, write an album of all my own songs and for some reason, I just never got around to it." Cash coproduced the album with his friend, recording engineer Charlie Bragg. The result is an album of songs that reflect what Cash had on his mind in 1974: the sad state of our country's affairs after the Watergate scandal, as well as water pollution, and his general observations on life, love, and God at the time. The album included one single and reached number 16 on the country album chart. The cover of *Ragged Old Flag* presents a denim-clad Cash pointing at a tattered American flag waving behind him.

"Ragged Old Flag" is the song that Cash says in his liner notes came the easiest to him. He writes, "I didn't even have control over it. It came out faster than I could write it down. You've heard of people who write songs in ten minutes. 'Ragged Old Flag' was one of those songs." While the song didn't become a hit (it only reached number 31 on the country chart), it has become one of his most identifiable compositions. Cash titled a chapter in his autobiography, *Man in Black*, after this song, and wrote, "I love my country so much and believe in it so strongly. A lot of family blood has been shed for it. It's that American heritage which compelled me to write 'Ragged Old Flag'" (58). It's an honest narrative about a man who happens upon an old man sitting on a park bench in a small town square and inquires about the ragged old flag hanging in front of the courthouse. The old man proceeds to explain to him what that flag symbolizes to him by taking the narrator on a virtual tour of the American past. It's a stunning recitation by Cash backed by Earl Scruggs's banjo and Chuck Cochran's lovely orchestration. It was recorded at a Columbia luncheon at the House of Cash on January 28, 1974, and the applause at the end of the song is from Columbia Records executives.

Cash recorded a dramatic recitation of "I Am the Nation" in 1974. It was originally written in 1955 as a public relations advertisement for the Norfolk and Western Railway company magazine and updated in 1976. The narrator personifies our country and takes us on a journey recalling America's hard-won freedom. It's an eternal poem of love to the nation. It's Cash channeling the ghost of Walt Whitman as he celebrates the sights, sounds, and individuals who make America so special. "I Am the Nation" appeared for the first time on the 2008 album, *Johnny Cash's America.*

Cash wrote the topical "Sold Out of Flagpoles" for his 1976 album *One Piece at a Time.* The song finds Cash conversing with his friend Lonnie, who runs a handy hardware store. They converse about the happenings of the day, specifically the bicentennial and the upcoming presidential election. Lonnie offers Cash his words of wisdom on various topics before informing him that "we're sold out of flagpoles." The song is a bit disjointed in its random cataloging of thoughts and observations, and there might have been a better choice for a follow-up single to "One Piece at a Time." "Sold Out of Flagpoles" made it to number 29 on the country chart, certainly a bit of a letdown after the two-week number 1 reign of "One Piece at a Time."

"Song of the Patriot," written by Marty Robbins and Shirl Milete, was recorded during the sessions for *Rockabilly Blues* in 1980, but not included on the album. Earl Poole Ball produced this track and it features Robbins on harmony vocals. The song was first listed on the recording ledgers as "Flag Wavin'" and is a whole-hearted patriotic effort that lets

The Johnny Cash Show with Bob Hope. *Courtesy of Sony Music Entertainment.*

Cash express his pride and passion for his country, as a self-proclaimed "flag-wavin' patriotic nephew of my Uncle Sam, a rough-ridin', fightin' Yankee man." Even though Cash always stood up for the underdog and expressed his own views without reservation, this is the kind of song that has led folks to view him as a staunch patriot, not unlike John Wayne. "Song of the Patriot" made it to only number 54 on the country chart in 1980, although it holds up well today and has been included in numerous patriotic music compilations.

In 1991, Sony Legacy released the Cash compilation album Patriot, featuring ten tracks culled from Cash's Columbia recordings. There's no doubt that two of Cash's favorite themes were God and country. He could always be counted on to write or record songs that expressed his deep-rooted faith in God and his unwavering love of country. The questions he posed and the topics he addressed helped define him as the most sincere type of patriot, who carried a torch and shone a light on all the injustice he witnessed in his beloved America.

Johnny Cash was more Jimmy Stewart than John Wayne, and his views and beliefs will continue to inspire and encourage generations to come to speak out and voice their views on equality and justice for all.

STEREO

STEREO
CS 8255

REGULAR
CL 1464

JOHNNY CASH
RIDE THIS TRAIN

A Stirring Travelogue of America in Song and Story

LOADING COAL
SLOW RIDER
LUMBERJACK
DORRAINE OF PONCHARTRAIN
GOING TO MEMPHIS
WHEN PAPA PLAYED THE DOBRO
BOSS JACK
OLD DOC BROWN

Chapter 4

THE BALLAD OF IRA HAYES

THE CONCEPT ALBUMS

A close examination of the unique concept albums
Johnny Cash recorded for Columbia Records

Johnny Cash had continued writing songs during 1958, but he was holding on to his best compositions, anticipating a move to Columbia Records later that year. Columbia Records offered Cash the freedom to record the songs, and most importantly the albums, he wanted to record. Sun was set up as a singles-oriented label, with albums only appearing at intervals to collect random singles together. Cash was thinking more holistically and conceptually at this point, and Columbia allowed him the opportunity to record cohesive concept albums based on subject matter he was interested in exploring. Add to that the superior sound quality of the recordings and

the money to spend on his various projects. Cash was conflicted about leaving behind Sam Phillips, the man who had taken a chance on him, and moving on to take charge of his career and write and record songs the way he envisioned them.

Don Law, who was head of Columbia Records' country division, brought Cash over to the label because he "was drawn to the sincerity and straightforwardness of Cash's voice as soon as he heard 'Hey, Porter'" (Hilburn, *Johnny Cash: The Life*, 133). Law had worked with blues artists such as Robert Johnson, and he had already produced hits for Ray Price and Marty Robbins. According to Robert Hilburn, Law was aware of

« Ride This Train. *Courtesy of Sony Music Entertainment.*

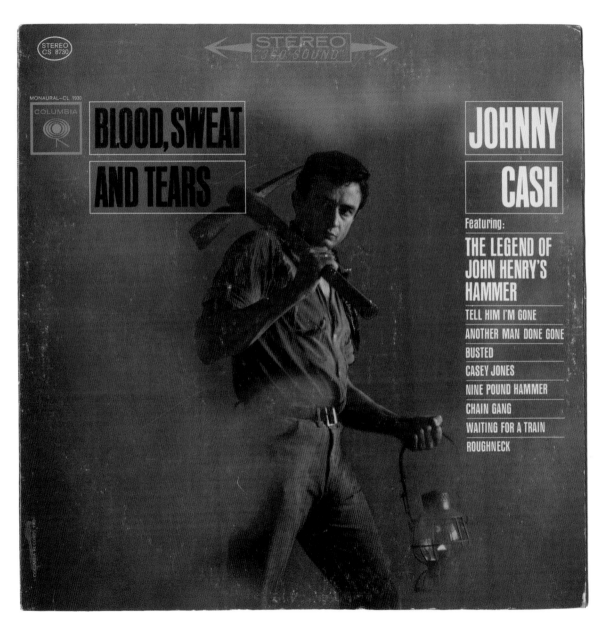

Blood, Sweat and Tears. *Courtesy of Sony Music Entertainment.*

Cash's contract with Sun Records expiring on July 31, 1958, but he wanted to sign him earlier because he believed other labels would be after him. He offered Cash "five cents per record in royalties, two centsmore than Sun, plus a $50,000 signing bonus. He also promised Cash total freedom in the studio" (Hilburn, *Johnny Cash: The Life*, 133). Cash was becoming more and more disillusioned with Sun, feeling that Sam Phillips had turned him over to Jack Clement, who was not as involved in his recordings as Cash would have liked. So Cash accepted Law's offer and signed with Columbia.

The Columbia years form the longest phase of Johnny Cash's recording career, and it was the period that produced his most innovative and successful recordings. The Mercury years would briefly breathe new life into Johnny Cash, and the American Recordings would produce his most compelling and haunting final works, but during the Columbia years Johnny Cash wrote, recorded, and produced some of the most popular albums of his career and some overlooked and underrated albums that deserve to be rediscovered and reevaluated.

A Stirring Travelogue

Cash was an important addition to the Columbia roster, and one of the first artists to record concept albums: musical portraits devoted to one subject. Cash relished the notion that he could compile soundtracks of songs he had written, revived, or discovered along the way. *Ride This Train,* released in September 1960, was Johnny Cash's first complete concept album, with the subtitle *A Stirring Travelogue of America in Song and Story*. Listeners meet coal miners, lumberjacks, cruel work bosses, and gentle, kind-hearted doctors. It's a potpourri of Americana in song and story. Years later, Johnny would include a popular segment on his television show based on this album called "Come Along and Ride This Train." Each song on the album begins with a narration that sets it up, and ultimately the whole album becomes one cohesive railroad journey through the heart and history of America. In *Cash: The Autobiography,* Cash states that he is most proud of the concept albums he recorded between 1960 and 1966, including *Ride This Train*; *Blood, Sweat and Tears*; *Bitter Tears*; and *Ballads of the True West.* He writes, "They brought out voices that weren't commonly heard at the time — voices that were ignored or even suppressed in the entertainment media, not to mention the political and educational establishments — and they addressed subjects I really cared about. I was trying to get at the reality behind some of our country's history" (Cash, *Autobiography*, 263).

Ride This Train opens with "Loading Coal," a Merle Travis coal-mining saga. Travis was born and raised the son of a coal miner in Muhlenberg County, Kentucky. He developed a unique style of guitar picking and later became a noted songwriter and guitarist who wrote the classic "Sixteen

Tons." Cash would cover that song years later on the album *Johnny Cash Is Coming to Town*. Cash had first heard Travis's music on the radio, as a boy growing up in Dyess, Arkansas. He had long admired Travis's authenticity and always wanted to record one of his songs. In "Loading Coal," Cash takes on the persona of a young boy from Beach Creek, Kentucky. He lives in a shotgun shack with his mother and father, a coal miner from Muhlenberg County. The boy and his mother wait for his father to come home from the mine every night with nothing clean but the whites of his eyes. Sadly, the boy can't wait to be a coal miner just like his Pa, when he's big enough to work in the mines. The song continues, informing us that at seventeen, a boy has no choice but to go work in the mines. The sad reality is infused with humor, as the narrator claims he's a "double first cousin to a dat-blame mole." And the song has an upbeat feel that defies the notion that working in the coalmines is a futile and frightening way to make a living. This song was released as the B-side of "Going to Memphis."

From the coalmines of Kentucky the train rolls west. In the song "Slow Rider," the narrator takes on the persona of John Wesley Hardin, the notorious outlaw who was thought to have killed forty men. Now he rides at night hoping to not get caught and maybe settle down in a small town. The song borrows the melody and some lyrics from the western folk ballad "I Ride an Old Paint."

Cash would record the more traditional version of "I Ride an Old Paint" for his concept album *Johnny Cash Sings the Ballads of the True West*.

"Dorraine of Ponchartrain" is one of Cash's finest story-songs. The spoken narration opens in Bogalusa, Louisiana. The narrator paints a beautiful portrait of the pristine lakes and landscape of southern Louisiana. He tells us he came down from Halifax, Nova Scotia, in 1788 with two hundred other Acadians. In their party was a beautiful girl named Dorraine. Sadly, the song itself tells of the ill-fated, tragic love affair and what became of the girl the narrator refers to as "my dark-haired little angel, my belle of Ponchartrain." The song seems to have a direct connection to the mournful A. P. Carter ballads that Cash knew all too well. It's stark, haunting, and unforgettable. This is among the undiscovered gems in the Cash catalog.

The narrator in "Going to Memphis" is from Pine Ridge, Mississippi. He tells of being in a knife fight in a bar in Natchez and ending up on the chain gang. Cash took an old folk song from Alan Lomax and Hollie Dew and added his own arrangement. The song opens with the sound of clanging chains and the singer begging for a drink of water. He wishes he were tied to his girl, Bertha, in Vicksburg, "instead of this ball and chain." He keeps repeating that he's going to Memphis, although he knows he's stuck on the chain gang, with little hope of escape. This song was released as the only single from this album, and it was Cash's first single

Bitter Tears. *Courtesy of Sony Music Entertainment.*

Johnny Cash Sings the Ballads of the True West. *Courtesy of Sony Music Entertainment.*

that failed to chart. Cash would revisit this song during his tenure at American Recordings, and it would be released posthumously as part of his *Unearthed* box set. The song is listed as "I'm Going to Memphis," and in the liner notes he admits that he wrote it after listening to a field recording Alan Lomax had made that contained references about going to Memphis. That's what inspired Cash to write the song, and it has held up very well over the years.

The narrator in Cash's "When Papa Played the Dobro" takes us to a county fair in Chester, South Carolina, for a more lighthearted song. It's about a boy being intrigued by his father's playing the dobro, a resonator guitar, in a dance band. In the song, Papa was a hobo when his son was born and didn't have enough money to pay a doctor, but when the going got real bad, all it took to make him feel better was to play a song on his dobro. This catchy, fun song could have been a single from the album, should they have opted to release it as such.

Country Music Hall of Famer Red Foley wrote "Old Doc Brown." He had written and recorded many hits through the years, including "Smoke on the Water" and "Tennessee Saturday Night." Foley was also Pat Boone's father-in-law and Debby Boone's grandfather. The train carries us to Pella, Iowa, where the narrator and others came in 1847 from Cork, Ireland, during the potato famine. They came to the new world and were lucky to have a doctor like old Doc Brown. His fees were small, if he took any money at all. It's an inspiring story of rural America during the nineteenth century. Although Doc Brown died almost penniless, beside each patient's name in his ledger he wrote "Paid in full." The song nicely sums up the true heart and spirit of our country and the people who helped make it what it is.

The John Henry Saga

In February 1963 Columbia released *Blood, Sweat and Tears.* It was another concept album that focused on songs about the American working man and how his muscle and spirit allowed him to persevere against all odds. Carter Family members Mother Maybelle, Anita, Helen, and June all appear on this album. From this point on, this famous family would become an almost permanent part of the Johnny Cash road show and appear as vocalists on many future albums. *Blood, Sweat and Tears* made it to number 80 on the pop album chart in 1963.

The first song on the album is "The Legend of John Henry's Hammer." From the opening clanging of the hammer to the rails, we are presented with Cash's saga of John Henry, the steel-driving man. June Carter helped Johnny arrange and adapt the song, and clocking in at over eight minutes, it became one of Johnny's most popular concert favorites. Johnny was so caught up hitting two steel bars together during the recording of the song that he didn't realize that his hands had become bloody by the end of the recording. He makes us feel the strength and power of the man who would ultimately beat the new steam drill machine with pure human energy. John Henry epitomized the soul of the American workingman. We get a lesson in humanity in this David-and-Goliath tale of technology versus humanity. When John Henry wonders "Did the Lord say that machines ought to take the place of livin' . . . do engines get rewarded for their steam?" we know the answer and we root for John Henry to beat the soulless steam drill. Other artists had recorded their version of this fable, including Harry Belafonte and Merle Travis, but Cash takes it one step further and makes it an epic tale of an American hero, a love story about John Henry and Polly Ann, and a folk song with a compelling message of hard work, human pride, and determination.

Cash's "Tell Him I'm Gone" follows "The Legend of John Henry's Hammer" with another hammer song that opens with the lines "You can take this hammer, take it to the captain." Cash had become a master of sequencing the songs on his albums, and this is the perfect track to follow "John Henry." The narrator in the song is determined not to take any more abuse, "kicks and whippings," from the captain. There was no room for intolerance towards man in Cash's universe, and he believed he had a podium to help right these wrongs, or at least shine a light on them.

Cash first heard the next song, "Another Man Done Gone," on musicologist Alan Lomax's 1959 documentary album *Blues in the Mississippi Night*, as performed by Vera Hall. This old folk song of persecution and injustice is brutal in its recounting of a man who is hanged from a tree with his children watching. We are never told what crime he committed to deserve such a harsh fate. Cash did not shy away from recording songs that held mankind accountable for its wrongful treatment of individuals. The call-and-response duet, with the great Anita Carter answering Cash's mournful pleas, cuts right to the bone. This type of ballad shows Cash's bravery in bringing to light subjects not usually addressed in popular song.

Harlan Howard's previously discussed "Busted" follows in the sequence, before Cash presents his adaptation of "Casey Jones." It's based on the true story of legendary railroad engineer Casey Jones, born Jonathan Luther Jones on March 14, 1862, in Kentucky. Casey was from Jackson, Tennessee, and worked on the Illinois Central railroad. His run was on the Canton Express, traveling between Memphis, Tennessee, and Canton, Mississippi. He became a folk hero on April 30, 1900, when he and his fireman Sim Webb roared around an S-curve right into the rear of another train. Casey tried hard to stop his train and save the people's lives. The song was written by a black engine wiper from Canton, Mississippi, named Wallace Saunders, and was first recorded in the 1920s by both Fiddlin' John

Carson and Furry Lewis. "Casey Jones" became a regular part of Johnny's concerts and one of his most requested story-songs. Legendary country crooner Eddy Arnold's single of "Casey Jones" made it to number 15 on the country chart in 1956.

Cash takes on another Merle Travis working man anthem in his version of "Nine Pound Hammer." He also returns to the theme of the hammer as a symbol of the workingman's ability and strength. Travis, as well as bluegrass legend Bill Monroe, had previously recorded the song. In fact, Cash first discovered the song on Travis' 1947 album *Folk Songs of the Hills,* in which Travis talked and sang about life in the coal country of his native Kentucky. That album also included the songs "Dark as a Dungeon" and "Sixteen Tons," which Cash would also record. In "Nine Pound Hammer" the narrator in the song is a coal miner who yearns for escape from the mines. We see the futility of such dreams as the singer rationalizes, "how can I go when my wheels won't roll?"

"Chain Gang" is another fine Harlan Howard song. This time the narrator is a kid roaming around a town, when he is arrested for vagrancy and placed on a chain gang. It's a hopeless situation, as the singer curses the day that he was born and believes that "it's better for a man to hang than to work like a dog on a chain gang." Cash's usual disdain for brutal authority figures is seen in the narrator's antagonistic relationship with the gun-toting, whip-cracking guard who makes his life a living hell.

Johnny next presents his version of the Jimmie Rodgers standard "Waiting for a Train." The song, written by the "Singing Brakeman," is also known by the title "All Around the Water Tank." It combines some of Cash's (and Rodgers's) favorite themes: trains, wanderlust, and, in this case, a hobo, who rides the rails heading from Frisco back to Dixieland. Fellow Sun recording artist Jerry Lee Lewis took the song to number 11 on the country chart in 1971.

Cash closes out this album with the song "Roughneck," which was written by Sheb Wooley, who scored a number 1 pop hit in 1958 with his novelty song "The Purple People Eater," and a number 1 country hit with "That's My Pa" in 1962. "Roughneck" is a decidedly more serious song, about the hard life of a disadvantaged roughneck who works hard labor laying pipe. Cash's empathy for the poor workingman is clearly evident in every song on *Blood, Sweat and Tears.* This final track sums it all up with the line, "born to be a roughneck, I'll never amount to nothin'." Cash wished that people could all have the same opportunities in life and railed against the discrimination that befalls those who are mistreated or beaten down for either their social status or personal beliefs.

The American Indian Connection

In October 1964, Cash released the album *Bitter Tears: Ballads of the American Indian,* and it proved to be one of Cash's most critically acclaimed concept albums. It focuses on the history and plight of the American Indian. For years Cash even insisted he was part Cherokee. In actuality, Cash's roots are Scottish, English, and Irish. On this album he brings to light the harsh treatment Native Americans endured at the hands of the white man. All the songs are written by either Cash or Peter La Farge, with the exception of the closing track, which was written by Cash and Johnny Horton. According to Cash's autobiography, Frank Jones had taken on production duties since Don Law retired, and even though Johnny got flak from the Columbia Records bosses while he was recording the album, Frank Jones "had the good sense and courage to let me go ahead and do what I wanted" (Cash, *Autobiography*, 265). Country music disc jockey Hugh Cherry, who served as the announcer on Cash's live recording *Johnny Cash at Folsom Prison*, wrote the liner notes for this album. The notes offer some general background information about Cash, and a brief history of America's shameful treatment of the American Indian. Cherry concludes his notes with the line, now known to be inaccurate, "Johnny Cash is proud of his Cherokee blood." *Bitter Tears* went on to sell over 100,000 copies and made it to number 2 on the country album chart and number 47 on the pop chart.

Peter La Farge wrote the opening track "As Long as the Grass Shall Grow." La Farge was a New York–based folk singer-songwriter who claimed he was distantly descended from the Narragansett tribe, although that claim has been refuted. He originally studied acting but then relocated to New York and began writing and performing his songs in Greenwich Village, with such contemporaries as Bob Dylan, Ramblin' Jack Elliott and Pete Seeger. "As Long as the Grass Shall Grow" was originally performed (but never recorded) by Bob Dylan at a Carnegie Hall "Hootenanny" in 1962. It tells of the flooding of the Allegheny Reservoir along the Pennsylvania–New York border against the wishes of the Seneca Nation of New York. The Seneca insisted the building of the Kinzua Dam violated the Treaty of Canandaigua, which was signed on behalf of the United States by George Washington.

"Apache Tears" is a sad tale set against a mournful drum background. The song recalls the hardships and persecution the American Indian faced in one of Cash's most gut-wrenching lyrics. He holds nothing back in detailing the cruel injustice faced by the women of the tribe as he moans, "Who saw the young squaw they judged by their whiskey law tortured till she died of pain and fear." The sheer brutality endured by the Native Americans is recounted here as Cash champions their cause, exclaiming "petrified, but justified, are these Apache tears."

Peter La Farge's "Custer" pointedly refutes the notion of General George Armstrong Custer as a heroic figure. Custer gained famed during the Civil War at the First Battle of Bull Run. After that war he was assigned to go out west and fight in the

Indian Wars. He suffered a major failure at the Battle of the Little Bighorn in 1876, fighting against a coalition of Native American tribes. Custer's last stand was a great victory celebration for the Indians, as Custer and the men under his direct command were killed. The Indians viewed him as a murderer who, as the song says, "With victories he was swimming, he killed children, dogs and women," and, we are informed, Native Americans perceive their victory as a "bloody massacre."

Cash's "The Talking Leaves" refers to the creation of the Indian alphabet. It tells of Sequoia, a young, sixteen-year-old Indian boy who walks at his father's side along the battleground where the American soldiers and Indians had fought the war. He notices the white paper with writing on it strewn all around, which he perceives as leaves that have fallen from the trees, strange snow-white leaves with markings on them. His father tells him they are talking leaves and, as such, "they weave bad medicine on these talking leaves." The boy reasons that if the white man can talk on leaves then why can't the Cherokee. His father banishes him for such thoughts, but he works on and on "till finally he cut into stone the Cherokee alphabet." Cash listed this song among his personal favorites for the 1999 *Reader's Digest* box set, *The Legendary Johnny Cash.*

Cash took a major gamble recording La Farge's protest song "The Ballad of Ira Hayes" and releasing it as a single. Gene Ferguson, Cash's friend and a promotion man at Columbia Records, brought Cash this song and told him he should record it. It tells the story of Ira Hayes, a Pima Indian who became a brave American Marine and helped raise the flag in victory on Mount Suribachi during the Battle of Iwo Jima in World War II. Ira Hayes became a hero, but soon turned to the bottle after the public forgot about him, and he eventually froze to death after a night of heavy drinking. Hayes was only thirty-two when he was found dead on January 24, 1955. "The Ballad of Ira Hayes" is a chilling tale of tragedy that opens with "Taps" playing before the singer begins telling the story. In the true folk idiom, the singer beckons us to gather 'round him as he relates the story of Ira Hayes.

Hayes's people were starving in the Phoenix Valley in Arizona because the white man once again stopped their water and let them go hungry. We are told that Ira forgot the white man's greed and joined the Marines to go fight in the war. He returned home a hero, but he was forgotten, began drinking hard, and often ended up in jail. When "The Ballad of Ira Hayes" was released, "radio stations around the country felt it was too controversial and, for the most part, refused to play it. It was only after Cash himself took out a full-page ad in *Billboard* magazine challenging disc jockeys to show some 'guts' that it finally got airplay" (Cash, *Autobiography*, 411). Thanks to Cash's efforts on behalf of the song, and despite its controversial subject matter, "The Ballad of Ira Hayes" made it to number 3 on the country chart.

Cash performed "The Ballad of Ira Hayes" at the Newport Folk Festival in 1964, where he was warmly welcomed. Pete Seeger also recorded the song one year earlier, and Bob Dylan would record it on his album *Self Portrait* in 1973. As a result of Cash's success with this song, Peter La Farge was offered a recording contract with MGM Records in 1965. Sadly, Hayes felt unworthy of the attention he was receiving, as other soldiers had given their lives in battle. "The Ballad of Ira Hayes" was another song Johnny considered to be one of his personal favorites, and he asked that it be included on *The Legendary Johnny Cash.*

Johnny closes the album with "The Vanishing Race," a fitting finale cowritten with Johnny Horton. It opens with Indian chanting before the singer begins recounting the sad reality of the disappearing Indian race and culture. It's a poetic lyric, and a sad farewell, proclaiming "I see an eagle in space, and my people will follow a vanishing race." This is a great summing up of the tragedy and tribulations of Native Americans, and one of Johnny's most profound albums.

Interestingly, prior to the *Bitter Tears* album, Cash had written and recorded the song "Old Apache Squaw" for his 1959 album *Songs of Our Soil.* While Cash had mentioned the American Indian in "New Mexico," "Old Apache Squaw" was Johnny's first Indian-themed song, and his first protest song. With an Indian drum introduction, the song questions how many hungry kids and bloody warriors the old Apache squaw has seen. It's a short narrative full of sadness for the hard life she's lived and the things she's witnessed. Cash lobbied hard to get this song released, and Columbia Records executives finally consented. Of course, Cash was ultimately allowed to record an entire album of songs about the American Indian.

"Navajo" is a standout track on the 1976 live album *Strawberry Cake.* Cash wrote this tender ballad about the Arizona Navajo Indians that harks back to his *Bitter Tears* album. However, whereas the songs in that earlier collection were predominantly pointed protest songs about the mistreatment of the American Indian through the years, this song is a celebration of the proud heritage of the Navajo Indian tribe. It's almost an antithesis of the bitter songs found on *Bitter Tears,* as Cash proclaims, "the Indian sun is rising instead of going down."

Cowboy Songs

September 1965 saw the release of the album *Johnny Cash Sings the Ballads of the True West.* Since Johnny had released his concept album *Bitter Tears* one year earlier, he decided to record this collection of western-themed cowboy songs. In his extensive liner notes for this album, Cash recalls that four years earlier his producer Don Law had suggested he record an album of western songs. Law brought Cash two books on western lore. Cash explains how he became fascinated with the subject, and to prepare for the recording of this album he followed trails in his Jeep and on foot while traveling throughout the West. It almost became an obsession for him, and the end result is a milestone album in the Cash catalog. The liner notes include pertinent information about many of the songs and a list of "Western Lingo" translations. It was originally released as a double album featuring twenty songs, some traditional western folk songs and others written specifically for the project by Cash and some of his favorite writers.

Cash opens the album with "Hiawatha's Vision." Hiawatha was the leader and cofounder of the Iroquois Nation, immortalized in literature by Henry Wadsworth Longfellow in his poem "The Song of Hiawatha." In the liner notes Johnny says he was inspired by this poem, particularly the part called "The White Man's Foot." Cash's recitation begins with the opening lines from the Longfellow poem before he adds his own lyrics about Hiawatha seeing the white settlers come in canoes to take over, conquer and develop the Indian land. And so begins the album proper with Hiawatha's "dark" vision foreshadowing what was to come, as the Indians were pushed aside in the name of manifest destiny, and their lands were taken over by the multitudes of white settlers.

June Carter wrote "The Road to Kaintuck," which concerns the settlers moving west to Kentucky, or "Kaintuck" as it's pronounced in the song, down

the Wilderness Road, the road to Moccasin Gap. This was an area very familiar to June, for it was located in the Clinch Mountains of Virginia where she grew up. Daniel Boone's Wilderness Road traveled north from the Holston River, located in southern Tennessee all the way to the Cumberland Gap, which borders Kentucky, Virginia, and Tennessee. After a banjo intro, Johnny sings the song and tells the story of heading west through Kentucky during the Indian wars. The narrative takes place in 1873, after Daniel Boone lost his son, Jim, to the fighting. The narrator is traveling with his wife and kids. The Statler Brothers are featured on vocals, warning the singer to turn his wagons back. And the Carter Family harmonizes with him as he insists on moving ahead. Johnny would include a new version of this song on his album *America: A 200-Year Salute in Story and Song*, and June would record a version for her own album *Wildwood Flower*.

Cash writes in the liner notes that "The Shifting Whispering Sands, Pt. 1" has special meaning for him. He explains that he often went to an abandoned ranch near Maricopa, California, that he discovered had been an old Indian burial ground. Johnny narrates the saga of a prospector stumbling upon the valley of the shifting, whispering sands. He sees the devastation all around him as he wanders for weeks aimlessly in the valley wondering where the bodies are. He escapes from the valley and recounts what he learned on the desert. The Carter Family and the Statler Brothers explain the mystery of the shifting, whispering sands. It was originally a number 5 hit on the pop chart for Billy Vaughn and His Orchestra in 1955, and a number 3 hit for Rusty Draper later that same year. Country singer Jim Reeves also recorded a moving cover of this song.

Former Sun colleague and lifelong friend Carl Perkins wrote "The Ballad of Boot Hill," a western ballad about the gunfight at the O.K. Corral in 1881 in Tombstone, Arizona, where Doc Holliday killed three gunmen. Johnny sets up the song with a narration explaining the history of Boot Hill. Tombstone, we are told, "is where the brave never cry, they live by a six gun, and by a six gun they die." The narrative is more like a panoramic tour of Boot Hill and all the tragic events that took place there. Cash originally recorded the song in 1959 and included it on *Johnny Cash Sings the Rebel-Johnny Yuma*. But it makes its first appearance here on an album, where it fits in perfectly.

Johnny was always fascinated by western folklore, and he did his research to compose the song "Hardin Wouldn't Run," about the notorious American outlaw, gunfighter and folk hero, John Wesley Hardin. In fact, in the liner notes for this album, Cash informs us that he wrote the song after reading the autobiography Hardin wrote just before he was killed. Hardin found himself in trouble with the law from an early age and was pursued by lawmen and federal agents throughout the West after the Reconstruction. He was eventu-

ally captured and sent to prison in 1878, where he wrote his autobiography and studied law. He was released from prison in 1894, only to be shot by John Selman one year later while in a saloon in El Paso, Texas. Cash puts Hardin's story into song and vividly recounts all the details of his life. Bob Dylan was also fascinated by Hardin's outlaw persona and wrote a song about him for his 1967 album titled *John Wesley Harding*. Cash named this as one of his personal favorite songs for *The Legendary Johnny Cash*.

Brooklyn-born folk singer Ramblin' Jack Elliott wrote "Mister Garfield" about the 1881 shooting of President James A. Garfield in broad daylight at a railroad depot. A man named Charles J. Guiteau shot Garfield, and the story is told from the point of view of a young man who is shocked to hear about the assassination. The boy talks his brother into going with him to see the ailing president. The boy is saddened to learn that the president ultimately died from his wounds. Elliott originally had presented the song to Cash as "The Ballad of Charles Guiteau," but Cash preferred the title "Mister Garfield." The song was the only single released from this album, and it climbed to number 15 on the country chart.

Johnny presents a reverential cover of the American cowboy ballad "The Streets of Laredo," also known as the "Cowboy's Lament." It was originally derived from a British ballad called "The Unfortunate Rake," about a young man dying of syphilis in a London hospital. This song has been recorded numerous times, by artists such as the Kingston Trio, Joan Baez, Willie Nelson, and Marty Robbins.

Mother Maybelle Carter cowrote "A Letter from Home" with Dixie Dean, the wife of country singer-songwriter Tom T. Hall. It's a sad lament about a young cowboy who rides into "San Antone" and asks the postmaster if he has received a letter from home. That night he's shot on the wrong side of town, and the narrator reaches for his Bible and hands it to the young cowboy, saying "Here is your letter from home." The Statler Brothers add beautiful harmony to this heartbreaking tale.

Johnny wrote "Mean as Hell," a tough-as-nails narrative about the brutal nature of the Wild West. He paints a lyrically descriptive picture of the devil asking the Lord if he had anything left when he made the land, and the Lord said He does, but it's all down by the Rio Grande, concluding that "the stuff is so poor, I don't think you can use it as a hell anymore." That sets up the notion of the West being the perfect metaphor for hell on earth. Overall, it's a fine piece of Western poetry.

Country star and movie actor Tex Ritter wrote "Sam Hall." Ritter had scored a number 5 country hit, and Top 20 pop hit with "I Dreamed of a Hillbilly Heaven" in 1961. Cash had earlier recorded Ritter's song "Boss Jack." "Sam Hall" is based on an old English folk song about an unrepentant criminal named Jack Hall. Tex's adaptation brings the action to the American West and makes Sam Hall an outlaw who is too ornery to die. Cash gives a theatrical reading, grunting and snorting and cussing his way through the song in one of his most animated performances. He seems to be really enjoying himself as he recounts the evil deeds of Sam Hall that have led to his eventual hanging, laughing hysterically and proclaiming, "I killed a man they said, so they said . . . and I smashed in his head, and I left him a-laying dead, well darn his hyde."

In "25 Minutes to Go," Cash takes on the persona of a man on death row counting down the minutes until he is hanged. Shel Silverstein, noted singer-songwriter, poet, cartoonist and author of children's books whose work regularly appeared in *Playboy* magazine during the 1960s and '70s, wrote the song. This was the first major recording of a Silverstein song, but he would go on to enjoy many more country and pop hits as a songwriter including, "The Unicorn" by the Irish Rovers, "Sylvia's Mother" and "Cover of the Rolling Stone" by Dr. Hook & The Medicine Show, "Marie Laveau" by Bobby Bare and "One's on the Way" by Loretta Lynn. Silverstein would write other songs that Cash would record through the years, including his giant hit "A Boy Named Sue." By so memorably putting us in the mind of a convict sweating out his final hours, it would become a highlight of Cash's Folsom Prison concert.

Cash turns in a convincing performance on Harlan Howard's great story-song "The Blizzard."

Originally a number 4 country hit for "Gentleman" Jim Reeves, Cash felt the song would nicely fit the theme of this album. Cash's sad, haunted vocal separates this version from Reeve's sweeter, more honey-voiced performance. The singer is counting down the miles until he gets home to his beloved Mary Ann. The thought of Mary Ann keeps him going through the driving blizzard winds. He struggles and fights to keep his horse going down to the last mile. Cash takes on the third person voice to close the narrative explaining they found the man frozen just one hundred yards away from Mary Ann.

Cash delivers a lighthearted performance of "Sweet Betsy from Pike," an American folk ballad about a tough pioneer woman named Betsy who crossed the big mountains with her lover Ike. They take everything they own —"two yoke of oxen, a big 'yeller' dog, two shanghai roosters and one spotted hog"— as they travel from Pike County, Missouri, across the hot desert on their way out west. Ike and Betsy eventually get married, but Ike getting jealous obtains a divorce, and Betsy moves on.

Cash arranged and adapted "Green Grow the Lilacs," a popular nineteenth-century Irish folk song, and shaped it into a mournful ballad about a young man missing his loved one, who has left him for someone new. One interpretation of the lyric is of an American soldier who is in love with a Mexican girl who does not return his feelings. He wishes to win her love and bring her to America, trading the green lilacs for the red, white, and blue.

Tex Ritter also helped popularize this ballad, and in the liner notes Cash claims that "the song was done best in our time by Tex Ritter," although Cash turns in a meaningful performance of his own.

After recording a number of Peter La Farge's songs for his *Bitter Tears* album, Cash included La Farge's "Stampede," a change-of-pace cowboy song about the wilder side of life on the range. Even though most songs romanticize the calmer, simpler life depicted in ballads like "Home on the Range," this song focuses on the more turbulent side of range life, where cattle can wildly stampede and wreak havoc. It's a wild and wooly performance by Cash with a chorus of shouting voices chiming in with him, screaming "stampede!" Cash even name-checks the song's author as he laments the plight of the trampled cowboy, explaining, "Now I ain't got no partner 'cause ol' Frank's done dead and gone, but just so he'd be remembered, Peter put him in this song."

Cash closes out the album's song cycle with "The Shifting Whispering Sands, Pt. 2." The sands still whisper to the narrator of the days of long ago as they cover up the memories of all that transpired. We are told that they found the body of the prospector we learned about in Part One. They crossed his hands and buried him. And his secret is still sleeping beneath the shifting, whispering sands. He encourages us to wander through this quiet land and discover for ourselves the stories hidden beneath the shifting, whispering sands.

An additional track recorded during the sessions for *Ballads of the True West* was "The Sons of Katie Elder" a song that was recorded for the John Wayne movie of the same name, and which appears on the soundtrack album of the Paramount motion picture, but was not included in the actual movie soundtrack. It tells the story of four brothers who were raised by the gun by their mother, Katie Elder. It's a warning to avoid the outlaw lifestyle and "to not live by a gun, and to not live like the sons of Katie Elder." Cash turns in a highly believable performance on a song that was released as a single and made it to number 10 on the country chart in 1965.

First Columbia Hit

Cash recorded many western-themed ballads over the years. Among his greatest was "Don't Take Your Guns to Town" in 1959; his first big hit on Columbia Records. This now classic story-song is about a young cowboy named Billy Joe who grew restless on the farm and left home, not heeding his mother's advice to not take his guns to town. It's a life lesson, a morality tale, and a great western ballad all rolled up into one. The tragic ending of the young cowboy falling dead after a gunfight only reinforces the message that one should always listen to one's parents' sound advice. It was Cash's second single for Columbia and his first for the label to reach number 1 on the country chart, and it remained there for six weeks. It also broke

February 1965, signing recording contract with Goddard Lieberson, President of Columbia Records and Don Law, Cash's producer. *Photo: Don Hunstein © Sony Music Entertainment.*

the Top 40 in pop, climbing to number 32. "I Still Miss Someone" was the B-side to the single, and together these two songs reflected the finest attributes of Johnny Cash, revealing the master storyteller and the tenderhearted troubadour. While Johnny began the year 1959 with a western-themed saga, his friend and fellow country star, Marty Robbins, closed the year out with his western classic "El Paso."

In 1959 Cash also recorded "The Rebel-Johnny Yuma," written by Richard Markowitz and Andrew J. Fenady. Cash was asked to perform the theme song to the TV western *The Rebel*, which starred Nick Adams and ran from 1959 to 1961. The theme of the series must have appealed to Cash. It was the tale of a young Confederate soldier who is left to wander aimlessly throughout the West two years after the Civil War had ended. The song perfectly captures the loneliness the soldier experiences as he wanders alone through a lawless land. And although Cash did not write it, you would never know it. The song made it to number 24 on the country chart in 1961, shortly before the series was cancelled. It was originally released as the title song of *Johnny Cash Sings the Rebel-Johnny Yuma.*

In 1963 Cash took another stab at a TV western theme song by cowriting and recording "Bonanza." This time, he and friend Johnny Western wrote their own lyrics to the musical theme, composed by Jay Livingston and Ray Evans, for the television series *Bonanza.* Cash's version was never used on the TV series about the Cartwright family, starring Lorne Greene, Pernell Roberts, Dan Blocker, and Michael Landon. But he did release it and include it on the *Ring of Fire* album. Interestingly, Cash would record a duet version of "The Shifting, Whispering Sands" with Lorne Greene. Greene enjoyed a number 1 pop and Top 20 country hit of his own with the song "Ringo" in 1964.

During the 1970s, Cash recorded songs that revealed a deep nostalgia for the fading cowboy mythology of his youth, such as 1977's "The Last Gunfighter Ballad," a sharply written song by Guy Clark. It's a narrative that finds the singer recount-ing the story of an aging gunfighter who is having trouble fitting into the modern world. He's old and relegated to living in the past. Cash empathizes with the old gunfighter, and it's not too much of a stretch to see this as a metaphor for Cash's trying to find his place in the then ever-changing country music landscape. The song takes a tragic turn when the old man wanders out where "there's ghosts in the street seeking revenge, calling him out to the lunatic fringe," and sadly, he's killed by a car as he goes for his gun. The ending may have been too disturbing for the song to succeed as a single. It only made it to number 38 on the country chart, another poor performance for a very good song.

In 1978 John Carter Cash made his recording debut on "Who's Gene Autry?" It was the elder Cash's self-penned ode to his childhood hero, cowboy star Gene Autry. When his son asks him, "Daddy, who's Gene Autry?" Cash proceeds to explain to him in detail how much the legendary actor, singer, and songwriter influenced him. Cash had already recorded Autry songs like "That Silver Haired Daddy of Mine," and the two icons respected each other so much so that Autry had presented Cash with one of his guitars (which Cash would ultimately loan to Bob Dylan). In his later years, Autry even pitched songs he had written to Cash to record. Furthermore, in 1995 Cash, Willie Nelson, Kris Kristofferson, and Waylon Jennings recorded a demo of Autry's classic "Back in the Saddle Again," which was released on the reissue of the Highwaymen album *The Road Goes On Forever.*

The Highwaymen all shared a love of the cowboy myth. Together they recorded "The Last Cowboy Song," an epic cowboy tune written by Ed Bruce and Ron Peterson. Singer-songwriter Bruce cowrote Waylon and Willie's hit "Mammas Don't Let Your Babies Grow Up to Be Cowboys." Bruce also had Willie join him on his original recording of "The Last Cowboy Song," which made it to number 12 on the country chart in 1980. The song tells about the disappearing ways of the American West and "the end of a hundred-year waltz." It's a sad commentary about the loss of values and the symbols associated with the birth of this country and the cowboys who forged ahead and settled it. Waylon opens the song, with Kris taking the second verse and Willie the third, explaining that, "Me and Johnny and Waylon and Kris sing about him and wish to God we could have ridden his trail." Johnny concludes with a spoken word narrative about how we've forgotten about the cowboy, "like living and dying was all that he did."

When Cash signed with American Recordings in 1994, "Oh, Bury Me Not (Introduction: A Cowboy's Prayer)" was the song that first caught Rick Rubin's ear when he was listening to Cash's repertoire while they were getting to know each other. When Rubin heard Cash recite the poem "A Cowboy's Prayer," he immediately turned on the record-

ing equipment and asked Cash to sing it again (Hilburn, *Johnny Cash: The Life,* 541). "A Cowboy's Prayer," expresses Cash's faith and belief that God's presence is everywhere, not only through a stained-glass window, but rather in the dim, quiet starlight on the plains. It's a moving recitation that segues into a tender version of "Oh, Bury Me Not on the Lone Prairie."

November 2003 saw the release of Cash's "Big Iron," a tribute to his dear friend Marty Robbins. The song was included on Cash's posthumous *Unearthed* box set. "Big Iron" was a Robbins western saga that Johnny had wanted to record his whole life. It was a number 5 country hit for Robbins in 1960, and was included on his classic 1959 album *Gunfighter Ballads and Trail Songs.* This cover works so well because Cash does not try to imitate Robbins's immaculate croon, but instead tells the story in his patented singing storyteller style.

And quite possibly the most interesting cowboy song Cash ever recorded was "The Greatest Cowboy of Them All." It was originally released on his *A Believer Sings the Truth* gospel collection. Cash wrote this western-flavored narrative describing Jesus as the greatest cowboy of them all. It's a churning ballad wherein Cash compares Christ to his cowboy heroes and calls Him the greatest of them all. This song creatively juxtaposes two recurrent themes in Cash's music: the American West and Cash's unwavering faith in Jesus Christ.

JOHNNY CASH
THE HOLY LAND

Prologue
Land Of Israel
A Mother's Love (Narrative)
This Is Nazareth
Nazarene
Town Of Cana (Narrative)
He Turned The Water Into Wine
My Wife June At Sea Of Galilee (Narrative)
Beautiful Words (Narrative)
Our Guide Jacob At Mount Tabor
The Ten Commandments
Daddy Sang Bass
At The Wailing Wall (Narrative)
Come To The Wailing Wall (Narrative)
In Bethlehem (Narrative)
In Garden Of Gethsemane (Narrative)
The Fourth Man
On The Via Dolorosa (Narrative)
Church Of The Holy Sepulchre (Narrative)
At Calvary (Narrative)
God Is Not Dead

Chapter 5

FAR SIDE BANKS OF JORDAN

THE GOSPEL ACCORDING TO CASH

The inspirational songs that reveal the
deeply spiritual side of Johnny Cash

Johnny Cash felt constrained at Sun, and Sam Phillips's reluctance to let Johnny record a gospel album at the studio also helped accelerate his departure from the label. After all, Don Law had promised Cash he could work on a gospel album as soon as he wanted to at Columbia Records. Law also offered Cash a higher royalty on his records and a fifty-thousand-dollar signing bonus. The first inspirational song Cash recorded for Columbia was Dorothy Love Coates's "That's Enough," which appeared on his LP *The Fabulous Johnny Cash.* The gospel-blues song expresses the singer's devotion to God by explaining that others may talk bad about him and push him down but he's got Jesus, and that's enough. He testifies, "You may scorn me and turn your back on me, God's got His arms wrapped all around me" and that's enough. The Jordanaires sing backup for him on this track. Cash so loved this song that he recorded it years later on his highly personal double album *A Believer Sings the Truth* with a more elaborate instrumental background and a more emphatic vocal delivery.

During his career Cash recorded over 150 inspirational songs, and nine gospel-themed albums.

« The Holy Land. *Courtesy of Sony Music Entertainment.*

And that's not including his reading of the entire New King James Version of the New Testament on sixteen CDs. Among numerous traditional hymns and spirituals, Cash wrote and recorded many observational commentaries concerning his own personal religious beliefs. The most personal being the *A Believer Sings the Truth* album, and his ultimate labor of love, *The Gospel Road,* which was both a movie and soundtrack. Initially, it was easy to see how the line was drawn between the devotional and the personal, but in later years the line was blurred when secular songs like "Hurt" would take on deeper, more spiritual overtones as performed by a more frail and elderly Johnny.

A Dream Fulfilled

After being allowed to record only a few inspirational songs at Sun, in May 1959, Columbia released *Hymns by Johnny Cash*. It was the album that Johnny had wanted to record since his initial signing at Sun Records, and in fact, it was a prerequisite to his signing with Columbia. It was the fruition of Johnny's dream and contains some very inspired and moving Christian recordings. Johnny's first gospel album includes twelve songs, five of which Cash wrote himself. The other seven tracks are either traditional favorites or more recent inspirational compositions. Cash's own compositions fit in perfectly with the more traditional ballads.

Hymns by Johnny Cash opens with "It Was Jesus," a self-penned song of praise. It had originally been intended for his prior album, *The Fabulous Johnny Cash,* but was ultimately left off. Johnny recounts the story of Jesus feeding the multitudes: "With just five loaves and two little fishes, five thousand had fish and bread." He repeatedly asks, "Who was it everybody?" and waits for the response from the gospel choir that it was "Jesus Christ, our Lord." Then he moves on to the story of the crucifixion, and so begins the album that Johnny felt he was destined to record.

Other standout songs on the album written by Cash include "Lead Me, Father," a powerful song of reckoning. Cash prays to God to lead him with the staff of life and "give me the strength for a song, that the words I sing might more strength bring to help some poor troubled weary worker along." This is exactly what Cash wanted to do from the start. He wanted to perform inspirational songs that might have a major impact on people's lives. This is his own personal plea to the Lord to keep his flame of inspiration lit and to help him write and sing songs that make a difference. Cash wrote this song after he signed his recording contract with Sun Records. In his 1975 autobiography, *Man in Black*, he recalls, "That night I went home and wrote a song which concerned 'tithing' my music and called it 'My Prayer.' It was recorded three years later on Columbia Records in my first hymn

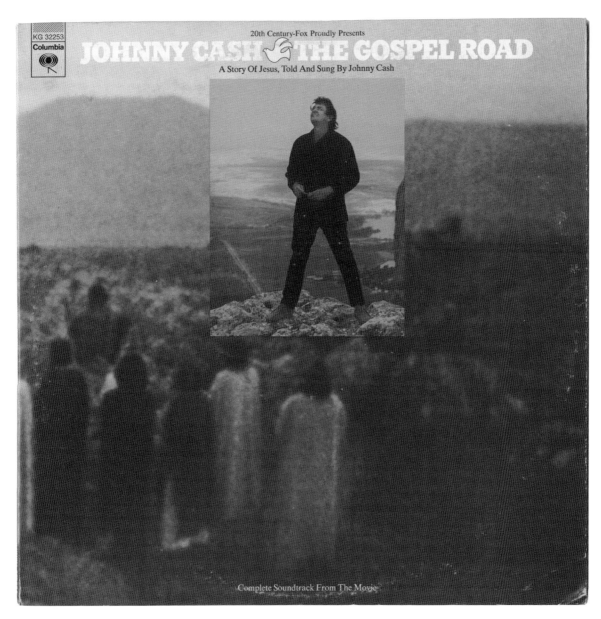

The Gospel Road. *Courtesy of Sony Music Entertainment.*

album and renamed 'Lead Me, Father.' It was never a big seller, but every few days for the last twenty years I have sung this song over in my mind, if not aloud" (68). In fact, none of Cash's religious albums were big sellers, although *The Holy Land* performed well enough due to its following Cash's extremely successful *Johnny Cash at Folsom Prison* album.

"I Call Him" is credited on the original album label to Johnny Cash and his brother Roy Cash Sr., but it was actually written by Johnny and his nephew Roy Cash Jr. Also, on the original album cover sleeve the song is referred to as "I Called Him." On the record label itself, it's listed as "I Call Him." Way beyond the blue of the water and the sky, the singer believes, there is someone watching over it all. And though Cash paints himself as having been a poor boy, he knows that God does not judge people, as he heeds his mother's life's lesson, stating, "I call Him when I'm troubled, and I call Him when I'm weak . . . He's always there to answer when I call Him."

Renowned instrumentalist Arthur "Guitar Boogie" Smith wrote "I Saw a Man." Smith's guitar work influenced performers such as Glen Campbell and Roy Clark. He was also a talented songwriter who went on to compose an instrumental banjo tune called "Feudin' Banjos." That song would find its way into the classic motion picture *Deliverance* under the more familiar title "Duelin' Banjos." (Originally not given credit for the song, Smith sued and was awarded a songwriting credit in a landmark copyright case.) "I Saw a Man" is a hauntingly beautiful ballad that finds the singer recalling a dream he had of an angel who appears to him in the form of Jesus Christ, beckoning the singer to come to Him. Upon waking he realizes he was not dreaming, but had truly found his Savior. The lyric offers sharp, vivid imagery of Christ's nail-scarred hands as the singer reaches to touch the hem of His garment.

South Carolina hillbilly singer-songwriter Marshall Pack wrote "Snow in His Hair." Pack composed the 1957 single "Henpecked Daddy" for Ralph Johnson and the Hillbilly Show Boys, and recorded his own gospel album *God, Country, Mother & Home,* with the Sierra Boys. In "Snow in His Hair," the singer is returning home to see his father after being away for many years. When he arrives home he finds his father aged and nearly blind, admitting "there's snow in his hair and I helped put it there." It's a powerful song of reckoning, as we all face the realization of our parents' growing older. The snow takes on the shine of a halo as the singer comes to terms with the inevitabilities of life.

But undoubtedly, the two strongest songs on *Hymns* are the traditional "The Old Account" and "Swing Low, Sweet Chariot." "The Old Account" is about settling life's account when we get to heaven to meet Jesus. Cash arranged this song of true forgiveness, about when a sinner believes that Jesus will forgive us our earthly imperfections. As the song proclaims, Christ died for our sins and so the old account was settled long ago, "and the record's clear today because He washed my sins away." The song is a call to all sinners to seek out Christ, knowing He will not judge them or turn them away, but rather embrace them and welcome them back to the fold. "Swing Low, Sweet Chariot" is the classic hymn rendered brand new in one of the finest recordings of the well-known gospel treasure. Cash's devotional performance and the tender backing choir make this one of his greatest inspirational recordings of all. It's always a revelation how Cash can not only breathe new life into songs that go back many years, but also make us listen to them again with fresh ears.

Traditional Hymns

In June 1962, Columbia released Johnny's second inspirational album, *Hymns from the Heart*. It was more traditional in both feel and song selection than Cash's prior *Hymns* album, with Cash arranging and adapting material, but not contributing any original songs to the set. Noteworthy tracks from *Hymns from the Heart* include B. Whitson's "When I've Learned," one of Johnny's best performances on the album, and one of his finest gospel recordings. It's the testament of a good man who

has seen heaven on earth by being a hard worker and living a good life. But the singer knows the fruits of this world are temporal, reasoning, "When I've learned enough to really live I'll be old enough to die." If ever the adage "youth is wasted on the young" holds true, it's here. The singer has grown "to kind of like this life," knowing the real payoff for his good works will be in the afterlife. This profound revelation coming from the young Johnny Cash attests to the fact that he always displayed wisdom far beyond his years.

Honky tonk singer and songwriter Eddie Noack wrote "These Hands," a superb recitation that Cash delivers with true devotion. It's one of Cash's strongest performances and is only matched by a later version of this same song he recorded live for *The Johnny Cash Show* album. Hank Snow reached number 5 on the country chart with his rendition of this song in 1956, but Johnny truly makes it his own and brings a sense of world-weary truth to the song about a man's hard-working hands that raise up to praise the Lord.

American gospel singer and songwriter Albert E. Brumley, whose many credits include the inspirational standard "I'll Fly Away," wrote "If We Never Meet Again." The song seems like the precursor to "Far Side Banks of Jordan," a song Cash would record years later. It's a comforting ballad of acceptance that explains, "if we never meet again this side of heaven, I will meet you on the beautiful shore." "I Won't Have to Cross Jordan Alone" is another song that parallels "Far Side Banks of Jordan." In this ballad the singer attests to the belief that Jesus will be there to help him cross the Jordan when his time has come. There's a fervent sense of hope and comfort knowing that the Lord will be there to personally meet him and guide him to life's other side.

"Far Side Banks of Jordan" made its first appearance on *The Last Gunfighter Ballad* album, and it is unquestionably one of the finest songs Johnny Cash ever recorded. This heartfelt duet with June is also one of Cash's best gospel songs. The lyric is profound and foreshadows the final outcome of Johnny Cash and June Carter's life together. In the song, June prophetically sings, "If it proves to be His will that I am first to cross, and somehow I've a feeling it will be." We can only hear this song as the final destination of these two iconic individuals. John always said that he'd be lost without June, and this song serves as a comforting reminder that she would be there waiting for him when his time would come. We can easily picture Johnny (who would pass away on September 12, 2003 just four months after June, who would die on May 15, 2003) arriving across the Jordan and seeing June sitting, awaiting his arrival while drawing pictures in the sand. While the song "Hurt" may be Johnny's epitaph, this is the song that best summarizes the love and life of John and June. Schoolteacher and songwriter Terry Smith who has written country and inspirational songs for artists ranging from Kitty Wells to the Oak Ridge Boys wrote the song. And it was from the Oak Ridge Boys that Cash first learned of the song.[1]

"I'll Cross Over Jordan Someday," included on the album *The Adventures of Johnny Cash,* is a gospel ballad from songwriter Peck Chandler. The opening lyric is a bit enigmatic, but the ultimate message is one of faith and hope. The song has elements that remind us of "Far Side Banks of Jordan," a theme Cash appeared to be drawn to throughout his career. The singer reminds us that he'll cross over Jordan someday and sing on that beautiful shore. Beginning to face his own mortality, in 1996 for the *Unchained* album, Cash wrote "Meet Me in Heaven" for June, with the title taken from the words carved on his brother Jack's tombstone. It is arguably the best song on that album. It's a lovely, poetic musing, written for his dear companion, about the end of life's journey, when their last song is sung, and the hope that they will meet up in heaven someday. The singer admits that he's not sure what will be there when they walk into the light, but his faith reassures him that they will find each other out there beyond the stars. This is Cash's personal prayer for himself and June, and the perfect bookend to their earlier recording of "Far Side Banks."

Cash's idealized notion of paradise is best expressed in "(There'll Be) Peace in the Valley (for Me)," one of his most popular gospel songs. He first recorded it in 1963 as the closing track of the *Ring of Fire* album. It's one of the songs that always brought him comfort because it was sung during his brother Jack's funeral. The Carter Family join him on the Thomas A. Dorsey standard, which was a number 5 country hit for Red Foley in 1951 and was also previously popularized by Elvis Presley. "Peace in the Valley" would close out many Cash concerts, most notably his recorded performance at San Quentin State Prison.

A Trip to the Holy Land

In January 1969, Cash released *The Holy Land.* He had always wanted to visit the Holy Land to see the places he had read about in the Bible. After he and June wed in March of 1968, they decided to take a trip to Israel to visit the places where Jesus had walked. They carried with them a cassette-tape recorder to capture all the spontaneous wonder of visiting this ancient land. What resulted was a travelogue of their journey interspersed with songs that Johnny had been inspired to write while there. *The Holy Land* was a radical departure from his previous albums but still managed to reach number 6 on the country album chart in 1969 and number 54 on the pop album chart. It also included one hit single, "Daddy Sang Bass," that helped in promoting the album. Riding on the wave of Cash's unexpected success with *Johnny Cash at Folsom Prison*, and the "Folsom Prison Blues" single, Columbia invested more money into *The Holy Land*, complete with a three-dimensional hologram cover for the original LP release. Every song and narrative was written by Johnny Cash, with the exception of "Daddy Sang Bass" by Carl Perkins, "The Ten Commandments," by Lew DeWitt, and "The Fourth Man," by Arthur "Guitar Boogie" Smith.

Standout tracks include "He Turned the Water into Wine," one of Johnny's finest inspirational compositions. With great devotion and reverence, he tells the story of Jesus's turning the water into wine. He would perform this song in concert continually over the years and it ranks right up there with the greatest contemporary gospel songs of the twentieth century. It was issued as the B-side of "Daddy Sang Bass."

Cash uses the story of Jesus's transfiguration on the Mount to segue into "The Ten Commandments," the story of Moses receiving from God the tablets bearing the Ten Commandments. Statler Brother Lew DeWitt wrote the song. DeWitt had written the Statlers' giant hit "Flowers on the Wall," and remained with the group until 1982, when he had to leave because he was suffering from Crohn's disease. Sadly, he passed away in 1990. The Statler Brothers recorded their own version of the song for their gospel album *The Holy Bible: The Old Testament.*

"The Fourth Man," is a spirited song that reinterprets a story from the Book of Daniel, offering the idea that Jesus delivered Shadrach, Meshach, and Abednego from the fiery furnace in which King Nebuchadnezzar II had thrown them. They were three God-fearing men whom Jesus saved by becoming the Fourth Man in the fire and rescuing them. It became a favorite of Cash's live shows, performed almost always as a duet with the Statler Brothers. In fact, the Statler Brothers recorded their own version of the song for their gospel album *The Holy Bible: The Old Testament.*

"God Is Not Dead" is the perfect finale to Johnny's journey through the Holy Land. His faith is reinforced as he humbly proclaims that "God is not dead, He never died." Cash goes on to ask "What man on earth can make one blade of grass, and who can make one seed then make it grow?" He bravely affirms his belief by trying to share with doubters what he had experienced and what his faith meant to him. It's a passionate lyric with an honesty and depth that Cash expresses eloquently.

The Preacher Said

During the 1970s and beyond, Cash included at least one inspirational song on most of his albums. He ushered in the decade with his album *Hello, I'm Johnny Cash*, which included the song "Jesus Was a Carpenter," a religious narrative about the life of Christ, written by author Christopher Wren. Wren was a senior editor at *Look* magazine and was working at the time on a biography of Cash called

Winners Got Scars Too. "Jesus Was a Carpenter" is stark, lyrical, and fervent all at the same time. It's also a plea for Jesus to return and be a carpenter among us once again. At the same time the singer wonders how Christ would be received if He were to return.

That same year Cash would include two devotional songs on *The Johnny Cash Show* album. The aforementioned "These Hands," and "Here Was a Man." "Here Was a Man" is a deeply moving recitation that Johnny originally recorded for *The Christmas Spirit* album in 1963. This version is even more inspiring by being presented in a live setting with Bill Walker's moving backing arrangement. Country stars Johnny Bond and Tex Ritter adapted the popular 1926 sermon "One Solitary Life" by Dr. James Allan Francis and added the hook, "Here was a man."

In 1971, Cash bookended his *Man in Black* album with religious songs. The record opens with "The Preacher Said, 'Jesus Said,'" featuring Billy Graham. Cash had befriended presidents and kings, but no relationship was dearer to his heart than his friendship with the Reverend Billy Graham. According to Michael Streissguth in his book *Johnny Cash: The Biography*, "Graham had courted Cash in late 1969, after witnessing his own son Franklin's enthusiasm for the singer. Seeking common ground with his son and alliances with public figures who could help him bring the Gospel to young audiences, Graham contacted Cash and initiated one of the most visible aspects of Cash's gospel career" (Streissguth, *Cash: The Biography*, 177). "The Preacher Said, 'Jesus Said'" finds Cash singing the praises of the preacher, while Graham reads scriptures from the New Testament. Cash and Graham remained lifelong friends, and Cash participated in many of Graham's popular crusades.

Cash included the song "Billy and Rex and Oral and Bob" on his 1974 album *The Junkie and the Juicehead Minus Me*. Cash lists the popular preachers of the day: Billy Graham, Rex Humbard, Oral Roberts, and Bob Harrington in the title, and goes on to list other evangelists such as Billy Sunday, James Robison, Kathryn Kuhlman, Garner Ted Armstrong, Tommy Barnett, Jimmy Snow, and Reverend Ike. This was Cash's tribute to the great super-preachers who were ordained for proclaiming the gospel of Jesus. Some of the many evangelists he mentions in the song, especially some of the televangelists, were scandalized in years to come. But others like Billy Graham have remained highly respected standard-bearers of their faith for many decades.

Johnny closed out the *Man in Black* album with a duet with June, "I Talk to Jesus Every Day," an inspirational song written by Glenn Douglas Tubb. Even though the singer has met many great people along the way, all those superstars seem small when compared to Jesus. Cash admits that he talks to Jesus every day and that "He's interested in everything I say." When Cash says that he may never be in any

hall of fame, we can only smile, knowing that he has already been inducted into many.

"I Talk to Jesus" is among many personal inspirational songs Cash wrote and recorded over the years. Among his finest is his self-penned "I'm Gonna Try to be That Way" from *The Johnny Cash Show* album. It's another inspirational song about a man who hopes to emulate Christ by living his life as best he can. It's a potent message, delivered with true devotion. The Statler Brothers add some wonderful harmonies as Cash attests to his desire to be an inspiration to others. It was released as the B-side of "Sunday Morning Coming Down." "Good Morning Friend," from Cash's *Ragged Old Flag* album is a similarly themed ballad, in which Cash sings the praises of talking to the Lord as a friend whenever he needs to. With the Oak Ridge Boys singing backup, Cash describes God as a friend who is available to us all and is always there to listen to our problems.

Another prime example of this type of personal admission is "One of These Days I'm Gonna Sit Down and Talk to Paul," from the 1986 gospel album *Believe in Him*. "One of These Days" expresses Cash's fascination with the story of St. Paul. Cash studied the teachings of the apostle Paul, who, as Saul of Tarsus, was converted by Christ on the road between Jerusalem and Damascus, Syria. Saul, who was born a Jew, was on his way to Damascus to seek out the Christians and persecute them. Along the way God blinds him with an amazing light and sends him on a different mission, and as St. Paul he would preach the gospel of Christ throughout the land. In 1986 Cash wrote his only published novel, *Man in White*, chronicling six years in the life of the apostle Paul. The novel was a moderate success, and it received mostly positive reviews. "One of These Days" explains Cash's desire to know St. Paul better and ask him about his journeys and the incredible life he lived. Additionally, Cash wrote the song "Man in White" about St. Paul after he had completed his novel *Man in White*. The song was released on cassette and available only to his fan-club members.

Cash recalled writing "My Children Walk in Truth," also from the *Believe in Him* album, after a terrifying accident landed his son John Carter Cash in the hospital. On Labor Day 1974, John Carter had been riding in his father's jeep with other kids. Johnny's sister Reba was driving and opted to take off the top of the vehicle. The jeep flipped over and John Carter was taken to Vanderbilt Children's Hospital, where he was placed in intensive care after suffering a concussion and a small skull fracture. He remained in the hospital for three days, and on the last night in the hospital Cash remembered picking up the Gideon Bible and turning to a verse of Scripture that expressed exactly what he felt. The verse was *I have no greater joy than to hear that my children walk, in truth* (3 John, verse 4). "I took a pen and a get-well card that had come to John Carter and wrote the song in a few minutes"

(Cash, *Man in Black,* 209). In the song, Johnny prays to know more joy in life but comes to realize that his greatest joy in his salvation is to know his children walk in truth. The better man he is, the more he knows his children will find their way in truth. Cash was a student of the Scriptures and had an amazing ability to find the kernels of truth, and great song hooks, sprinkled throughout the Bible.

Cash also recorded inspirational songs that he did not write, but which espoused his personal ideology in such a way as he had intended. "I'm Just an Old Chunk of Coal," included on his 1979 *A Believer Sings the Truth* album, is one of these songs. Billy Joe Shaver wrote the now-classic ballad about having faith in God and believing that although "I'm just an old chunk of coal, I'm gonna be a diamond someday." It's a priceless motif and a song that Cash delivers with sincerity. It should have been among Cash's biggest hits. Unfortunately, his recording of it was never released as a single and, ultimately, the song was recorded by then up-and-coming singer John Anderson who took it to number 4 on the country chart in 1981. This is one of the most unfortunate missed opportunities in Cash's recording career.

Student of the Bible

Cash was a student of the Bible, and did not hesitate to explore his ideas about and understanding of the scriptures in song. Johnny takes on the role of apocalyptic preacher in his prophetic reading of "Matthew 24 (Is Knocking at the Door)," from his 1973 album *Johnny Cash and His Woman.* It's a catalog of what Cash believes to be the signs of the times he was living in. It's a frightening call for change that explains, "today or one day more might be our last." Cash recalled in *Man in Black* that "Having been to Israel three times, studying the life and words of Jesus, and on the third trip doing a film about Jesus, with His words always on my mind, I wrote a flood of songs, one of them being [this one]" (14). Cash holds nothing back as he asserts what might happen if we do not change our errant ways. If Cash's goal was to frighten listeners and make us think about what's ahead, he certainly succeeded.

In February 1993, while touring in Ireland, Cash was invited by the rock group U2 to join them in a Dublin recording studio to record "The Wanderer." Bono had long been a fan of Cash and was especially inspired by his Sun recordings. He saw Cash as a mystical preacher and originally had called this song "The Preacher," before changing the title to "Wanderlust" and finally "The Wanderer." Bono recalled, "Ecclesiastes is one of my favorite books. It's a book about a character that wants to find out why he's alive, why he was created. He tries knowledge. He tries wealth. He tries experience. He tries everything. You hurry to the end of the book to find out why, and it says, 'It's good to work,' 'Remember your Creator.' In a way, it's such a letdown. Yet it isn't. There's something of Johnny Cash in that"

(Turner, 191). Cash believed the song was like "a post-apocalyptic search. It's the search for three important things: God, that woman, and myself" (Turner, 191).

Cash sang the lead vocal as U2 backed him up. This would foreshadow Cash's career resurgence as an icon for a younger generation. The song is about a prodigal son who wanders away from his home with nothing but the thought of someone he loved. He wanders around the world with nothing but her memory. He goes out searching for experience, as much as he could find before he would repent. It's a potent lyric with Cash as preacher, relating his own worldly-wise journey solely for us to learn from. "The Wanderer" was included as the closing track on U2's *Zooropa* album.

In 1976 country singer Bobby Bare had a Top 20 hit with Paul Craft's "Dropkick Me, Jesus," a song that cleverly utilized football metaphors to describe the singer's view of phony "righteous, upright" Christians. That same year, Cash recorded his own take on the subject with "No Earthly Good." The Oak Ridge Boys originally recorded it with Cash for their *Old Fashioned, Down Home, Hand Clappin', Foot Stompin, Southern Style, Gospel Quartet Music* album. Cash performed it solo on his 1977 album *The Rambler*, and the end result is a well-done inspirational song with a mighty hook, "You're so heavenly minded, you're no earthly good." The song is filled with great lines that show off Cash's prowess as a songwriter in any genre. Regarding this song, Cash has said, "Once a Christian puts himself above the world, or in his fervor becomes 'holier than thou' or too good to associate with people of questionable character, then he has alienated the very people who need what he has to share, which is why I wrote [this song]" (Cash, *Man in Black*, 204). Cash would revisit this gospel gem while at American Recordings. It was eventually released on the *Unearthed* box set. In the liner notes to *Unearthed*, we are told that "No Earthly Good" was written by Cash as a social commentary about "phony, pious Christians," who he believed give Christianity a bad name. Hence the hook line, "You're so heavenly minded, you're no earthly good." Cash took such comfort from his faith that it truly troubled him to see people denigrate it in any way. This acoustic version on *Unearthed* includes a previously omitted fourth stanza.

In 1973 Cash did a session which songwriter Albert Hammond produced. Hammond was still riding high from the success of his hit song "It Never Rains in Southern California" one year earlier. Hammond and collaborator Mike Hazlewood wrote "Praise the Lord and Pass the Soup," and it features guest turns by the Carter Family and the Oak Ridge Boys. In fact, this was the Oak Ridge Boys' first charting single and in just three years they would begin an extremely successful career as an award-winning country group. This song is an inspirational shout-out to the mission down the street where everyone can get something to eat. It's a humanitarian plea to help the less fortunate, with a gospel-choir background that emphasizes this point. It's a fully produced, overtly religious single, and maybe that's why it failed to gain any measure of commercial success. Whereas a song like "Daddy Sang Bass" captured a universal notion of family and childhood, the message in this song is sincere but ultimately too pious and preachy. It managed to make it only to number 57 on the country chart, a very weak showing for a Cash single at the time.

One of Cash's finest religious-commentary songs appeared on the album *Believe in Him.* Songwriter Mark Germino wrote "God Ain't No Stained Glass Window," asserting his belief that God is more than just a stained-glass window we see in church. It's a tender ballad that lets Cash reaffirm his faith by presenting a list of things that he doesn't understand, juxtaposed against something he does wholeheartedly believe, that "God ain't no stained glass window because He never keeps His window closed." Country star Kathy Mattea first released the song on her debut album *Kathy Mattea* in 1983.

Gospel Journey

In February 1973, Cash attended the premiere of his movie *The Gospel Road* in Charlotte, North Carolina. In April, Columbia released the Larry Butler–produced soundtrack album. In his autobiography, Cash called *The Gospel Road* the most ambitious project he ever attempted. He remembered, "The idea of going to Israel and making a movie emerged one morning when June woke up and told me about a dream she'd had in which she saw me on a mountain in the Holy Land, talking about Jesus" (Cash, *Autobiography*, 308). He was also inspired by his friendship with Billy Graham; so in May 1972, Cash returned to the Holy Land with forty associates and spent thirty days filming a Twentieth Century Fox motion picture following the footsteps of Jesus Christ. Cash would cowrite the dialogue with Larry Murray, who had worked with Cash on his television show, and compose much of the music for the movie and two-LP soundtrack album. The soundtrack also includes songs written by Kris Kristofferson, Larry Gatlin, John Denver, Joe South, and Christopher Wren.

The director was noted cinematographer Robert Elfstrom, who had also worked on the earlier 1969 Cash documentary, *Johnny Cash: The Man, His World, His Music.* Elfstrom also took on the role of Jesus, with June Carter playing Mary Magdalene; Cash's sister Reba Cash Hancock played the Virgin Mary, and songwriter Larry Murray portrayed John the Baptist. From 1972 to 1973, Larry Butler was Cash's studio manager, producer, and pianist. *The Gospel Road* was the last of five Cash albums that Butler would produce until 1978, when he and Cash would reunite for *I Would Like To See*

You Again. During that time Butler served as head of United Artists Records in Nashville, where he would go on to produce a series of giant hits and million-selling albums for Kenny Rogers. *The Gospel Road* made it to number 12 on the country album chart and included only one charting single, "Children." Twentieth Century Fox released *The Gospel Road* on DVD in 2005. The soundtrack album was not released on CD until Sony issued *The Complete Columbia Album Collection* in 2012.

Author and songwriter Christopher Wren, who had written "Jesus Was a Carpenter" for Cash, composed the song "The Gospel Road." Cash divides it up into four segments, with the first recalling how the evangelists Matthew, Mark, Luke and John told about Jesus on the Gospel highway. The second part speaks of John the Baptist proclaiming the coming of Jesus and going to see Him at the Jordan River. The third section explains how the word goes out to Nazareth that Jesus is coming. And the final verse of this song finds Jesus's remaining disciples walking in His footsteps down that Gospel road. A new recording of "Jesus Was a Carpenter" is also included, with lyrical changes to help tell the story.

Highlights include Larry Gatlin's song of praise "Help," that was first released as part of Kris Kristofferson's critically acclaimed album *Jesus Was a Capricorn.* "Help" is broken up into four segments. The first part is the original track featuring Kristofferson and Gatlin singing the opening verse. Kristofferson sings the second part of this tender inspirational favorite of the original recording. Then Cash takes over with a newly recorded third verse, before he concludes the song with the final stanza asking God's help to let him see how he fits into the Lord's master plan. The song would become a number 6 charting country hit for Elvis Presley in 1974, and has become a modern inspirational standard. On both the Kristofferson release and the Elvis single, the song is titled "Help Me."

Interestingly, it was Gatlin's "Help Me" that inspired Kris Kristofferson to write "Why Me." Cash had originally recorded a version of "Why Me, Lord" in 1977, but never released it. He finally got around to rerecording it for his *American Recordings* album. The song was Kristofferson's biggest charting single. Kris wrote the song after being in church and hearing Gatlin perform "Help Me." Kris was so moved by the experience that he wrote his own song of praise to the Lord. Cash delivers a poignant rendition of his own. When he sings "Lord help me Jesus, I've wasted it, so help me Jesus, I know what I am," there is a sense of personal salvation rendered with truth and conviction.

Cash recites "The Lord's Prayer" on *The Gospel Road,* before being joined by the Carter Family and the Statler Brothers for the "Amen Chorus." Then he introduces June, in the role of Mary Magdalene, who speaks about her love for and devotion to Christ. June sings "Follow Me," the John Denver–penned ballad, to explain Mary Magdalene's love and devotion to Jesus. Aside from Denver's own fine version of the song, Mary Travers of Peter, Paul and Mary released it as a single in 1971. The song fits perfectly into the fabric of this album and June delivers one of her finest vocal performances.

Johnny includes the tender ballad "Children," written by singer-songwriter Joe South, about the wonder and innocence of little children. South had enjoyed two hits on the pop chart with "Games People Play" in 1969 and "Walk a Mile in My Shoes" in 1970. He also released his own single of "Children" in 1970 that reached number 51 on the pop chart. Cash's version, backed by the Carter Family, fared a little better, making it to number 30 on the country chart in 1973.

With "Burden of Freedom," an outstanding ballad by Kristofferson, Cash explains the high price Christ had to pay for our salvation. Kris had originally included it on his third Monument album *Border Lord,* and Rita Coolidge, his wife at the time, also recorded it. In his first autobiography, *Man in Black,* Cash recalled, "Kris sang 'Burden of Freedom,' and throughout the song I could see Jesus carrying His cross, falling, struggling, making the long, torturous journey to Calvary" (199). Cash brings his own solemnity to the song, as it dramatically captures the events surrounding the final days of Jesus's life on earth.

Harold and Don Reid composed the lovely "Lord, Is It I?" a tender meditation performed by the Statler Brothers. "The Last Supper" is a song Larry Gatlin wrote especially for this project. It describes what might have been the mood around the table for the Last Supper. Gatlin recalls, "Johnny asked Kris to write a song for the Last Supper scene, and he wrote 'Jesus Was a Capricorn.' I wrote 'The Last Supper,' which Johnny sang for the soundtrack. Kris later recorded 'Capricorn' as the title song of his new album" (Gatlin, 93). And *The Gospel Road* concludes with "Ascension, Amen Chorus," a sacred rendition of the "Amen Chorus" performed by the Carter Family and the Statler Brothers, as Jesus ascends into heaven.

Dedicated to Jack

With Columbia Records still letting Cash do whatever he wanted, in 1976 he released *Johnny Cash Sings Precious Memories,* an album of his favorite traditional songs of inspiration. With elaborate arrangements and full orchestration, Cash selected eleven gospel standards and recorded them the way he wanted them to sound. The result is an outstanding album of everlasting spirituals that ranks among his greatest inspirational recordings. Cash dedicated the album to his beloved older brother Jack.

Cash turns in a first-rate performance of the album's title song, "Precious Memories." This gospel hymn has been credited to J. B. F. Wright, and it dates back to 1925. Many artists have recorded it, but no one sings it quite like Cash, who imbues it with notable sincerity. The same goes for "Rock of Ages," the popular Christian hymn credited to the Reverend Augustus Montague Toplady, who wrote it in 1763. Thanks to Bill Walker's rich arrangement, Cash turns in an evocative performance of this inspirational standard.

Many country and folk performers have recorded the song "Farther Along." From Pete Seeger and Roy Acuff to Elvis Presley, Linda Ronstadt, and Emmylou Harris. The Byrds even titled their final album *Farther Along.* The song was written in 1911 by Reverend W. A. Fletcher, and tells of what all the faithful might have to look forward to in heaven. J. R. Baxter Jr.'s arrangement of this song affords Cash the perfect background accompaniment for his memorable performance of the devotional lyric.

"Amazing Grace" is arguably Cash's finest performance on this album. It says a great deal about Cash that he was able to take the greatest of Christian hymns and turn in a performance that ranks among the very finest. English poet and clergyman John Newton published the hymn in 1779, and its message of grace and redemption has inspired and comforted people for centuries.

A Dream Come True

In December 1979, Cash released *A Believer Sings the Truth*. Johnny called this double album his "dream gospel album," and has called it his most ambitious project aside from *The Gospel Road*. It took the better part of six months to complete, with some very extensive overdub sessions. He brought on board his family and friends to help him sing his favorite inspirational songs, old and new. Cash and Jack Clement were the driving forces behind this project, and the result was one of Johnny's most impassioned inspirational albums. However, Columbia refused to release it. Cash kept the masters and released them on a small label, Cachet (pronounced "Cash-et") Records. Interestingly, despite having no major-record-label promotion, the record still managed to make it to number 43 on the country album chart.

Cash opens the album with "Wings in the Morning" a profound, original gospel composition about the joy of finally arriving in heaven after having lived a rich, full life. Cash paints a pretty picture of life's other side, where all the faithful weary travelers will find rest and relief from their "old aching bones" and earthly constraints. This is a sturdy inspirational song that ranks among Johnny's finest-written and -recorded gospel songs.

Johnny delivers a preacher-like performance of "Gospel Boogie (a Wonderful Time up There),"

Southern gospel writer Lee Roy Abernathy's rousing 1947 standard, which Pat Boone took all the way to number 4 on the pop chart in 1958. After listening to Johnny testifying about what awaits us in heaven, we are totally convinced that we can look forward to something wonderful in the Promised Land. This was the song that he first sang for his mother as a young boy, and after she heard him sing it he recalled, "My mother's eyes were full of tears. 'You sound exactly like my daddy,' she said....'God has his hand on you, son,' said mama" (Cash, *Man in Black,* 56).

Whenever Johnny sings with Anita Carter, something magical happens. Her angelic voice is the perfect complement to Cash's rugged, worldly-wise musical minister. "Over the Next Hill" is a tender ballad about what awaits us over the next hill when we'll be home. Cash echoes evangelicals when he relates how, according to his reading of the prophets, the end may be near but that we have nothing to fear, and "there will come a great redeeming, and over the next hill we'll be home." Cash begins his first autobiography *Man in Black,* by discussing the inception of this song. Cash recalled that, "We were doing a concert in Laramie and were driving there from Denver. The land surrounding us was mountainous — massive, rolling hills — and the sunset in the big sky up ahead was beautiful. 'Looks like songwriting time,' June said. 'Don't know if we'd have time,' I said. 'By the way the land is layin',

I think I'd be safe to say that just over this next hill we'll be in Laramie.' 'There's your song,' she said. 'Why don't you make that 'Over the Next Hill, We'll Be Home.' And so I did" (Cash, *Man in Black*, 13).

Southern Christian songwriter Don Francisco wrote "He's Alive," a song about the Apostle Peter describing the events just after Christ's crucifixion. Johnny does an exemplary job interpreting this account of Jesus's resurrection. This is a duet with June, in which she takes on the role of Mary. In 1989 Dolly Parton included this song on her *White Limozeen* album and released it as a single. Dolly's cover made it to number 39 on the country chart.

Cash revisits "I Was There When It Happened (So I Guess I Ought to Know)," an old favorite from his Sun days. It's a reassuring, first-person proclamation told from the perspective of someone who was there with Jesus and was saved by Him. This song would be one of the last to feature original Tennessee Two member Marshall Grant on bass and vocal. In 1979, Grant left the Cash show, and in 1980 he filed a lawsuit against Cash for wrongful dismissal and embezzlement of retirement funds. The lawsuit was later settled out of court and the two men eventually reconciled. Grant went on to manage the Statler Brothers for many years until his retirement, and he reunited with Cash and the Tennessee Three in 1999. He borrowed the title of the song for his 2006 autobiography, *I Was*

There When It Happened: My Life with Johnny Cash. Sadly, Grant passed away while attending a Johnny Cash tribute concert in Jonesboro, Arkansas, on August 7, 2011, at age eighty-three. Grant sings with Cash on this updated version of "I Was There When It Happened," just as he did for the original Sun recording.

While the specific origins of "This Train Is Bound for Glory," first recorded in 1925 are unknown, Sister Rosetta Tharpe, the first black artist signed to a major label, recorded it in the late 1930s. Cash had long referred to Tharpe as his favorite singer. It was her version that Johnny had first become familiar with and on which he based this arrangement. The rousing spiritual also became a folk-music staple and served as the inspiration for Woody Guthrie's autobiography, *Bound for Glory*. Many artists have recorded it including Pete Seeger, Peter, Paul and Mary, Mahalia Jackson, and the Seekers. Johnny and June turn in a solid performance testifying about the pulse-pounding train that's picking up passengers and bound for the Promised Land.

Songs His Mother Taught Him

In 2003, "My Mother's Hymn Book" was the title given to the fourth disc in the *Unearthed* box set. In April 2004, it was released as a separate album comprised of songs Cash originally learned from his mother. She had an old book called *Heavenly*

Highway Hymns from which Cash selected the songs on this album. It's just Johnny and his guitar singing the songs that formed the foundation of his remarkable career in music. After all those years, Cash closed out his career just as he had begun it, with a desire to record an album of the music his mother had taught him. Cash always expressed his deep love for inspirational music and in the liner notes says this is his favorite of all the albums he has made.

Cash says that his mother, Carrie Rivers Cash, was a big fan of the Carter Family. He goes on to explain that the songs they sang were songs they'd been singing in church all their life. Of course, heaven is the land "Where We'll Never Grow Old," and to hear Cash sing this James C. Moore tune is beautiful and heartbreaking at the same time. There is a sense of pure acceptance as Cash sings, "All our sorrows will end and our voices will blend, with the loved ones who've gone on before." John Carter Cash sums it up best in the liner notes when he writes, "In terms of soul and spirit, that record's going to be it, just him and his guitar and the boy in his heart singing his Mother's Hymn Book."

Cash refers to V. O. Fossett's "I Shall Not Be Moved" in the liner notes as the white church version of the black gospel standard "We Shall Not Be Moved." Cash is in exceptionally fine voice on these songs and this track in particular. When he sings, "Just like the tree that is planted by the water, I shall not be moved," we hang on every syllable and believe every word he sings.

Cash writes that "I Am a Pilgrim" is an old country gospel classic that his mother sang, which he knew he would record one day. He speculates that a younger generation might have become familiar with the song from the Byrds recording on their classic *Sweetheart of the Rodeo* album. That historic album fused country and rock music together for a popular audience. But Cash says that he knows it as a Merle Travis song, and he delivers an outstanding reading of another song about the lovely home that awaits us in "that yonder city" that lies across the Jordan River.

Cash admits that "When the Roll Is Called Up Yonder," which was sung at his brother Jack's funeral, is a precious song to him. Originally recorded with a full orchestra backing on *Sings Precious Memories,* it is certainly more sentimental to hear Cash sing it on *My Mother's Hymn Book* in the twilight of his years.

In the liner notes Cash talks about how he originally wanted to be a gospel singer, and how he first introduced himself to Sam Phillips as "Johnny Cash, gospel singer." Albert E. Brumley's "If We Never Meet Again This Side of Heaven," originally included on the *Hymns from the Heart* album, is one of the songs that led Cash in that direction. This cover of "If We Never Meet Again" takes on added significance as Cash sings about coming to the end of his journey and preparing to gather in heaven's bright city. Cash takes a solo turn on Brumley's uplifting "I'll Fly Away," another cover of a song he had originally recorded on *The Survivors* album.

"Where the Soul of Man Never Dies" is another gospel standard that talks about what awaits us in our heavenly home where the soul of man never dies. And Cash relates a very moving story regarding the song "Let the Lower Lights Be Burning" in the liner notes. When his father was dying, having been in a coma for days, all the family had gathered around him. Johnny's sister Louise suggested they sing to him and chose this song. His father's lips started moving and he started singing along with them, and they cried upon hearing his voice. Cash had originally recorded this song on *Hymns from the Heart*. And "When He Reached Down His Hand for Me" is yet another song originally recorded for *Hymns from the Heart*, and a song that Cash calls one of his mother's all-time favorites.

"In the Sweet By and By" is a song that was sung at his brother Jack's funeral. Cash originally recorded it with a full-orchestra arrangement on *Sings Precious Memories*. This ranks among the best performances on *My Mother's Hymn Book*, and that's saying a lot, considering they are all impressive. Cash explains in the liners how "I'm Bound for the Promised Land" has always offered him comfort knowing that he was bound for the Promised Land. Even when Jerry Lee Lewis said they were doing the devil's music back during the Sun days, Cash always knew he would make it all right.

"In the Garden" is another lovely performance of a song about the beauty of heaven. It precedes two songs that were all originally recorded with full arrangements for *Sings Precious Memories*. Cash refers to "Softly and Tenderly" as a song of invitation. He explains how it brings him comfort and embodies the healing power of music. And Cash says that the previously discussed "Just As I Am" is a song he's sung all his life. He also refers to it as another song of invitation, inviting us to church. He says through all his "years in the wilderness," and through past drug addictions, he finally accepted the fact that God thought there was something worth saving in him. Though Cash always thought this, he often had trouble acting like the good Christian he thought he should be.

Whereas *My Mother's Hymn Book* is made up of songs that were inspired by Cash's mother, "Family Bible," from the 1990 album *Boom Chicka Boom,* features Carrie Rivers Cash singing along with her famous son. "Family Bible" is one of the songs Willie Nelson wrote and sold for fifty dollars back when he was starting out in Nashville and struggling to make ends meet as a songwriter. The song is still credited to Walt Breeland, Paul Buskirk, and Claude Gray. Country singer Gray took the song to number 10 on the country chart in 1960.

The Johnny Cash Show with his mother Carrie Rivers Cash. *Courtesy of Sony Music Entertainment.*

It has become a modern-day inspirational standard. Cash puts his own stamp on it here and is joined by his mother on harmony vocal. Mrs. Cash introduced her son to gospel music and this poignant pairing was certainly a milestone in Cash's recording career. When Cash sings, "I can hear my mother softly singing, 'Rock of Ages,' 'Rock of Ages,' cleft for me," Mrs. Cash joins in to make this one of the standout songs in Cash's career. One year later, on March 11, 1991 Carrie Rivers Cash passed away. She had been the single biggest influence in her son's life, and Cash would feel her loss for the rest of his life.

Stereo
CAN ALSO BE PLAYED
ON MONO EQUIPMENT
CS 9639
COLUMBIA

JOHNNY CASH
AT FOLSOM PRISON

Folsom Prison Blues
Orange Blossom Special
The Long Black Veil
Jackson
(With June Carter)
Green, Green Grass of Home
I Got Stripes
Dirty Old Egg-sucking Dog
The Wall
25 Minutes to Go
Dark as the Dungeon
I Still Miss Someone
Cocaine Blues
Send a Picture of Mother
Give My Love to Rose
(With June Carter)
Flushed From the Bathroom of Your Heart
Greystone Chapel

Chapter 6

I GOT STRIPES

THE LEGENDARY PRISON RECORDINGS

The albums Johnny Cash recorded live at
Folsom Prison, San Quentin, and På Österåker

May 1968 saw the release of *Johnny Cash at Folsom Prison,* the album that Johnny had wanted to record for six years while at Columbia Records. His original producers at the label, Don Law and Frank Jones, were not supportive of such an endeavor, nor were Columbia label executives at the time. But in 1967 the label underwent organizational changes, and Johnny was assigned a new producer named Bob Johnston. Johnston was known as a creative loose cannon who had also been working with Bob Dylan. Writer Michael Streissguth has written a definitive account of

everything that went into the making of this prison concert and resulting album in his book *Johnny Cash at Folsom Prison: The Making of a Masterpiece.* He explains that after he began working with Johnston, Cash saw an opportunity to pitch his idea of recording a live album at a prison. "From Cash's perspective, this Texas speculator with New York bite appeared to be the gatekeeper who could admit him to a recording date in prison" (Streissguth, *Johnny Cash at Folsom Prison*, 60-61). According to Robert Hilburn, Cash felt that the label relented to let him record the album because they had pretty much given up on Cash. His last

« Johnny Cash at Folsom Prison.
Courtesy of Sony Music Entertainment.

Columbia
Stereo
CS 9827

JOHNNY CASH AT SAN QUENTIN

A Boy Named Sue
Wanted Man
I Walk the Line
Wreck of the Old 97
San Quentin
Darling Companion
Starkville City Jail
Folsom Prison Blues
Peace in the Valley

Johnny Cash at San Quentin. *Courtesy of Sony Music Entertainment* few albums had not sold as well as the label had hoped, and Cash's behavior was erratic as he battled "with too many pills, too many missed shows, too many troubled recordings sessions" (Hilburn, *Johnny Cash: The Life*, 26).

On January 10, 1968, Cash, June Carter, the Tennessee Three (Marshall Grant, Luther Perkins, and W. S. Holland), Carl Perkins, the Statler Brothers, Johnny's father Ray Cash, and Bob Johnston arrived in Sacramento, California. The troop would gather and rehearse for the next two days. On January 12, California governor Ronald Reagan would visit the group, say hello, and offer his best wishes. This was Johnny's fourth visit to perform at Folsom Prison, as he writes in his descriptive liner notes for the album. He recalls, "I brought my show to Folsom. Prisoners are the greatest audience that an entertainer can perform for. We bring them a ray of sunshine in their dungeon and they're not ashamed to respond, and show their appreciation."

On January 13, 1968, two complete performances were recorded at Folsom Prison, the first at 9:40 AM and the second at 12:40 PM. The album *Johnny Cash at Folsom Prison* was released just four months later and included sixteen songs, fourteen of which were taken from the first concert and two ("Give My Love to Rose" and "I Got Stripes") edited in from the second show. The original album became a landmark recording for Cash and helped revive and revitalize his standing with Columbia Records and his career in general. *At Folsom Prison*

remained at number 1 for four weeks on the country album chart, and climbed to number 13 on the pop album chart. It was certified double platinum by the RIAA, and was named the 1968 Country Music Association's Album of the Year. The album also won Cash a Grammy Award for Best Album Notes in 1969.

Sony released what they had then called the complete concert recording in 1999, with three previously unreleased tracks added for a total of 19 songs. Then in 2008, Legacy released a newly revised two-CD-plus-DVD box set including both concert performances in their entirety without editing, and featuring solo performances by the other artists on the bill.

Columbia Records had just about given up on Cash at this point and unceremoniously released his live recording of "Folsom Prison Blues" without any great expectations as a single. They didn't count on the thrill and excitement the song generated as the opening track of what is now regarded as a Cash milestone. There's something electrifying about hearing Cash render a line like "I shot a man in Reno, just to watch him die," before a group of over one thousand incarcerated men. From the opening introduction of "Hello, I'm Johnny Cash," we know something special is about to take place. The whoops and hollers of the inmates made this record take on a life of its own, and even though this is the third released version of "Folsom Prison Blues," following the original Sun hit single and the studio rerecording for Columbia included on the 1964 album *I Walk the Line*, this one feels brand new, as if we're hearing it for the very first time. Although it might be effusive to call something magical, there is really no other term that appropriately describes the impact of this particular recording. Ironically, Gordon Jenkins, who had written "Crescent City Blues" on which Johnny based his version, saw how successful the song had become for Johnny this time around, and finally confronted Cash and drew a settlement that approached $100,000. Cash did however get to keep his songwriter credit (Streissguth, *Folsom Prison*, 49). The song remained at number 1 on the country chart for four weeks and reached number 32 on the pop chart. Cash won the Grammy Award for Best Male Country Vocal Performance for this song in 1969.

Cash follows an edited version of "Busted" with a somber performance of Merle Travis's "Dark as a Dungeon." That is until a surge of laughter erupts as the prisoners detect the correlation of the dark, dreary mine with the prison they're in. Cash breaks down during the song, laughing along and saying to the audience, "No laughing during the song, please, it's being recorded I know, hell. Don't you know it's recorded?" Hearing Cash utter a mild profanity drives the prisoners wild as Cash finds new ways to relate to his audience. When the song is over he informs them that the show is being recorded and they can't say things like "hell or shit

or anything like that." On the original release the word shit was bleeped out, but reinstated for the 1999 reissue.

Merle Travis wrote "Dark as a Dungeon," about the hardships of being a miner and the toll the job will take on your health and happiness. It's a brutal, haunting tale of struggle and strife. Even when he's dead and gone, the narrator will look down from his heavenly home and pity the miner digging his bones. Merle Travis wrote the song from his own experience growing up around the coalmines of Kentucky, where his father and brothers were coal miners. Cash originally released it in 1964 as the B-side of the single "Understand Your Man," and managed to make it to number 49 on the country chart. This version was not included on an album at the time. Cash recorded the song again for the 2003 *Unearthed* box set. He explains in the liner notes that "Dark as a Dungeon" is a song that he always thought he should have written. And he has recorded it a few times over the years. He admits that he promised the song's writer, Merle Travis, that he would keep on trying until he got it right. Well, on *Unearthed* he got it right.

We can see the care Cash has taken to select precisely the right songs for this performance. "I Still Miss Someone" certainly resonated with this audience, as everyone must have been missing someone they couldn't forget. We hear total silence from the prisoners as he sings this song, and that's quite a feat in itself. Johnny wrote "I Still Miss Someone" with his nephew, Roy Cash Jr. Roy had written the first draft of the song as a poem for a college writing assignment. He showed it to his uncle and they worked together on the lyric and added the melody. It's considered by many to be the ultimate jewel in the Cash songwriting canon. It's a simple, sparse, cathartic expression of romantic grief. The singer mourns the love he's lost and rationalizes that "there's someone for me somewhere, and I still miss someone." It's poetic, personal, and profound in its simplicity. It is the perfect country song. When Cash sings "I never got over those blue eyes, I see them everywhere, I miss those arms that held me, when all the love was there," we can feel his sense of loss and devastation. The song would resonate with fans and fellow performers alike. Emmylou Harris would record an outstanding version of the song; Bob Dylan would duet with Cash on the song during their unreleased Nashville session; and Cash would revisit it frequently over the years on various albums and in concert.

Next, Cash reinstates the proper title and lyric to "Cocaine Blues," which originally appeared on *Now, There Was a Song!* as "Transfusion Blues." The song, written by T. J. "Red" Arnall in 1947, is a western swing tune about a man who gets crazy on a transfusion and ultimately shoots his woman down. It's a reworking of the traditional ballad "Little Sadie," and it's a cautionary tale that Cash would revisit over the years. The song was originally written as "Cocaine Blues," but Cash had to change it to the less controversial "Transfusion Blues," making it a song about alcohol abuse. He changed the title back to the original "Cocaine Blues" when he performed it live at Folsom. Years later he slowed the tempo down for a more sedate version on his 1979 album *Silver*. Cash had readily admitted to his battle with substance abuse. This song describes the worst possible outcome of drug addiction, and Cash clearly desires to warn people of what might happen if they stay hooked on drugs or alcohol. Interestingly, in the song "Folsom Prison Blues," the narrator shot a man just to watch him die; in this song the narrator shoots his woman because she was cheating on him, reasoning, "I thought I was her daddy but she had five more." Needless to say, the audience goes wild from the very start of the song about a drug addict who took a shot of cocaine before he shot his woman down. It's a full-speed-ahead roller-coaster ride as the man flees and tries to escape the law until he's finally captured. He's taken to jail and eventually ends up in Folsom Prison for murder in the first degree. This raucous live rendition even ends with him showing no remorse and proclaiming, "I can't forget the day I shot that bad bitch down."

What Johnny Cash prison album would be complete without a song about a hanging? Johnny revisits the Shel Silverstein–penned "25 Minutes to Go," which originally appeared on *Sings the Ballads of the True West*. Johnny slyly snickers as he sings the opening line, "Well, they're building a gallows outside my cell," as he begins the count-down to his own execution. The audience claps and shouts along until the end when they erupt in deafening applause.

"I'm Here to Get My Baby Out of Jail" was not included on the original album release, and it was also omitted from the 1999 Sony reissue. It made its first appearance on the 2008 Sony Legacy box set. It's the first time Cash ever recorded this song, which was from the 1930s and had previously been recorded by the Everly Brothers. It's about an old woman who comes to a jail and tells the warden of the penitentiary that she's just there to get her baby out of jail. The woman had searched far and wide for her son until she finally found him locked up in jail. Unfortunately, Cash, admittedly, forgets the words to the final verse and we never really learn how the song ends or if the mother ever managed to get her baby out of jail.

Cash dives full throttle into a stirring rendition of his hit "Orange Blossom Special." The song is best when performed live and Cash does not fail to deliver a first-rate performance. The audience can't contain their excitement and enthusiasm as Cash sings and ad libs his way through this harmonica-infused favorite. Many artists had per-formed "Orange Blossom Special," but it was Cash's recording that helped popularize it. Thanks to Mother Maybelle Carter, Johnny learned that the song's author was Ervin T. Rouse, and for the first time Rouse received songwriting credit. The song is about a passenger train. The first recording of the song was by Ervin and Gordon Rouse in 1939, and it went by the title "The Special." Bill Monroe originally popularized the song and performed it as an instrumental with a fiddle breakdown. Johnny replaced the fiddles with a pair of harmon-icas and turned it into a number 3 country hit in 1965. That recording also reached number 80 on the pop chart. The narrator is excitedly anticipat-ing the Orange Blossom Special bringing his baby back to him. He also informs us that he's ready to ride the train to either Florida or California to get some sand in his shoes. It's all in good fun and shows off Cash's less serious side. He makes us want to ride along with him on the fastest train on the line. Boots Randolph played the saxophone on "Orange Blossom Special," and Johnny would record this song many times over the years, most notably at his shows at Folsom and San Quentin. Willie Nelson and Sheryl Crow would perform the song in tribute to Cash in 1999 at the Hammerstein Ballroom in New York City.

Cash follows "Orange Blossom" with another old favorite, "The Long Black Veil." Cash slows things down to perform this somber tale of cheating and murder that he first recorded for his *Orange Blossom Special* album. "The Long Black Veil" is a haunting murder ballad written by Marijohn Wilkin and Danny Dill, who cowrote the Bobby

Bare hit "Detroit City," which Cash would later cover in a medley on *The Johnny Cash Show* album. "The Long Black Veil" was originally released by country legend Lefty Frizzell, and the single made it to number 6 on the country chart in 1959. Cash turns in an unsurpassed rendition of this ghostly tale of mistaken identity. The story tells of a murder that took place ten years before as the singer recalls the events from the grave. He could have saved his own life if he had told the truth, but the truth was never revealed, for he had been in the arms of his best friend's wife. Now, "she walks these hills in a long black veil, and visits my grave when the night winds wail, nobody knows, nobody sees, but me." So, the secret remains and the end result is one of country music's greatest story-songs. Johnny selected the Folsom Prison performance of the song as one of his all-time favorite recordings for *The Legendary Johnny Cash.* "Long Black Veil" is the perfect song for the Folsom inmates, who remain silent throughout his performance until he reaches the line "I'd been in the arms of my best friend's wife." Cash breaks down laughing along with the audience, asking, "Did I hear somebody applaud?"

The studio version of "Send a Picture of Mother" was originally issued as the B-side of the single "Busted." It makes its first appearance here on a Cash album, and fits nicely into the program. The song is about a prison friendship of seven years.

The singer's friend is going to be freed, while he remains behind bars. He begs his friend to send a picture of his mother if he can. The song addresses the idea of friendships forged behind bars and how these men truly come to rely on the only human interaction they have. Cash studied his subject matter well and in the line, "The hardest time will be on Sunday morning," we can feel the sad sense of loss as one man mourns not only his own lack of freedom, but also the loss of his best friend.

"The Wall" is another Harlan Howard song from the *Orange Blossom Special* album. It's a prison tale about an inmate who robbed and stole from his girl for simply naming her wedding day. Now he just sits staring at the wall all day, saying he will be the first to climb over it. One year later, the singer recounts how the newspapers called it a jailbreak plan when the inmate was killed trying to climb the wall. But the narrator knows better; it was suicide because he just couldn't stand being in the prison any longer. Once again, Cash breaks down in laughter and omits a verse from the song. That's what makes Johnny Cash so distinctive: he's not afraid to mess up a performance and still include it on an album.

Cash knows that humor is one of the best ways to win over this particular audience, and he wisely includes a few novelty songs in his Folsom Prison shows. The first two are written by Jack Clement. "Dirty Old Egg-Sucking Dog" first appeared on

Cash's *Everybody Loves a Nut* album. It's a funny story about a shaggy dog that keeps on killing the narrator's chickens. It's an amusing cartoon of a song, wherein the narrator is threatening to send the dog to that big chicken house in the sky. Cash wryly introduces it as a "love song," and it elicits shouts of laughter from the crowd. "Flushed from the Bathroom of Your Heart" was originally recorded in 1966 but never released. It makes its first appearance here and serves as a hilarious takeoff on a country breakup ballad. The narrator complains of being swept out of his darling's life. It's full of silly, clever wordplay, and the audience devours it. It says a lot about Cash that he can sing a silly lyric with the same confidence that he exhibits on a serious ballad.

Johnny brings June out to perform the couple's recent smash hit "Jackson." The song was written by country songwriter Billy Edd Wheeler, and pop hit-maker Jerry Leiber (using the pseudonym Gaby Rogers) who cowrote many hits with Mike Stoller, including "Hound Dog," "Don't," and "Jailhouse Rock" for Elvis Presley. Johnny and June deliver an uplifting, spirited performance that has the prisoners clapping and singing along. Next they perform "Give My Love To Rose," which was taken from the second show and incorporated into the original album. Johnny delivers a gentle, sensitive performance of one of his finest ballads. Interestingly, although June is credited on the song, she does not seem to be on it, or her vocal was mixed so far back that it's almost inaudible.

Johnny's hit song from 1959 "I Got Stripes" makes its first appearance on a Cash album in live form. It was taken from the second show and included on the original album release. It fits in nicely here, as Cash sings about being a prisoner with stripes around his shoulders and chains around his feet. This song elicits the loudest response from the audience. "I Got Stripes" was originally recorded at the sessions for *Songs of Our Soil*, and though it was released as a single, it was not included on the album. It was cowritten by Cash and his friend, California disc jockey Charlie Williams, who also wrote Gene Watson's 1979 hit "Farewell Party." "I Got Stripes" is one of Cash's best prison songs. It was also one of his biggest singles, reaching number 4 on the country chart and number 43 pop in 1959. Cash may have been influenced by Lead Belly's 1943 recording, "On A Monday." In short order the narrator is arrested on a Monday, locked up in jail on Tuesday, has his trial on Wednesday, and is found guilty on Thursday. If only the courts still moved as quickly! The chorus says it all, "I got stripes, stripes around my shoulders, I got chains, chains around my feet." While the subject matter is somber, the song has a lively tempo that keeps it from being maudlin. During the performance of this song at Folsom, Cash nervously breaks down laughing, omitting the final verse.

Johnny Cash performing at the Tennessee State Penitentiary in Nashville, 1968.
Courtesy of Sony Music Entertainment.

After an exceptional performance of "Green, Green Grass of Home," Cash introduces a song written by an inmate at the prison. Glen Sherley was a songwriter who had a song for Cash and passed it on to a California pastor who regularly visited the inmates to give to Cash. Cash liked what he heard and learned the song so that he could surprise Sherley with it during the concert. "Greystone Chapel" is a gospel song about the one place inmates could go for some measure of comfort. The hope was that the song might be released as a single, although it never was. The song was the perfect closing number for the set and did manage to gain Sherley some acclaim. He was offered the opportunity to record his own album and, upon being freed from prison, Johnny invited him to be part of his touring show. Eddy Arnold recorded Sherley's song "Portrait of My Woman" and released it as a single in 1971. Sadly, Sherley continued to exhibit erratic and threatening behavior, until Cash had to let him go. His career waned and in 1978 he died from a self-inflicted gunshot wound.

On August 5, 1968, tragedy struck when guitarist Luther Perkins died of injuries sustained in a fire when his house burned down. Cash, along with Marshall Grant, W. S. Holland, and Carl Perkins were pallbearers at Luther's funeral on August 7. Carl filled in for Luther on the Cash show until the following month, when a young guitarist named Bob Wootton would be hired as Luther's permanent replacement in the Tennessee Three.

The San Quentin Recordings

In June 1969, after a detour to the Holy Land, Johnny followed up his immensely successful Folsom Prison album with the release of *Johnny Cash at San Quentin,* an edited version of the concert he had performed on February 24, 1969. The original *At San Quentin* album included ten songs, presented in a sequence different from the original show. The album was a huge success, bigger than *Johnny Cash at Folsom Prison.* It remained at number 1 on the country album chart for an incredible twenty weeks, and stayed at number 1 on the pop chart for four weeks. It was named CMA Album of the Year in 1969, and it contained Johnny's most successful pop single, "A Boy Named Sue." The album was certified gold on August 12, 1969, platinum and double platinum on November 21, 1986, and triple platinum on March 27, 2003. Sony issued what was described as the complete concert recording in 2000. While it did move most of the songs back into their original performance order and added eight more songs from the concert, it wasn't until the two-CD Legacy edition of 2006 that the entire concert was finally released.

On January 1, 1959, Cash performed his first concert for the inmates of San Quentin Prison in California. During that show, Cash greatly inspired a twenty-year-old Merle Haggard, who was in the audience. Haggard had been incarcerated in March 1958 for attempted burglary. He and a friend were drunk and tried breaking into the back door of Fred & Gene's Café on Highway 99 in Bakersfield, California, with the intent of robbery, not realizing that the diner was still open for business.

Haggard could not believe the reception Cash received from the inmates, and decided that when he was freed he would pursue a career in country music. Though Haggard did not meet Cash that day, they would ultimately become friends and record together in the years to come. Interestingly, during a concert at Madison Square Garden Cash gets his facts a bit confused when he claims that Merle Haggard was in the front row of the audience at San Quentin when he played there in 1964. In his autobiography Haggard recalled, "Cash wasn't nearly as famous as he is today, but it was easy to see the raw talent in that tall, hungry-looking dude from Arkansas" (Haggard, *Sing Me Back Home,* 176).

Cash chose to open his headlining segment of the San Quentin concert on February 24, 1969, with "Big River." The song was not part of the original album and made its first appearance as the proper show opener on the 2000 Sony reissue of *Johnny Cash at San Quentin.* It's a shorter, sped-up version of the song, but a good choice for opening the show. Then Cash slows things down with "I Still Miss Someone." The song made its first appearance on the 2000 Sony reissue, and it's perplexing why this fine rendition was left off the original album. The only possible explanation might be that it had

been included on *At Folsom Prison,* and the record label preferred not to duplicate it here.

"Wreck of the Old 97" was the second song on the original San Quentin album. It was reinstated to its proper place in the show's sequence on the 2000 CD reissue. Anywhere you put it, it's a terrific, energized performance of the great train song. And ever the defiant rebel, Johnny tells the inmates that the show is being recorded to be televised in England, and they (the record label) warned him that, "you got do this song, you got to do that song, you know you got to stand like this, or act like this, I just don't get it, man, I'm here to do what you want me to and what I want to do, so what do you want to hear?" And the deafening response of the inmates is clear, they want to hear "I Walk the Line," the third track on the original album.

The medley "Long Black Veil/Give My Love to Rose" was not included on the original album release of *At San Quentin,* nor was it added to the 2000 CD reissue. Possible reasons for the omission from the original album are that both songs in the medley were featured on the Folsom Prison album. Also, the abbreviated versions of these two particular songs do not do them justice. We really want to hear the whole story of "The Long Black Veil."

The complete San Quentin version of "Folsom Prison Blues" in its proper sequence did not surface until the 2006 Legacy edition. No doubt another case of choosing not to duplicate a song that figured so prominently on the earlier prison-concert recording. Otherwise, this is quite a dynamic, riveting performance that the audience responds to enthusiastically. "Orange Blossom Special" is another song that duplicates one found on *At Folsom Prison.* And, as such, it was not included on the original album release and was also left off the 2000 Sony reissue. And "Jackson" is yet another great performance that did not surface until the 2006 Legacy Edition reissue. The song was such a big hit for Johnny and June that he simply had to perform it. But, since it was featured on *At Folsom Prison,* the thought was to leave it off the San Quentin album.

Johnny and June recorded their duet of the John B. Sebastian song "Darlin' Companion" for the first time on the original San Quentin release. Sebastian was a member of the sixties pop group the Lovin' Spoonful, and a gifted songwriter as well. He had composed many of the Spoonful's hits, including their classic "Do You Believe in Magic." On his own, Sebastian enjoyed a number 1 hit in 1976 with "Welcome Back," the theme song for the popular television series *Welcome Back, Kotter.* "Darlin' Companion" is a saucy love ballad that Johnny and June perform effortlessly.

Mother Maybelle and the Carter Sisters perform the George Hamilton IV hit "Break My Mind" while Johnny is faintly heard on background vocals. The song "I Don't Know Where I'm Bound" made its first appearance on the 2000 Sony reissue. As with the song "Greystone Chapel" from *At Folsom Prison,* an inmate, T. Cuttie, had written this song, but this time at San Quentin. It's a song about an incarcerated man's sense of confusion, not knowing what his future has in store. Johnny admits to making up his own melody to the lyric he was handed. It was a noble effort, but not the success "Greystone Chapel" was.

There has always been a misconception that Johnny spent time in prison. Maybe it was because of his empathy for prisoners and his highly successful prison concerts. In fact, he only spent seven nights in jail during his lifetime, for minor offenses. He was arrested once for being caught carrying one thousand pills across the border from Mexico, which resulted in a night in the El Paso county jail. In 1967 he was arrested for public drunkenness in LaFayette, Georgia, which also resulted in a night in jail, and another time in Carson City, Nevada, where police found Cash passed out naked in his car. The story was that he had fallen into a creek and taken his clothes off to dry. Cash also was arrested for breaking curfew and being publicly intoxicated in Starkville, Mississippi. For that he spent three hours in jail. That episode gave Cash the inspiration to write "Starkville City Jail," a lighthearted, humorous narrative about the consequences of being caught "picking flowers" in Starkville, Mississippi.

The second side of the original *At San Quentin* album opened with "San Quentin," a brand-new song Johnny had written the day before, especially for the inmates. What resulted was a powerful song that received such thunderous applause that Johnny had to perform it two times in a row. When he sings "San Quentin may you rot and burn in hell, may your walls fall and may I live to tell," the audience erupts with thunderous screams and shouts. The original album contained both performances of the song and there might have been plans to release it as a single, since it ended up as the B-side of the runaway hit, "A Boy Named Sue."

Johnny introduces the song "Wanted Man," which he wrote with Bob Dylan, by calling Dylan "the greatest writer of our time." Having recently spent time writing and recording with Dylan in Nashville, this song was one they wrote together while Dylan was visiting at Johnny's house. Cash and the record label had so much faith in this song that it was selected to open the original album. And it truly is a fine song about a man on the run, as it lists locations throughout the country where the wanted man is hiding out from the law and the women he has left behind. Cash would record the song a few years later for the soundtrack to the movie *Little Fauss and Big Halsy,* and again in 1991 for the album *The Mystery of Life.*

"A Boy Named Sue" was the fifth and last new song Johnny included on the original release of San Quentin. Shel Silverstein wrote the hilarious story-song. Silverstein may have been inspired to write it because of his friend, humorist Jean Shepherd, who had a feminine-sounding name, and by male

attorney Sue K. Hicks from Madison, Tennessee, who was a prosecutor during the "Scopes Monkey Trial." Publisher and future record producer Don Davis called Cash the day before he was to leave for San Quentin. He told him he had a song that Cash would like. Davis recalls in the preface to his book *Nashville Steeler,* that "when Shel Silverstein, a well known song writer and author, came into my office at Wilderness Publishing Co. and played and sang me a song he had written on his old guitar, I knew immediately the only person who could cut it was Johnny Cash. The song was 'A Boy Named Sue.' I knew Johnny needed a hit song at that time, so I called him and said, 'John, I know you get a lot of songs and I wouldn't bother you if I didn't know you'd want this song. It's called 'A Boy Named Sue.' Shel Silverstein wrote it.' John said, 'Bring it out now.' The song wasn't even demo-ed, so when I took Shel out to John's house, he sang it to him live. When we left, all John had was the lyrics."

Cash played "A Boy Named Sue" for the first time during the San Quentin concert, reading it off the lyric sheet. The result was magnetic and the audience responded with thunderous applause for the tale of a man who has to struggle his way through life because his daddy named him Sue. Ultimately, father and son meet and fight it out, before the father tells his son he would not have been so tough and strong if he had not named him Sue. It's an inspired piece of writing and an incredible performance by Cash. It's interesting to note that back in 1969 the word "bitch" had to be bleeped out in the song when the father informs his son that, "I'm the son of a bitch that named you Sue." The bleep was removed for the 2000 reissue, although for many that bleep was as much a part of what made the song so unique. Johnny won CMA Male Vocalist of the Year in 1969 for his performance of "A Boy Named Sue." He also won the Grammy Award for Best Country Vocal Performance, Male, for this song in 1970. The song stayed at number 1 on the country chart for five weeks and made it all the way to number 2 on the pop chart, becoming Johnny's highest-ranking pop single of all.

Billy Edd Wheeler's "Blistered" was still a work in progress when Cash recorded it at San Quentin, and it made its first appearance on the 2006 Legacy Edition. After a shaky attempt at San Quentin, Johnny would ultimately rework the song about a woman driving the singer crazy with desire, and record it in the studio. It would ultimately be the first single release from his next album, *Hello, I'm Johnny Cash*, making it to number 4 on the country chart and number 50 pop. Cash sings it in a lower register here, and the lyric would undergo some major changes.

It was at the San Quentin concert that a young man named Lou Robin saw Johnny perform for the first time. Robin would go on to play an enormous role in Cash's life. He was a well-respected concert promoter from California, who along with his partner, Allen Tinkley, had created one of the most successful promotion companies in the country. Robin had come to see Johnny Cash perform as his company was expanding to include country artists. He was greatly impressed by what he saw. Initially, Robin became the booking agent for Cash's shows and, ultimately, his company, Artist Consultants, would take over all of Cash's promotion. And in just a few short years, Robin would take over managing Cash from Saul Holiff.

Inside a Swedish Prison

In December 1974, CBS Records released the album *På Österåker*, then titled *Inside a Swedish Prison*. It was only released in Sweden at the time. Produced by Larry Butler and Charlie Bragg, the original LP contained twelve songs edited from a live concert Cash and his troop — Carl Perkins, Larry Butler, W. S. Holland, Marshall Grant, and Bob Wootton — performed at a prison in Stockholm, Sweden, on October 3, 1972. It was not released in the United States, though the concert was filmed to be shown in Europe. In 1982, Bear Family Records of Germany released the album under the title *Inside a Swedish Prison*. In 2007 Sony Records released the complete concert for the first time on CD. *På Österåker* is a very good live album that mixes some new songs along with some Cash standards and is quite a bit different from Cash's other live albums.

The Tennessee Three open the show with a full instrumental version of "I Walk the Line." This is followed by Cash's introduction and his performance of "A Boy Named Sue." It's an animated, rushed rendition, as Cash appears to be trying to move on to other favorites. He's in fine voice, and the inmates respond with wild applause. Next, he performs Kris Kristofferson's "Sunday Morning Coming Down." Johnny's original single of this song was recorded live at the Grand Ole Opry. This is a great new version of one of Johnny's finest songs. It's interesting to note that in this version he watches a small boy "cussin' at a can," as opposed to "playin' with a can that he was kickin'." Also, after the lyric "And then I stopped beside a Sunday school and listened to the songs that they were singin'," he adds "like 'Bringing in the Sheaves.'"

Johnny changes the lyric to "San Quentin" by substituting the name "Österåker." Of course, the inmates respond with great enthusiasm. Then Johnny converses with the audience in Swedish before diving into Kristofferson's "Me and Bobby McGee." It's a wonder Cash had never recorded this song before. Roger Miller originally recorded it, and his version reached number 12 on the country chart in 1969. Janis Joplin's classic version climbed to number 1 on the pop chart in 1971. Kristofferson wrote the song after producer Fred Foster suggested the title to him. Foster had signed Kris to his first recording contract at Monument Records. In Michael Streissguth's book *Outlaw: Waylon, Willie, Kris, and the Renegades of Nashville,* Foster explains that he shared a small office building with legendary songwriters Felice and Boudleaux Bryant. The Bryants had a secretary named Bobby McKee. Boudleaux playfully accused Foster of coming downstairs to his office to check out Bobby McKee. Surprised by this, Foster replied, "'What? Bobby? What're you talking about?' He said, 'Barbara. Bobby. Bobby McKee.' I said, 'Oh yeah. . . . Haven't you heard about me and Bobby McKee?'" (Streissguth, *Outlaw*, 57). When Foster relayed the story to Kristofferson, Kris thought he heard him say Bobby McGee, and proceeded to write a song around the title while flying helicopters over the Gulf of Mexico.

Kris first played "Me and Bobby McGee" for the Statler Brothers, who said they wanted to record the song as soon as they could book studio time. But less than a week later, Kristofferson informed the group that he had gone to Los Angeles over the weekend, sung the song to Roger Miller, and Roger had already recorded it for release as his next single. In the book *The Statler Brothers: Random Memories,* Don Reid says that "Me and Bobby McGee" is "possibly the best country song ever written. It has it all: story, intimacy, tenderness, poetry, simplicity" (161). Cash turns in an inspired performance of this incredible song about loving someone so much that you are willing to set them free. The line "freedom's just another word for nothing left to lose," made it into *Bartlett's Familiar Quotations.*

Dick Feller wrote "Orleans Parish Prison," for Cash, and Cash performs the conversational prison song with spirit and drive. The lyric questions if we've seen the singer's dark-haired girl, green-eyed son, and brother, who are all doing time in Orleans Parish Prison in Louisiana. Cash thought so much of this song that he released it as a single in 1974. Unfortunately, it was not successful and only reached number 54 on the country chart. Interestingly, the single version differs from the album version. In the album version the dark-haired girl, we are told, took money from a "whorin' world" as opposed to a "hungry world" in the single release. The album performance of this song is much more subdued than the more frenetic, fiery, fiddle-laden single, and fiddle music was rare for a Cash song.

Johnny introduces "Jacob Green" as a true story he wrote about a man who was arrested for possession of marijuana in the state of Virginia. It's a brutally frank tale of what happens to an incarcerated man when he is sentenced to prison. They cut his hair, shame him, and ultimately he hangs himself. It's a blistering commentary on the injustices of the penal system at the time (which still continue today), and the harsh penalties certain minor crimes induced. And "Life of a Prisoner" is another prison ballad. Jimmy Lee Wilkerson wrote this song. Wilkerson had worked on a prison farm in Georgia and wrote from firsthand experience about prison life as he knew it. He calls the prisoner a forgotten man who's there to stay, "who

lives on faith and hope and courage and a few old dreams of yesterday."

"The Prisoners Song" was popular in the early twentieth century. Singer-songwriter Vernon Dalhart originally recorded it. His cousin, Guy Massey, wrote it. And it went on to become the best-selling song of the 1920s. Interestingly, in 1924 Dalhart had enjoyed a massive hit with his version of "Wreck of the Old 97," a song Cash would record over thirty years later. "The Prisoner's Song" is a natural for Cash, and one wonders why it never found its way onto an earlier Cash prison record. In his introduction Cash says that this is the oldest prison song that he's heard, and that a prisoner wrote it. In fact, Massey may have learned the song from his brother Robert, who did serve time in prison. The song captures the anguish and frustration of the daily prison routine with the concluding line, "If I had the wings of an angel, over these prison walls I would fly, I would fly to the arms of my darling, and there I'd be willing to die."

When Cash asks the Swedish prisoners what they would like to hear, the answer comes across loud and clear, "Folsom Prison Blues." He follows "Folsom" with "City Jail," a somewhat silly song that was written by Cash. It makes its first appearance here and seems to serve the purpose of lightening things up a little. Cash would record a studio version of it five years later for *The Last Gunfighter Ballad* album. It's always entertaining to see Cash reveal his sense of humor and truly have fun with a song. The song does receive a strong response from the audience.

Cash next performs a solo version of the Kristofferson classic "Help Me Make It Through the Night." He had originally recorded it as a duet with June. It works nicely as a solo male vocal, and in 1980 Willie Nelson would take his version to number 4 on the country chart. Then Johnny presents his first recording of the Gene Autry classic "That Silver Haired Daddy of Mine," which he dedicates to his then seventy-five-year-old father, Ray Cash.

"The Invertebrates" is a poem written by a man in an American prison. It's a searing, firsthand account of the hardship and emptiness of prison life, explaining, "As long as there are two such roads a man can look upon / As long as some men linger deep within the twilight zone / The weak will always take the road that leads to wall of stone." And Cash turned to former convicts Glen Sherley and Harlan Sanders for "Looking Back In Anger," a song about the torment and rage a prisoner feels as he looks back in anger at the time he spent behind bars. Cash explains in the introduction that Glen Sherley could not be with them because the parole board would not allow him to leave the country. He also says that Sherley had been a free man for a year and a half at that time, the longest he'd ever been out of prison and that he had bought himself a farm and was raising cows outside of Nashville. Sadly, as mentioned earlier, Sherley would die five

years later from a self-inflicted gunshot wound at the age of forty-two.

Cash reaches back to 1959 for the inspirational gem "I Saw a Man," from his original *Hymns* album. It sounds as good live as it did when he first recorded it. And after mentioning the prisons he has played at, Cash introduces Carl Perkins, who had been with him for all those shows, and he calls him the most underrated performer he knows. Carl Perkins offers two solo performances, "High Heel Sneakers" and "Blue Suede Shoes."

"Nobody Cared" is a song that June had written for Johnny the week of the Österåker performance. He goes on to explain that he's never sung it before nor had the time to rehearse it. It's about the singer watching his wife carry on in a club downtown before he gets drunk and burns the club to the ground. He ends up in solitary confinement where "nobody cared." It's unconventional to say the least. And Cash closes out the show with a reprise of "San Quentin," this time with the original lyric, and the Tennessee Three conclude the concert with a brief instrumental finale of "Folsom Prison Blues."

Prison Songs

Cash included prison songs on his albums as far back as *The Sound of Johnny Cash* in 1962. Johnny made it to number 8 on the country chart with the Jimmie Rodgers classic "In the Jailhouse Now." Interestingly, Jimmie Rodgers took it to number

14 on the pop chart in 1928, and honky-tonk country star Webb Pierce landed a number 1 country hit with his version in 1955. It's a lighthearted, up-tempo song about Bill Campbell who, as the title suggests, ends up in jail. It's all in good fun and a nice change of pace radio record for Cash. He doesn't actually yodel in the song, but encourages listeners to join in and yodel along with him. Cash so admired Jimmie Rodgers that at one point he was rumored to have been trying to acquire the rights to play the part of Rodgers in a movie. For the second prison song from the album Johnny picks up the tempo on the Jimmie Rodgers ballad "I'm Free from the Chain Gang Now," written by Lou Herscher and Saul Klein. Cash infuses the song with a sense of defiance as he sings of his being freed from the chain gang where he was known by a number and not a name. He's optimistically hoping to return to the girl he will marry. This song is a good example of Cash tailoring a song to fit his own particular style and vision.

Cash explains in his liner notes to the 1968 album *From Sea to Shining Sea,* that he wrote "The Walls of a Prison" after performing his regular show at Folsom. "After leaving the prison that day, I wrote the words to "The Walls of a Prison." The same melody was used in the late 1890's for 'The Streets of Laredo.'" He explains in the intro that "The Walls of a Prison" is about a man's attitude toward his fellow man and toward this land. A convict walks up to a ninety-nine-year man who informs the new inmate that tomorrow he will break out of prison through a tunnel he is digging beneath his cell, proclaiming, "The walls of a prison will never hold me." Sadly, the old man tries to escape, but he's ultimately shot down. So, true to his claim, he is finally free of the prison walls. Interestingly, this song was never featured on any of Johnny's prison albums, although it certainly would have fit in nicely.

Cash cowrote "Dear Mrs.," a moving narration about a prisoner who could only talk about the woman he loved. The song is from the *Man in Black* album, and it is in the form of a letter addressed to the wife after the narrator's friend, the inmate, has passed away. It's a persuasive account of the loneliness and heartbreak the prisoner suffered as the narrator admonishes the prisoner's wife for not sending him a letter while he was alive. He always waited for one but never received any. And the narrator goes on to inform her that the man had died many times waiting to hear anything from home. She is told that no one was there to claim his body and he would end up in a pauper's grave. It's a sad commentary on prison life and, as Cash recounted in the song "Man in Black," the prisoner who has long paid for his crime.

What would a self-penned Cash album like *Ragged Old Flag* be without at least one prison song? Well, "Please Don't Let Me Out" is it, and it's a good one. The narrator explains that he's been in jail for eleven years, and his parole has just come through. But he insists on staying put because it's the only life he knows. Rather than face the big unfriendly world he'd rather remain in jail. It's an interesting twist on a subject Cash covered from many different angles. Similarly, "Michigan City Howdy Do," from the *One Piece at a Time* album, is based on the true story of Johnson Van Dyke Grigsby, who served a sixty-nine-year prison sentence before ultimately being paroled at eighty-nine years old. The song details what he finds once he's released and "breathed the first free breath of air he'd breathed since 1908."

Johnny wrote "In Your Mind" for the soundtrack to the 1996 movie *Dead Man Walking* starring Susan Sarandon and Sean Penn. The movie, based on a true story, was about a nun, Sister Helen Prejean, who develops a special relationship with Matthew Poncelet (a fictionalized composite of actual prisoners), a prisoner on death row in Louisiana. The song was produced by multi-talented guitarist and recording artist Ry Cooder. It begins as an acoustic arrangement with Cash singing about a man "living on the bottom of the stairs of life . . . with one foot on Jacob's ladder and one foot in the fire." Cash immerses himself in the fabric of the story of the inmate on death row and even references his song "What Is Truth." "In Your Mind" builds to a full gospel choir backing as Cash delivers an enigmatic sermon about salvation and redemption.

Even though many of the songs that Cash would write or record for American Recordings were not necessarily about prisons with cells and bars, they were about the physical prison the increasingly weak and frail Cash faced during the late 1990s. While his mind was still as sharp and creative as ever, his body was breaking down. And for the first time, Cash could not outrun his demons, as his own mortality was closing in on him.

STEREO
"360 SOUND"

STEREO
CS 8853

MONAURAL—CL 2053
COLUMBIA

RING OF FIRE
THE BEST OF
JOHNNY CASH

THE REBEL—JOHNNY YUMA
BONANZA!
THE BIG BATTLE
REMEMBER THE ALAMO
TENNESSEE FLAT-TOP BOX
RING OF FIRE
I'D STILL BE THERE
WHAT DO I CARE
I STILL MISS SOMEONE
FORTY SHADES OF GREEN
WERE YOU THERE
(When They Crucified My Lord)
(There'll Be) PEACE IN THE VALLEY
(For Me) — With The Carter Family

Chapter 7

RING OF FIRE

SONGS FOR JUNE

The timeless songs Johnny Cash recorded
with and about June Carter Cash

n his second autobiography, Cash says that he first laid eyes on June Carter when he was eighteen, on a Dyess High School senior-class trip to the Grand Ole Opry. He recalls, "I'd liked what I heard of her on the radio, and I *really* liked what I saw of her from the balcony of the Ryman Auditorium. She was singing with the Carter Family that night, but also doing her solo comedy act, using Ernest Tubb as her straight man. She was great. She was gorgeous. She was a star. I was smitten, seriously so. The next time I saw her was six years later, again at the Opry but this time backstage, because by then I was a performer too. I walked over to her and came right out

with it: 'You and I are going to get married some-day'" (Cash, *Autobiography*, 212). So began a love story that has become a legend. That was in 1956, and the only problem with that original declaration was that both Johnny and June were married to other people at the time.

Johnny was a lifelong fan of both Jimmie Rodgers and the Carter Family. The original Carter Family consisted of Alvin Pleasant "A. P." Delaney Carter, his wife Sara Carter, and A.P.'s sister-in-law, Maybelle Addington Carter. The family was from Maces Spring, Virginia, and they made their first historic recordings in 1927 for record producer Ralph Peer at his studio in Bristol, Tennessee. Among the

« Ring of Fire. *Courtesy of Sony Music Entertainment.*

Carryin' On With Johnny Cash and June Carter. *Courtesy of Sony Music Entertainment*

Carters' classic recordings are "Wildwood Flower," "Keep on the Sunny Side," "My Clinch Mountain Home," and "Wabash Cannonball." Maybelle was married to A. P.'s brother Ezra Carter, and they had three daughters: Helen, June, and Anita. The second generation of the Carter Family—consisting of Maybelle, Helen, June, and Anita—would ultimately join Johnny Cash's road show in the early sixties, and record with him for over thirty years.

In October 2002, Cash contributed his song "Tears in the Holston River" to the Nitty Gritty Dirt Band album *Will the Circle Be Unbroken, Volume III.* In weakened voice Cash explains in this song's spoken introduction that, though he never met A. P. Carter, the man had a lot of influence on his music. But it's Mother Maybelle and Sara that he knew well, and for whom he sheds his tears in the Holston River. Cash begins the song by confessing that on October 23, 1978, he "cried over the loss of a loved one" and that, in the joyous celebration of the lady and her music, "there were tears in the Holston River when Maybelle Carter died." The song is an overlooked gem among Cash's later recordings.

According to Cash, on December 5, 1961, his manager, Saul Holiff, hired June Carter to perform with Cash's show on the *Big D Jamboree* radio program out of Dallas, Texas. A few months later, on February 11, 1962, Holiff booked June again, and by the end of the tour Cash asked Holiff to make her a permanent part of the Johnny Cash Show. While at first their relationship was more of a flirtation,

as time went on they could scarcely hide their feelings for one another. Telltale signs of the impending romance may have been revealed in Cash's 1958 recording of the classic folk ballad "Frankie and Johnny," as it was listed on the original album sleeve of *The Fabulous Johnny Cash.* It was released as the third Columbia single with the title changed to "Frankie's Man, Johnny." It reached number 9 on the country chart and number 57 pop. The story-song is about a cheating "Johnny" who is caught messing around by his sweetheart Frankie's sister. Frankie's redheaded sister dresses up and catches him off guard proclaiming "I'm Frankie's sister and I was checking up on you; if you're her man, you better treat her right." Johnny's a long-legged guitar picker in this version, and it might be a foreshadowing of Cash's future relationship with June. The song, made the pop chart in versions by Brook Benton in 1960, Sam Cooke in 1963, and Elvis Presley in 1966, as part of the soundtrack to Elvis's movie *Frankie and Johnny.* Cash might have inspired them all to revisit this popular folk ballad.

A strong case can also be made that Cash's heartbreaking "I Still Miss Someone" was inspired by his love for June. After all, the lyric clearly states "I never got over those blues eyes, I see them everywhere." June had blue eyes, while Vivian's eyes were brown. There's an ache and a longing in the song that mirrors Cash's conflicting emotions volleying between his feelings for Vivian and his growing, burning passion for June. During a performance of the song on his TV show, Cash introduced it by saying, "You know everybody needs somebody, seems like most everybody misses somebody. This song is for everybody that might be secretly in love with somebody else."

Johnny and June's first official collaboration was on "The Legend of John Henry's Hammer," on June 7, 1962. The song was listed as being arranged and adapted by Johnny Cash and June Carter. This was also the first song for which the Carter Family is listed as background vocalists. June, Maybelle, Helen, and Anita all appear on the *Blood, Sweat and Tears* album, and from this point forward, the Carter Family would contribute to many Cash recording sessions.

In July 1963, the album *Ring of Fire: The Best of Johnny Cash* was released. It gathered together some of Johnny's finest songs and recent singles. It reached number 26 on the pop album chart. In 1964 *Billboard* debuted its country album chart and this album was Cash's first to appear on it, where it remained at number 1 for fourteen weeks. It was also his first album to be certified "Gold" by the RIAA (Recording Industry Association of America), denoting sales of 500,000 units. Although production credit lists Don Law and Frank Jones, Jack Clement had a lot to do with the production on *Ring of Fire.*

There was growing pressure at the record label for Cash to release a hit record. And he certainly came through with "Ring of Fire," his biggest hit since "Don't Take Your Guns to Town" five years earlier, and one of his greatest recordings overall. It remained at number 1 on the country chart for seven weeks in 1963, and made it to number 17 on the pop chart. It became a jukebox staple and the song many believe to be a personal commentary on his relationship with June Carter. June, in fact, wrote the song with renowned songwriter Merle Kilgore, who also penned the country standard "Wolverton Mountain," and served as Hank Williams Jr.'s manager for many years. "Ring of Fire" was originally written for and recorded by June's sister Anita Carter, and released as a single on Mercury Records. Anita's version, "Love's Ring of Fire," was a slow, melancholy ballad about hopelessly falling in love. Cash heard the song and had a dream that it opened with a Mexican trumpet horn section. This was unheard-of in country music at the time, but he was able to convince (unbilled) producer Jack Clement to find a horn section and rearrange the song as a mid-tempo song about the ramifications of falling so deeply in love. It's unapologetic and intense in its message, and, overall, one of the greatest love songs ever recorded. The chorus of the song is iconic and imbued with smoldering passion as Cash sings, "I fell into a burning ring of fire, I went down, down, down, and the flames went higher." June has said that the inspiration for the song came to her while she was driving around pondering her relationship with the married Cash. Interestingly, in her book, *I Walked the Line,* Vivian Cash refutes the claim that June wrote "Ring of Fire." She writes, "To this day, it confounds me to hear the elaborate details June told of writing that song for Johnny. She didn't write that song any more than I did. The truth is, Johnny wrote that song while pilled up and drunk, about a certain private female body part" (V. Cash, 294). Regardless, if "I Walk the Line" was Johnny's declaration of fidelity to his first love and first wife Vivian, "Ring of Fire" captured the intense emotions and helplessness of his blossoming relationship with future wife June Carter.

For his follow-up single to "Ring of Fire," Johnny and June collaborated on "The Matador." They tried to replicate the sound and arrangement of the prior hit. The same Mexican horns open the track. The song recounts the story of the tempestuous love of the bullfighter for Anita, who is watching with her new love from the stands. The bullfighter is saddened to know that the rose she wears is not for him tonight. His one last chance is to impress her with his bullfighting prowess. June and the Carter Family perform on the track. The song was not included on an album at the time, although it reached number 2 on the country chart and number 44 pop. June and Jan Howard wrote two songs for Cash's *The Christmas Spirit* album: "Ringing the Bells for Jim," and the previously discussed "Christmas as I Knew It."

With The Carter Family

In March 1964 Cash was featured on the album *Keep on the Sunny Side: The Carter Family with Special Guest Johnny Cash.* Johnny is billed as a "special guest" on this Carter Family album, but he appears on almost every track, alongside Mother Maybelle, Helen, June, and Anita. Cash takes on the parts that were performed by A. P. Carter on the original Carter Family recordings. All songs in the original recording ledger are credited to A. P. Carter, however most are folk songs that A. P. adapted and the original Carter Family recorded and made popular.

One of the standout tracks from this collection is "When the Roses Bloom Again." The original Carter Family recorded it in 1929. Johnny takes the lead on this tragic tale of a wounded soldier asking his captain to promise that he will convey the soldier's dying request to tell his darling that if he does not die in battle he will be with her when the roses bloom again. The haunting lyric goes, "Yes, when the roses bloom again beside the river, and the robin red-breast sings its sweet refrain / As in days of Auld Lang Syne I'll be with you sweetheart mine, I'll be with you when the roses bloom again." This is a sublime song of farewell, and the perfect finale to a wonderful collaborative album.

In 1965 June Carter sang with Cash on "When It's Springtime in Alaska," a former number 1 hit for Johnny Horton. It was included on the *Orange*

Blossom Special album, and it is their first true duet, in which June can be heard singing solo. The song's author, Tillman Franks, cowrote the Johnny Horton hit "Honky Tonk Man" with Horton. "When It's Springtime in Alaska," tells of an Alaskan prospector who travels from Point Barrow to Fairbanks, Alaska, where he strolls down to the Red Dog Saloon. He falls hard for Red Headed Lil, the singer at the saloon. He proceeds to dance with her, inciting the jealousy of her lover, Big Ed, reinforcing the song's conclusion that "when it's springtime in Alaska, I'll be six feet below."

Also from the *Orange Blossom Special* album, June sings harmony with Cash on "It Ain't Me, Babe." And from those same sessions, Cash and Carter collaborated on "Time and Time Again." It was issued as the B-side of "It Ain't Me, Babe." We learn that time and time again the narrator's girl keeps leaving him and he keeps taking her back. It has a sound that harks back to Johnny's earlier records. It's more reminiscent of his Sun singles than what he was recording at the time for Columbia. That same year, June wrote the aforementioned western saga "The Road to Kaintuck" for *Sings the Ballads of the True West.*

In September 1966, the Carter Family officially joined the Johnny Cash Show, and in October Johnny's album *Happiness Is You* was released. Two songs in particular from this album celebrate the state of their relationship at the time. Johnny and June wrote "Happiness Is You." It's a straight-forward love song for Cash and seems to capture their burgeoning romance. It's simple, sweet, and honest, as it explains the singer's frustrations in love until he found his one true love. The lyric is well-written and quite expressive, as he sings, "No more chasing moonbeams or catching falling stars, I know now my pot of gold is anywhere you are." When he sings "I tried to doubt you and live without you, tried to deny that I love you like I do," we feel the singer's anguish at falling into a difficult situation with someone he can't live without.

Merle Kilgore and June Carter reteam with Johnny for "Happy to Be with You," a positive affirmation of the joys of being in love. Once again, one can't help but read into it the personal nature of Johnny and June's situation at the time, and the fact that they were truly enjoying each other's company. This was the only single released from the *Happiness Is You* album, and it reached number 9 on the country chart.

A third song from the album also appears to mirror Cash's deep feelings for June. "You Comb Her Hair" is an outstanding song from the pen of two master songwriters, Harlan Howard and Hank Cochran, that Cash delivers with sincerity. He tries to soothe his lover's doubts and fears that there's someone else by explaining that she's the only one he dreams about, explaining, "You comb her hair every morning . . . and put her to bed every night." George Jones made it to number 5 on the country chart with his version of this song in 1963.

John and June's First Duet Album

In August 1967 Columbia released *Carryin' On with Johnny Cash & June Carter*. Johnny and June had become songwriting partners, and June had already appeared on Johnny's albums as part of the Carter Family. Johnny and June would wed seven months after the release of this, their first all-duets album. Interestingly, despite their success as a duo, they would only release two full-length duet albums over their careers, this one and *Johnny Cash and His Woman* in 1973. However, June would be featured in duets with Johnny on many of his solo albums. And they would continue to issue singles together over the years. *Carryin' On* also features the other members of the Carter Family—Maybelle, Anita and Helen—on background vocals. This was the last Cash album to be produced by Don Law before he retired. It reached number 5 on the country album chart and number 194 on the pop album chart in 1967. After the major success of their song "Jackson," the album was retitled and reissued as *Jackson*. Carl Perkins wrote the humorous liner notes for the reissued album, recalling his "many long miserable years" knowing Johnny Cash and accusing the unsuspecting record buyers of making Cash the "biggest damn thing in country music." The cover photo for the original album told a different story. Cash was deep into his pill addiction at the time, and he looked skeletal in the picture.

Cash had begun taking pills ten years earlier. He recalls in his autobiography, "I took my first amphetamine, a little white Benzedrine tablet scored with a cross, in 1957, when I was on tour with Faron Young and Ferlin Husky, and I loved it. It increased my energy, it sharpened my wit, it banished my shyness, it improved my timing, it turned me on like electricity flowing into a light-bulb" (Cash, *Autobiography*, 191). So began a vicious cycle that would torment and haunt Cash for most of his life. And the impending divorce from Vivian, missing his four young daughters, and falling helplessly in love with June only added to the strain. He was deep into his addiction by 1967.

Marshall Grant wrote the opening track for *Carryin' On*. "Long-Legged Guitar Pickin' Man," is a gritty, playful song that lets Johnny and June literally carry on together as they appear to genuinely have fun with the silly lyrics. It's a lighthearted romp with a catchy hook that made it to number 6 on the country chart in 1967.

Other highlights from the album include "Pack Up Your Sorrows," a first-rate ballad that was cowritten by folk singer-songwriter Richard Fariña. The Brooklyn-born Fariña was an up-and-coming author and friend of Thomas Pynchon. He was also married to Joan Baez's sister Mimi. Fariña was tragically killed in a motorcycle accident when he was just twenty-nine years old. This song is an affirmation of true devotion when the singer asks his lover to "pack up your sorrows and give them all to me." This is the most overlooked song on this album and certainly would have made for a fine single.

"Jackson" is the song that turned Johnny Cash and June Carter into a full-fledged hit-making duo. Everyone knows to sing along when they hear the opening line, "We got married in a fever, hotter than a pepper sprout / we've been talkin' 'bout Jackson, ever since the fire went out." Their performance of this song is flirty and catchy. It would become a staple of Cash's live show. The single made it all the way to number 2 on the country chart in 1967 and became the duo's signature song. The song was cowritten by songwriter Billy Edd Wheeler, who also cowrote "The Reverend Mr. Black" for the Kingston Trio and Kenny Rogers's giant hit "Coward of the County." In fact, Cash may have first heard this song while listening to the Kingston Trio's 1963 album, *Sunny Side!*. Steel guitarist and record producer Don Davis also takes credit for introducing the song to June. In his book *Nashville Steeler,* Davis recalls hearing the song on the radio while driving down Sixteenth Avenue South in Nashville. It was a duet performed by the song's coauthor Billy Edd Wheeler and a singer named Billie Joan Scrivner. Davis was married to June's sister Anita at the time and passed the song on to June, who in turn played it for Johnny. Johnny liked it, and he and June began performing it together in concert. Davis was Anita's second husband. She had previously been married

to fiddler Don Potter, and she then married Bob Wootton after divorcing Davis. That marriage also ended in divorce. "Jackson" also made it to number 14 on the pop chart courtesy of Nancy Sinatra and Lee Hazlewood in 1967. Johnny and June won the 1968 Grammy Award for Best Country & Western Performance Duet, Trio, or Group for "Jackson."

In January 1968 Cash and Vivian Liberto were officially divorced after fourteen years of marriage. The relationship had suffered over the years, and Johnny's open love affair with June didn't help matters. That same month saw the release of another concept album. *From Sea to Shining Sea* is a collection of songs about the people and places he had seen all across the United States. It's a loosely constructed concept album, but Cash deserves credit for writing every song on the album and singing, or narrating, them in the first person. Since the album was recorded before Cash's divorce was finalized, he took a more indirect approach. But it was no mystery who he was in love with. In the liner notes for the album, Johnny writes, "'You and Tennessee' I wrote for someone in particular." It's not hard for us to guess who that someone is, and the result is a love letter in song to June Carter. It tells of his staying away too long from the one he loves who resides in Tennessee. He sees her face everywhere he goes and longs to be back with her in Tennessee. Another song on the album can be viewed as a defense of leaving Vivian for someone who more readily understands the lifestyle he leads. "Another

Song To Sing" is the only single released from the album, and it failed to chart. It's a light, breezy song wherein the narrator wonders if someone he knows remembers him as he travels on, because that's what he has to do. It's the rambling, folk-flavored type of song that Cash enjoyed singing, and the autobiographical aspect makes his performance even more compelling.

On February 22, 1968, Cash surprised June with a proposal on stage at London Gardens in London, Ontario. On February 29, while accepting the Grammy Award for "Jackson," Cash thanked the audience and said, "This will be a fine wedding present." On Friday, March 1, Johnny and June married in a private ceremony at the Methodist Church in Franklin, Kentucky. Merle Kilgore was Johnny's best man and June's friend Micky Brooks was her matron of honor. June's daughters, Carlene and Rosie, also attended the ceremony. Just over a week after their wedding, Johnny and June headed back out on the road to perform concerts in the South and Midwest.

For Cash's next single, June, Anita, and Helen Carter joined together to write "Rosanna's Going Wild" for Cash. It's about a male narrator's girl cheating and running around on him. It's a lighter, up-tempo tune that Cash sings with abandon. The horn arrangement, similar to that on "Ring of Fire," adds flare to a song that hit number 2 on the country chart and number 91 pop. This was the first record that Bob Johnston produced for Cash.

The song was a sizeable hit for Cash, but it was never included on an album.

One of Cash's most revealing songs about his anguish over his love affair with June is "I Tremble for You," a song that might have been written out of desperation, during a fight. Cash and Statler Brother Lew DeWitt collaborated on this bleak, dark ballad that was first recorded by Waylon Jennings for his 1967 album *Love of the Common People*. It's a scathing song that's filled with remorse and regret, as the singer tries to fight his misery over losing his lover by returning to his old reckless ways. We feel the hurt and anguish as he tries to drown her memory in liquor. The lyric is poetic, with lines like "The world that I live in is empty and cold / the loneliness cuts me and tears at my soul." Cash's performance is nothing short of electrifying.

After Johnny and June wed, there was a true sense of joy and relief that both exhibited. After all, the public had accepted them, and "Jackson" made it clear that they were now officially a couple, both personally and professionally. They appeared to revel in their newfound freedom, traveling to the Holy Land together to record an album, and on songs like "Darlin' Companion," from the *At San Quentin* album.

Then *The Johnny Cash Show* television series debuted on ABC. It was a weekly variety series that ran from June 7, 1969, to March 3, 1971. It was recorded at the Ryman Auditorium in Nashville, and fifty-eight episodes were produced in total. The show featured Johnny along with June, the Tennessee Three, the Carter Family, and the Statler Brothers. It also was the first series to showcase legendary artists like Bob Dylan, Joni Mitchell, Neil Young, James Taylor, and Linda Ronstadt. Cash's guests on the first show were Bob Dylan, Joni Mitchell, and Doug Kershaw. Johnny and June performed duets together on almost every episode.

With the release of the album *Hello, I'm Johnny Cash* in 1970, Cash was at the peak of his popularity. The album featured two standout performances from Johnny and June. Together they turned acclaimed songwriter Tim Hardin's folk ballad, "If I Were a Carpenter," into a defining country duet. The back-and-forth exchange between Cash and Carter is full of fun and energetic. It's an outstanding performance of a solid piece of material. The song originally reached number 8 on the pop chart for Bobby Darin in 1966. Johnny and June took it all the way to number 2 on the country chart and number 36 pop. "If I Were a Carpenter" earned Johnny and June a 1971 Grammy Award for Best Country Performance by a Duo or Group with Vocal. The album also included Cash's "'Cause I Love You," a lovely duet with June that was released as the B-side of "If I Were a Carpenter." It's a tender reaffirmation of their love for one another, and they perform it with warmth and sincerity.

Cash had a very prolific year in 1970; he recorded the soundtracks for two major movies (*I Walk the Line* and *Little Fauss and Big Halsy),* that were both released in November. *I Walk the Line* was the soundtrack album to the John Frankenheimer film starring Gregory Peck and Tuesday Weld. The movie was based on the book *An Exile* by Madison Jones. Johnny wrote almost all the songs for the film. The album made it to number 9 on the country chart. The first song on the album, "Flesh and Blood," is one of Cash's greatest achievements as a writer and performer. Johnny wrote it after driving out to DeKalb County, Tennessee, to have a picnic with June and daughters Carlene, and Rosie Nix, June's daughter with ex-football player and garage owner Edwin "Rip" Nix. Cash was so taken with the beauty of the countryside that he was inspired to write "Flesh and Blood." Johnny began performing this song a few years earlier and had originally recorded it in 1969, under the title "You Are What I Need." After revising some of the lyrics (it was a mockingbird that sang for him in the original, not a cardinal) and taking it back into the studio, what emerged was one of the most penetrating and perfect songs in his entire catalog. The tender lyric says it all, as we find the narrator sitting by a singing mountain stream, lost in reverie, and pondering all the wonders of nature that surrounded him. Ultimately, he comes to the realization that in amongst all this beauty, the love of his woman mattered to him most of all, because "Flesh and blood needs flesh and blood, and you're the one I need." If ever there was a song of devotion written especially for June, this is it. It deservedly became a number 1 country hit and reached number 54 on the pop chart.

Johnny and June performed two duets on 1971's *Man in Black*. The previously discussed "I Talk to Jesus Every Day," and "Look for Me," which was cowritten by Glen Sherley, whom Cash was then employing at his publishing company, House of Cash, and songwriter Harlan Sanders, who cowrote the George Jones classic "If Drinkin' Don't Kill Me (Her Memory Will)." "Look for Me" is an inspirational evocation of the redemptive powers of love, if we only look for Jesus in places we may not expect to find Him.

In 1972 Cash released the album *A Thing Called Love*. Country singer-songwriter and actor Jerry Reed wrote the title song, and it sounds like it was tailor-made for Johnny Cash. Producer Larry Butler found the song for Cash, and if ever there was a love song that detailed the true measure of what love can do, this is it. When Cash sings, "you can't see it with your eyes, hold it in your hand . . . this thing called love," we believe every word he says. "A Thing Called Love" was released as a single and made it to number 2 on the country chart. On the same album, Cash wrote "I Promise You," a sweet, tender declaration of love and commitment. It's addressed to the one he loves about the day when they will wed and what she can look forward to from him thereafter. It's a simple proclamation, but Cash imbues it with a sense of pro-

found urgency. The song was written for June on their wedding day, and the marriage vow never sounded more sincere.

Also included on *A Thing Called Love* is "Mississippi Sand," a descriptive story-song written by June, about a stranger who comes to town with two-tone shoes upon his feet, and proceeds to woo Ruby Colter, the girl the singer loves. The lyric is infused with June's sense of humor in lines like "she was a rose just right for pickin', and he nipped her in the bud." The stranger takes advantage of poor Ruby, just before the singer and his friend Carl gave him a beating. It's a fun caricature of a song, and Cash appears to be having a good time singing it.

In 1973 Cash and Carter performed two duets on Cash's *Any Old Wind That Blows* album, "The Loving Gift," and "If I Had a Hammer." Kris Kristofferson presented "The Loving Gift" to Johnny and June upon the birth of their son John Carter Cash. Well, this song was written from the heart, and Johnny and June sing it with true devotion. It was the third single released from *Any Old Wind That Blows*, and it reached number 27 on the country chart. Interestingly, the B-side of the single was another Kristofferson classic, "Help Me Make It Through the Night."

Folk icons Pete Seeger and Lee Hays wrote the American classic "If I Had a Hammer." Both Seeger and Hayes were members of the Weavers, who scored many hits during the 1950s. Peter, Paul and

The Johnny Cash Show with The Tennessee Three — Bob Wootton, Marshall Grant, and W. S. Holland. *Courtesy of Sony Music Entertainment.*

The Johnny Cash Show with June Carter Cash, Mother Maybelle Carter and The Statler Brothers — Harold Reid, Don Reid, Phil Balsley, and Lew DeWitt. *Courtesy of Sony Music Entertainment.*

Mary enjoyed a Top-10 pop hit with their recording of this song in 1962, and Trini Lopez took it to number 3 on the pop chart in 1963. In 1972 Johnny and June's duet made it to number 29 on the country chart. They were nominated for a Grammy Award for Best Country Vocal Performance by a Duo or Group for "If I Had a Hammer."

The Second Collaboration with June

August 1973 saw the release of *Johnny Cash and His Woman,* a duet album for which they were billed as "Johnny Cash and June Carter Cash." Six of the songs are duets with June and four are solo Cash recordings. It's a mixed bag of material, with a few standout tracks. For this album Cash brought back Don Law as producer. It made it to number 32 on the country album chart, and only one single charted from the set.

This album contains two songs by Billy Edd Wheeler, who provided Johnny and June with their classic hit "Jackson." The first, "The Color of Love," is a churning give-and-take, with Johnny and June trying to explain what the color of love means to them. It's a lighthearted romp and shows off the fun side of both performers. Wheeler's "The Pine Tree," finds Johnny and June comparing their troubles to different kinds of trees, ultimately realizing that their "love is a pine tree, 'cause that's the only tree that's true." There's a genuine charm and charisma between the two as they volley back and forth on the verses and meet up together for the chorus.

Songwriter Chris Gantry wrote "Allegheny." Among his many credits is the Glen Campbell classic "Dreams of the Everyday Housewife." Gantry's friend Kris Kristofferson immortalized him in his song "The Pilgrim-Chapter 33." This wild and wooly story-song finds Cash chasing after his half-French, half-Cherokee bride as she takes him on the ride of his life. The song is solid, however June's Indian war-whoops are a bit distracting. That may be why the single charted so poorly. Cash's singles were struggling in 1973, and this one made it to only number 69 on the country chart. It was his poorest showing on the chart thus far.

Johnny and June perform a fine rendition of the Margaret Ann Rich composition "Life Has Its Little Ups and Downs." Her husband Charlie Rich, Johnny's labelmate at Sun, originally recorded it. The song was written during a time when the Riches were struggling. Charlie had found early success as a songwriter at Sun Records, and in 1960 had a minor hit with his song "Lonely Weekends." But it would be over twelve years before he would achieve major acclaim with his number 1 hit "Behind Closed Doors." Margaret Ann stood by her husband through all the hard times, and this song is a brutally frank account of what they endured. But it's also a tender love ballad about what the singer wishes he could give his woman, and her understanding and contentment with whatever he's able to afford. He's confident knowing that she can take it with a smile and not a frown because she knows that life has its little ups and downs.

Johnny's sister Reba Hancock cowrote "We're for Love" for her brother and June. It was released as a single but failed to chart. This is a country song that lets the couple express their devotion for each other. Together they can weather anything the world throws at them because of their love. Johnny and June conclude the album with the David "Cuz" Powers song, "Godshine," an inspirational plea for the healing powers of God's celestial light. Johnny takes on those who question Jesus's divinity and His ability to spread His "Godshine." By this point in his career, Cash was not afraid to proudly proclaim his faith and salvation in Jesus Christ.

For *Ragged Old Flag,* Cash wrote a song about the state of his relationship with June at the time. "While I've Got It on My Mind" is a slice-of-life narrative about Cash's everyday life with June. He voices his happiness and contentment with his wife and how he likes to get his lovin' while he's got it on his mind. The song describes the perfect day of just laying around the house with his "queen of womankind."

In 1976, just prior to the release of *The Last Gunfighter Ballad* album, Johnny and June released the duet single, "Old Time Feeling." It's a tender song of devotion that finds them praising each other for still evoking that old-time feeling in each other. It's a lovely duet that ranks among their finest performances together. It only managed to climb to number 26 on the country chart, however, and was ultimately not included on the album. It would also be the last charting duet single from Johnny and June. Interestingly, the B-side of the record was "Far Side Banks of Jordan," which was included on the *Last Gunfighter Ballad* album.

For the 1978 album *I Would Like to See You Again,* Johnny and June recorded "You and Me," written by producer Larry Butler and songwriter Roger Bowling. It's a pretty duet tailor-made for Johnny and June. It's a sweet affirmation of their true love explaining how they always knew they would make it together and how good it is being together. Johnny and June would not have another duet released until 1983, when they included songwriter Paul Kennerley's "Brand New Dance" on the *Johnny 99* album. It's a lovely waltz that they perform with tenderness and affection. It's a song about reaffirming their love for one another and starting a brand new dance to point to what's ahead for them. Emmylou Harris covered it in 1990 on her album *Brand New Dance.* After being married to Brian Ahern, who produced the *Johnny 99* session, from 1977 to 1984, Harris married Paul Kennerley in 1985, but they divorced in 1993.

In 1988 Cash released *Water from the Wells of Home,* an all-star duets project for Mercury

Records. It featured an array of friends and family performing with Cash including Paul McCartney, the Everly Brothers, Hank Williams Jr., Emmylou Harris, Waylon Jennings, Tom T. Hall, Rosanne Cash, John Carter Cash, and, of course, June. "Where Did We Go Right," is a well-written ballad celebrating their love. Dave Loggins ("Please Come to Boston") and Don Schlitz ("The Gambler") composed the song about how, in a world where everybody's falling apart, Johnny and June's love keeps them together, wondering, "Where did we go right?"

Johnny never stopped writing love songs to June. On his *Boom Chicka Boom* album Cash included "I Love You, I Love You," a simple song of devotion written for June. It feels like a back-to-basics song he might have written during his Sun days. The narrator will do anything to win his lover's heart as he expresses his deep feelings for her. "Poor Valley Girl" is a buried gem of a story-song written by Cash about June Carter and the Carter Family. It was included as a bonus track on the 1993 release of *Return to the Promised Land,* which was an intended sequel to the album *The Holy Land.* It's a love letter in song, as Johnny sings, "Her laughter was infectious, her music was pure joy." He describes June with love and affection and thanks God that He gave him this sweet "poor valley girl."

This song is the revelation on this album and certainly deserved to be more widely heard and appreciated.

Cash produced June's first album, *Appalachian Pride,* in 1975. It contained ten solo tracks from June. Prior to this, Cash had produced June's 1971 single "A Good Man," which made it to number 27 on the country chart. The entire *Appalachian Pride* album, along with various singles and duets, was reissued by Sony in 2005 in the two-CD set *Keep on the Sunny Side: June Carter Cash–Her Life in Music.* John Carter Cash produced the project, which spans June's entire career from 1939 to 2003.

Additionally, Cash recorded "The Road to Kaintuck" and "Temptation" with June for her album *Wildwood Flower.* John Carter Cash also produced this record, and it contains some of his mother's final recordings. Valerie June Carter Cash, the love of Johnny Cash's life, passed away on May 15, 2003, less than six months after the release of *American IV: The Man Comes Around.* June's health had been failing, and the deaths of her beloved sisters Helen in 1998 and Anita in 1999 had certainly taken a toll on her. These final duet recordings conclude an amazing chapter in country music history, and there's something incredibly moving in listening to *Wildwood Flower,* the final chapter in June's remarkable life.

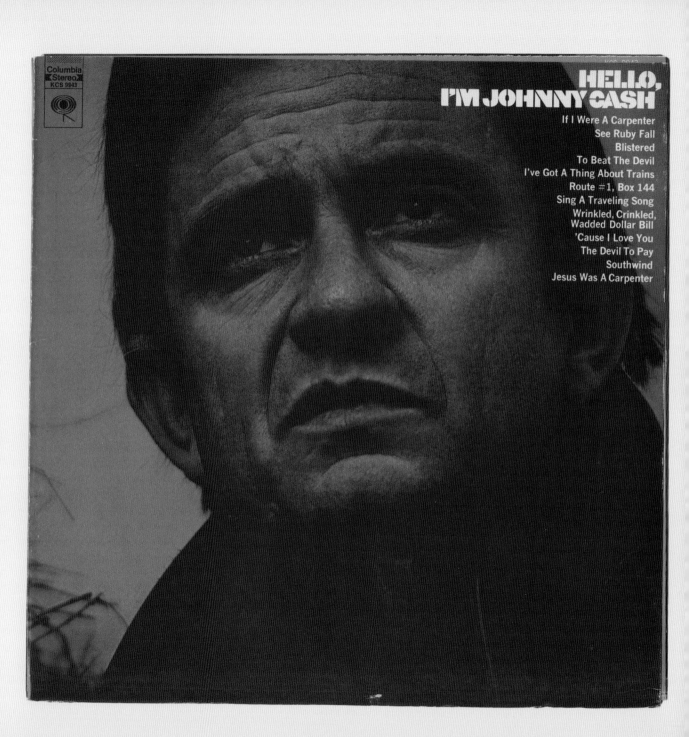

Chapter 8

SUNDAY MORNING COMING DOWN

KRIS KRISTOFFERSON AND THE
GREAT SINGER-SONGWRITERS

An appreciation of the songs Johnny Cash recorded that were written by legendary songwriters such as Kris Kristofferson, John Prine, and Bruce Springsteen

Sunday Morning Coming Down," is one of the most defining songs of Cash's career. It was written by Kris Kristofferson and epitomized the finest attributes of both artists. Kristofferson's words evoke the lonely feeling that permeates the soul of an individual who is somewhere alone and searching to find a measure of success. Kristofferson had come to Nashville to be a songwriter, and gave up so much to see his dream come true. The song is autobiographical and the lyric is pure poetry. Kristofferson wrote the song while he was living in a small apartment in Nashville following his divorce from his first wife. Kristofferson brought a new standard of songwriting to Nashville and popular music. Each word counted, and his imagery was rooted in the Romantic poetry of William Blake that he admired so much. Even though pop and country performer Ray Stevens had released the song as a single earlier that year, Kristofferson wanted Cash to record it. The onetime Army helicopter pilot, working for an oil firm, decided to fly his helicopter onto Cash's property to give Cash a copy of the song. Legend has it that Kris landed the helicopter, got out with a beer in one hand and a demo tape in the other, and walked up to Cash and handed him the tape.

« Hello, I'm Johnny Cash.
Courtesy of Sony Music Entertainment.

Kristofferson has since clarified the story, admitting he did make the trip to Cash's house but he never flew a helicopter while drinking a beer, and that Cash wasn't even home at the time.

Cash did eventually record "Sunday Morning Coming Down," in which Cash embodied the soul of the struggling songwriter in Kristofferson's song. During a taping for Cash's television show, he was asked to change a lyric from "I'm wishing Lord that I was stoned," to the more acceptable "I'm wishing Lord that I was home." Cash asked Kristofferson what he thought and Kristofferson preferred the lyric as originally written, because changing it would change the meaning of the song. When Cash recorded the song for his show, nobody knew what he would do. As usual, the rebel in Cash won out; he looked up at Kristofferson in the balcony of the Ryman Auditorium and bravely sang the words as they were written. The song remained at number 1 on the country chart for two weeks in 1970, and made it to number 46 pop. Johnny was nominated for the 1971 Grammy for Best Male Country Music Performance for this song.

"The Devil to Pay," from *Hello, I'm Johnny Cash,* holds the distinction of being the first Kris Kristofferson song Cash ever recorded. On the original album release it is erroneously credited to Merle Travis and Leon Rusk. The lyrics leave no doubt that this is an exceptional Kristofferson ballad with a potent, poetic message about being left behind by a woman who is cheating on the narrator. He warns her that the consequences of the "high life she's living" will ultimately leave her lonely with only the devil to pay for her actions. And, furthermore, the narrator won't be there to pick her up when she falls. The lyric has great imagery and Cash imbues it with the proper sense of empathy and forewarning. Kris regained his rightful songwriting credit when he released his own version of the song on his brilliant 1981 album *To the Bone* (not to be confused with his reflective 2009 album *Closer to the Bone*).

"To Beat the Devil," also on *Hello, I'm Johnny Cash,* further emphasizes the monumental relationship between Cash and Kristofferson. Kristofferson was a young man from Brownsville, Texas, who earned a Rhodes scholarship to Oxford University, became a captain in the U.S. Army, learned to pilot a helicopter, and ultimately gave it all up and moved to Nashville to be a songwriter. He had sent some songs to songwriter and publisher Marijohn Wilkin, who offered him encouragement. He ultimately got a job working as a janitor at Columbia Recording Studios. This allowed him to meet artists like Johnny Cash who would eventually record many of his songs. "To Beat the Devil" was the second Kristofferson song Cash recorded, and it is an outstanding story of a songwriter who sells his songs, along with his soul, in order to survive. In fact, Kris wrote the song in 1967 with Cash in mind as the troubled singer-songwriter who ultimately beats the devil. Cash turns in an indelible performance, and despite all his success and status, we believe beyond a doubt that Cash is the lonely singer in the song who is struggling to find his way. Kris Kristofferson's songs found the perfect voice in Johnny Cash.

Cash's introduction of Kristofferson at the Newport Folk Festival in Newport, Rhode Island, in July 1969 helped gain him a wider audience, and paved the way for Kristofferson's own future stardom. Cash so believed in the young Kristofferson that he gave him a spot during his set, allowing him to perform two songs, one of which was a new song Kristofferson had written called "Sunday Morning Coming Down."

The other songwriter Cash brought along to Newport was Vince Matthews, who never achieved the measure of success he deserved. Cash covered Matthews's "Wrinkled, Crinkled, Wadded Dollar Bill" on *Hello, I'm Johnny Cash.* Matthews's credits include Gene Watson's hit "Love in the Hot Afternoon," and Gordon Lightfoot's "On Susan's Floor." "Wrinkled, Crinkled, Wadded Dollar Bill" is the first Vince Matthews song Cash recorded, and it paints a stark picture of a vagrant trying to survive on his last dollar bill. He's cold and hungry and needs food and clothing, but still refuses to be bound to the precepts of his wrinkled, crinkled, wadded dollar bill. In his final act of defiance, he throws the bill into the chilly waters of Lake Michigan. The song is based on the true events of Matthews's almost giving up as a song-

writer before returning to Nashville to give songwriting another try. No doubt Vince's song must have appealed to Cash on many levels.

Cash included Matthews's "Melva's Wine" on his album *A Thing Called Love.* "Melva's Wine" is unequivocally one of the most moving songs in Cash's catalog. Matthews wrote it for an album he was working on called *The Kingston Springs Suite*, with the help of Cash and friends Kris Kristofferson and Shel Silverstein. This ballad is about the singer's love for his wife Melva, whose memory is tied around the wine she would make for him every year in Kingston Springs. The lyric is as sweet as the wine Melva made him before she passed away. The sense of loss permeates the ballad and once you've heard it you cannot forget it.

Johnny and June were among the first to hear Kristofferson's now-classic ballad "Help Me Make It Through the Night." It would have made the perfect country hit duet for them had Sammi Smith not had such a big hit with it two years earlier. But ultimately it still sounds as if it belonged to Johnny and June. Kristofferson has said that he wrote this sensual tune after reading an interview with Frank Sinatra, who said he used a bottle or a lover to help get him get through the night. Kristofferson was not afraid to use sexual imagery in his songs, and the lyrics were so veiled that he could get away with it. Maybe Cash was hesitant to release it initially for the same reason Dottie West was. She felt it was too suggestive and too controversial for country radio at the time. Sammi Smith did not feel any such hesitation and "Help Me Make It Through the Night" proved to be her career-defining performance.

In 1974 Cash recorded "The Junkie and the Juicehead (Minus Me)" as the title song of his new album. Offbeat title aside, it is a very good Kris Kristofferson song. Cash takes on the persona of a songwriter stumbling down the Music City sidewalks with a junkie and a juicehead that offer words of wisdom as they share their world-weary views. The story the starving songwriter tells feels like a sequel to "Sunday Morning Coming Down" if the narrator's luck had run out. That might be what drew Cash to the song, a worthy follow-up to one of his most critically acclaimed recordings. While the minimalist production on the song would lend itself nicely to an intimate acoustic performance, as a single it feels too sparse. Cash's reading of Kristofferson's lyric is spot on, but it just might have been too honest for country radio at the time. While "Sunday Morning Coming Down" benefits from Bill Walker's lush arrangement, "The Junkie and the Juicehead (Minus Me)" is stark and terrifying. By the time we get to the ending where the singer chooses to leave his sordid lifestyle behind, we are still reeling from the narrator's harrowing tale. Cash deserves credit for taking a chance on a "songwriter's song," so brutally frank that most producers would have steered him away from it.

In the end, this is another Kristofferson gem in the Cash catalog.

The Junkie and the Juicehead Minus Me may just be the most bizarre album in Johnny's catalog. It was produced by Cash and Charlie Bragg, and spotlighted members of Cash's family. June, her daughters Carlene and Rosie, and Johnny's daughter Rosanne Cash are featured. Interestingly, Rosanne selected "Broken Freedom Song," another strong Kristofferson ballad for her recording debut. Kristofferson originally included it on his 1974 album *Spooky Lady's Sideshow*. Rosanne's version omits the first verse about a soldier returning home from war with his sleeve pinned to his shoulder, and instead begins with the second verse about a poor girl waiting somewhere by a phone for a man who left her pregnant and alone. That verse is juxtaposed with the next one about Jesus feeling lonely and alone and wondering why His Father left him bleeding on the cross. It's weighty subject matter for a young girl and certainly foreshadows the remarkable songs Rosanne herself would write and record in years to come. In 1979 Rosanne would have her first charting single, "No Memories Hangin' Round," a duet with Bobby Bare, and she would go on to chart eleven number 1 country hits during the eighties, including her classic "Seven Year Ache."

One of the most disappointing chapters in Cash's recording career is that "The Last Time" did not achieve the success it so readily deserved.

Kristofferson, arguably the greatest songwriter in country music after Hank Williams, wrote this intimate account of the dissolution of his second marriage and it remains among the most profoundly moving songs in Kristofferson's catalog. Cash performs the lyrics with genuine emotion, having himself experienced the devastating cost of such a separation. The lyric is pure poetry, and when he sings, "All that is left of our love is a little girl's laughter, let her keep makin' believin' as long as she can," our hearts melt away. Kris recorded his own version of the song for his critically acclaimed album *To the Bone*, and this Cash single from 1980's *Rockabilly Blues* album unquestionably deserved better than to crawl in at number 85 on the country chart.

In May 1985, the *Highwayman* album was released featuring Cash, Kris Kristofferson, Willie Nelson and Waylon Jennings. In September 1985, Cash filmed the television movie *The Last Days of Frank and Jesse James*. The movie starred Cash in the role of Frank James and Kris Kristofferson as Jesse James. Also appearing in the film were Jennings, Ed Bruce, and David Allan Coe. And that same month the Highwaymen appeared at the first Farm Aid concert in Champaign, Illinois, with Glen Campbell filling in for Kristofferson who was unable to appear. In October, all four appeared on the Country Music Awards ceremony performing "Highwayman."

December 1985 also saw the release of *Rainbow*, Cash's last solo album on Columbia Records after more than twenty-five years. Record label politics, lack of label support, and loss of interest on the parts of both Cash and Columbia led to dwindling record sales and, ultimately, Cash's unceremonious departure from Columbia Records. This was the album that Cash had begun working on before the trip to Montreux which resulted in the *Highwayman* album. Cash and Chips Moman believed strongly in this project, but without label support, it was doomed from the start. *Rainbow* failed to chart, as did "I'm Leaving Now," the one single released from the album. It's a clever lyric about someone angrily leaving someone behind. The song could be viewed as Cash's final kiss-off to Columbia Records. Both Chips Moman and Kris Kristofferson, who had written the title song of the album, never even knew the album was officially released. Columbia did release the album. But Cash speculated that less than twenty thousand units were manufactured, and the label ultimately buried the album through lack of advertising and promotion.

Kris Kristofferson wrote "Here Comes That Rainbow Again," a lyrical masterpiece inspired by a scene in John Steinbeck's *The Grapes of Wrath*. Kristofferson had released his own version as a single in 1981, though it never charted for him. It did end up as part of the 1982 album *The Winning*

Hand featuring Kristofferson, Willie Nelson, Brenda Lee, and Dolly Parton. In his autobiography Cash states, "I don't think I've performed a concert without singing a Kristofferson song. 'Sunday Morning Coming Down' is the one people identify with me most strongly, but if I had to pick the one I love best, I think it would be 'Rainbow.' In fact, that might be my favorite song by any writer of our time" (Cash, *Autobiography,* 382–383). Kris paints a poetic portrait of a remarkable act of human kindness that takes place in a small roadside café. A kindhearted waitress lies about the cost of the candy on display so that two poor Okie kids can buy two pieces of candy for a penny. A truck driver drinking his coffee overhears this random act of kindness and leaves the waitress a very generous tip. It's a beautiful sentiment captured in song, which Cash conveys without sentimentality and with sheer honesty.

It seems appropriate that Cash waited for his final session to record "For the Good Times," Kristofferson's greatest song of parting. The song was included on Cash's *American VI: Ain't No Grave* album in 2010. The late, great Ray Price topped the country chart with his lovely rendition of this song in 1970. Kristofferson had begun writing the song in 1968 while driving from Nashville to the Gulf of Mexico where he piloted helicopters for offshore oil rigs. When Cash sings "Don't look so sad, I know it's over," we can't help but feel the sadness of losing one of our greatest purveyors of popular music.

Of course, Kris wrote the song about lovers coming to the end of their romance and ending their relationship with grace and gratitude. But Cash makes the affecting lyric a metaphor for life, as he calms and soothes us with the knowledge that "life goes on and this old world will keep on turning." But we know intrinsically that it will never turn in quite the same way again.

The significance of the relationship between Johnny Cash and Kris Kristofferson cannot be overemphasized. In his autobiography Cash wrote, "Kris is kind and funny, and honorable; he stands up for his beliefs and he won't let you down" (*Autobiography,* 383). Cash saw something in the Oxford-educated young man that he knew he had to help him fully realize. Kristofferson gave up a prestigious career and family life to purse a dream as a songwriter in Nashville. Maybe Cash saw a reflection of himself in Kristofferson, had he been afforded the opportunity to pursue an education, should he have wanted to, and not struggle through those blistering days in the Arkansas cotton fields. Both men had a calling to write and record songs that would change the perception of what country music was. Harlan Howard has been quoted as saying that a country song is three chords and the truth. If that's the case, Cash and Kristofferson brought a newfound truth to the standard themes of what country music represented during the generations before them. Kris's songs are brutally frank ballads filled with bold-faced truths, naked emotions, and unparalleled honesty. That's precisely what drew Cash to this brave, young songwriter, and the songs he couldn't stop himself from recording. Cash had forged a brotherly bond with one of his musical disciples that would last the rest of his life.

Marty Robbins

Johnny Cash was a songwriter first and foremost. The importance of his extensive catalog of self-penned songs cannot be denied. But that didn't stop Cash from searching far and wide to find songs that he wanted to record. He was the songwriter's best friend in so many ways. From Jimmie Rodgers and A. P. Carter to Dylan and Kristofferson, Cash knew precisely the caliber of song he wanted to record. If he did not write the songs himself, he always strived to find the best ones possible. He knew the value of a Marty Robbins song early on, as well a song by Jerry Reed, Johnny Horton, or Harlan Howard.

Cash recorded Marty Robbins's "I Couldn't Keep From Crying" twice, first at Sun, and then again for one of his first Columbia albums. Cash especially admired Robbins's beautiful voice and songwriting abilities. This song was a number 5 hit for Marty in 1953. Cash's Columbia version has a fuller, more elaborate arrangement. We feel the singer's pain and heartbreak as he sees his loved one walking with someone new before he has his ultimate breakdown. Cash would turn to Robbins for other songs through the years, and there were songs Robbins wrote that he would offer exclusively to Cash.

During the seventies, Robbins provided Cash with two impressive singles: "Kate," and "Song of the Patriot." Taking a page from murder ballads like "Delia's Gone," "Kate" also involves a remorseless narrator who cold bloodedly shoots his girl with a 38 and is charged with murder in the first degree and put in prison. He blames her for cheating on him, forcing him to shoot her. Interestingly, Marty Robbins, known for his tender ballads and story-songs, wrote this one and gave it to Cash, because only Cash could get away with a song like this. His delivery is free of any guilt or pathos, convinced that Kate is responsible for his unfortunate fate. It was the third single released from *A Thing Called Love* and made it to number 2 on the country chart and number 75 pop.

Interestingly, Cash also recorded an alternate, longer version of "Kate" that was released in Canada, but not in the United States. The fascinating thing about it is that in this version the singer does not shoot Kate with his .38, but rather the guy she was cheating on him with, with his .44. This changes the entire dynamic of the song, and makes the singer seem a bit more sympathetic. He still blames Kate for putting him in prison, but when the jury passes sentence, he tells them not to look down on him and that he's there to take the blame.

Willie Nelson, Tom T. Hall, and Merle Haggard

Cash had always admired Willie Nelson and, quite frankly, felt very competitive toward him because both shared the same basic philosophy about songs and songwriters. Willie's star rose as Cash's dimmed, and that's quite likely the reason Cash did not record more of Nelson's songs during his career. For his *Rainbow* album, Cash recorded Nelson's "They're All the Same." In the liner notes Cash wrote for the album *The Winning Hand,* Cash said that he had a dream that Willie Nelson had sung him the song "They're All the Same" years before. Cash recalls in detail how Willie had sung him this song and then sent him a demo of it. Cash misplaced the demo and years later asked Willie to send him another copy of the tape. Well, Willie must have eventually gotten the song to Cash, and he finally recorded it for this album. The song lyric fits Cash, being that it's about the high-and-mighty and the lowly people he has met and known over the years, and the realization that "they all need wine and they all need love and to me they're all the same." It may have taken Cash awhile to get around to recording a Willie Nelson song, but it was better late than never.

For his part, Nelson recorded Cash's "I'm a Worried Man." On *VH1 Storytellers: Johnny Cash & Willie Nelson,* Willie introduces "I'm a Worried Man" as a song that Cash wrote and he (Willie) recorded for a reggae album he was working on at the time. The album *Countryman* would not be released until 2005, and the song "Worried Man" would be included on it. Cash then proceeds to tell Willie the story of how he was inspired to write the song after walking down a street in Jamaica and having a man come up to him and say, "Mr. Cash, I'm a worried man." The song was originally included on Cash's album *Ragged Old Flag.*

Cash wrote and recorded two songs that proved his admiration for Nelson. He closed out his 1975 *Look at Them Beans* album with "Down at Dripping Springs" a song Cash wrote about Willie Nelson's Fourth of July Picnic concert in Dripping Springs, Texas. Cash enthusiastically chronicles the sights and stars that performed at the concert.

Similarly, Cash opens *Boom Chicka Boom* with "A Backstage Pass," a lighthearted look at what really goes on behind the scenes at a Willie Nelson concert. Willie's shows have that rare ability to attract people of all ages and from almost every walk of life. Cash made note of this and succeeded in writing a firsthand account of what he witnessed backstage at a Willie concert. The song was originally recorded under the title "Whackos and Weirdos," which is specifically the audience Cash describes in the song's opening lines, along with "dingbats and dodos, and athletes and movie stars and David Allan Coe."

Cash was always interested in songs that established songwriters like Merle Haggard and Tom T. Hall were sending him. Cash had included Hall and Dave Dudley's "There Ain't No Easy Run" as part of a medley on *The Johnny Cash Show* album in 1970. Ten years later, for *The Last Gunfighter Ballad* album Cash recorded Hall's "Give It Away." It's an inspirational little honky-tonk tune about the value of a smile, a kind word, or a song; they're easy things for us to share with others and they can mean so much to someone else. Hall always had a way with making the simple sound profound. Just listen to Hall's own hit "I Love," to see how so few words can say so much. That's why he's regarded as one of the greatest songwriters in country music.

In 1982 Cash guest-starred on his daughter Rosanne's *Somewhere in the Stars* album performing Hall's "That's How I Got to Memphis." Rosanne was born in Memphis, and so the lyric of this song would certainly have appealed to her. It's a splendid version of the Hall classic that Rosanne sings with great emotion. Her sultry voice suits this song perfectly, and having her father make a guest appearance on the last verse of the song makes this a truly memorable performance in so many ways.

Cash always admired Merle Haggard's songwriting. He may have refused to perform "Okie from Muskogee" at Nixon's White House, but he always loved Haggard's songs. In 1982 he recorded Haggard's "Good Old American Guest," for *The Adventures of Johnny Cash*. It's a great train song that serves as a perfect vehicle for Cash. For his part, Haggard always acknowledged his respect and admiration for Cash. This song finds the singer yearning to ride on a freight train in order to get away from all his troubles and cares. When Cash sings "the pressures of life got to me," we believe him, and he turns in a persuasive performance on this song about wanting to return to a simpler way of life where he can be a "good old American guest." Haggard had recorded his own version one year earlier for his Epic Records debut album *Big City*.

Fourteen years after Cash first recorded "I'm Leaving Now," he still believed in the song and rerecorded it for *Unchained*. He appeared to summon up more energy for it than the other songs on the album. Maybe it was because Merle Haggard is alongside him for their first duet together. It's hard to believe that Cash and Haggard had never recorded a song together before. Cash and Haggard did perform duets together when Haggard appeared on *The Johnny Cash Show*, but they had never released an official recording. Thankfully, they were able to join forces here, making this one of the standout tracks on *Unchained*. And Tom Petty and Marty Stuart join Cash on Haggard's "The Running Kind" on the *Unearthed* box set. Haggard took the song to number 12 country in 1978, and Cash delivers a sturdy performance as the narrator who is perpetually leaving and wandering off.

Marty Stuart, Rodney Crowell, and Guy Clark

Cash took special pride in championing the works of up-and-coming writers on the music scene. He mentored and recorded songs by many young artists, including Marty Stuart. Cash helped Stuart's career when the latter married Cash's daughter Cindy. Stuart always revered classic country, and the Carter Family in particular. "Mother Maybelle" features a young Marty Stuart performing a duet with Cash on a touching tribute to Mother Maybelle Carter. The song was recorded in 1979 and would later appear on the Marty Stuart compilation album *Once Upon a Time,* released in 1992. The song incorporates Carter Family song titles into a lovely salute to the revered Carter Family matriarch. When Marshall Grant was fired from the Cash show in 1980, Stuart joined the group. No longer the Tennessee Three, they were now known as "Johnny Cash and the Great Eighties Eight." The group consisted of Stuart, Bob Wootton and Jerry Hensley on guitars, W. S. Holland on drums, Joe Allen on bass, Earl Poole Ball on piano, and Jack Hale and Bob Lewin on horns.

Cash recorded Bob Nolan's "One More Ride" in 1981 for Marty Stuart's 1982 album *Busy Bee Cafe,* Stuart's second solo release issued on Sugar Hill Records. Cash contributed vocals on three tracks; this one, "Hey Porter" and "Get in Line." This is one joyous ride as Cash and Stuart layer their vocals throughout this first-rate guitar and mandolin driven rendition of the Sons of the Pioneers and early Cash favorite. Next, Cash sings a bluegrass-infused cover of his first Sun single "Hey Porter." Stuart ably backs him up on guitar along with the late, great Clarence White, who was a revered bluegrass and country guitarist. White played guitar for the Kentucky Colonels before joining the Byrds. This is a solid new bluegrass reinvention of the rockabilly classic. Cash and Stuart also duet on the gospel ballad "Get in Line," written by bluegrass legend Lester Flatt. Stuart played with Flatt early in his career and this song is a sedate, somber almost a cappella tribute to Stuart's esteemed mentor.

For Cash's 1981 album *The Baron*, Stuart wrote "Hey, Hey Train," a driving, up-tempo train song that Cash seems to enjoy performing. Again, the production is a bit overwhelming, but the song is catchy and Cash's performance is spirited and lively. There's nothing like a good train song about a girl leaving him behind and taking off on that train to get Cash excited in the studio. Ten years later Cash reunited with Stuart for the duet "Doin' My Time," for Stuart's album *This One's Gonna Hurt You.* Richard Bennett and Tony Brown produced the track, and it features Marty on the first two verses and chorus, before Johnny joins in on the third verse. It's a great arrangement and a first-rate production of a spirited duet by two artists who truly respect each other.

Like Marty Stuart, singer-songwriter Rodney Crowell is another son-in-law Cash promoted and turned to for musical inspiration. Crowell, born in 1950 in Houston, Texas, was married to Rosanne Cash from 1979 to 1992. Crowell moved to Nashville in 1972 after being discovered by Jerry Reed. He befriended singer-songwriter Guy Clark, and eventually became part of Emmylou Harris's Hot Band. Harris recorded Crowell's "Till I Gain Control Again," for her *Elite Hotel* album, and in 1977 Crowell released his first solo album *Ain't Living Long Like This.* The album contained songs that would be recorded by other artists, including the title cut by Waylon Jennings. Crowell met Rosanne at a party hosted by Jennings. Crowell and Rosanne started dating and eventually moved in together. Crowell recalled in a 2009 interview in *Uncut* magazine the time he and Rosanne were invited to visit Johnny and June at their home in Jamaica, "There was a confrontation between John and Rosanne about sleeping arrangements, so I with drunken bravura, I cut into the conversation. I said, you know I'd be a hypocrite if I changed my lifestyle—trying to be a puffed up man and hold my own with one of the world class

icons—and he kind of looked at me, and he said: 'Son, I don't know you well enough to miss you if you were gone'" (McCay, "Part Two"). Crowell was intimidated, but the two grew close over the years. Crowell produced six albums for Rosanne, including the best-selling *Seven Year Ache* in 1981, and the critically acclaimed *King's Record Shop* in 1987. The two also scored a number 1 country hit with their duet "It's Such A Small World." Crowell's own critically acclaimed 1988 album *Diamonds & Dirt* included five consecutive number 1 country singles, including the Best Country Song Grammy Award–winning "After All This Time."

The first Crowell song that Cash recorded was "Song for the Life," a brilliant character study about a man looking back on his younger days. Cash turns in a haunting performance of the poetic lyrics. Interestingly, Cash changed the opening lyric of Rodney's song to reflect his change from his wilder days, rather than his youth. The original lyric reads, "I don't drink as much as I ought to, lately it just ain't my style, and the hard times don't hurt like they used to, they pass quicker like when I was a child." Cash changed it to "I don't drink the way that I used to, lately that just ain't my style, and the hard times don't hurt like they once did, they pass more quickly like when I was wild." But either way it works, and although the meaning may be slightly altered, it remains one of the finest songs on Cash's 1978 album *Gone Girl.* And daughter Rosanne joins her father on background vocals, making this a truly meaningful performance.

In 1979 Cash recorded Crowell's "Bull Rider," a fine rodeo song that tells about what a bull rider has to endure. He turns in a convincing performance singing about the hard life of a rodeo rider, with the refrain "live fast, die young, bull rider." We're taken for a ride of our own on this clever song about what really goes on at a rodeo, and the high cost the riders have to pay to participate in this sport. "Bull Rider" was the third single released from the *Silver* album, and Cash's first charting single of the eighties. Unfortunately, it did not fare very well on the country chart, only making it to number 66. Crowell also appeared as a guest vocalist on Cash's "You'll Get Yours (And I'll Get Mine)" from the *A Believer Sings the Truth* album, and he coproduced *The Survivors Live* in 1982.

In October 1998, Cash was admitted to Baptist Hospital suffering from pneumonia, and in November 1998, he found himself back on the country chart after nearly eight years, as part of a Rodney Crowell tribute single referencing "I Walk the Line." In "I Walk the Line (Revisited)," Crowell reminisces about the first time he heard Cash sing "I Walk the Line," while driving in his father's '49 Ford in 1956. Cash comes in and sings his song as if it were coming out of Crowell's car speakers. Crowell recalls how hearing that song changed his life, as Cash picks up the second verse of "I Walk the Line." And Crowell completes his homage to his musical hero and former father-in-law by stating "I've seen the Mona Lisa, I've heard Shakespeare read real fine, just like hearing Johnny Cash sing 'I Walk the Line.'" The song reached number 61 on the country chart.

Another young Texas songwriter would soon attract Cash's attention. Guy Clark was born and raised in Monahans, Texas, and was a key architect of the Outlaw movement in country music. He influenced many songwriters, such as Crowell, Steve Earle, and Lyle Lovett, to name a few. Clark himself had been influenced by the legendary Texas songwriters Townes Van Zandt and Jerry Jeff Walker. Clark emerged on the scene during the early seventies, and Cash could not help but take notice. Clark had previously written the Jerry Jeff Walker ballad "L.A. Freeway," and had just released his debut album, the critically acclaimed *Old No. 1.* Cash immediately took a shine to Clark's "Texas-1947," the vivid recollection of a six-year-old boy anticipating the arrival of the first streamline train to pull into the depot of his small Texas town. Cash imbues the song with a sense of wonder and amazement at the sight of the train passing through town like a mad-dog cyclone, and the ultimate reward for the boy of getting a nickel smashed flatter than a dime. It was released as the second single from the *Look at Them Beans* album and it made it to number 35 on the country chart.

In 1977 Cash recorded Clark's aforementioned "The Last Gunfighter Ballad," and used it as the title of one of his albums. In 1983 Cash included Clark's "New Cut Road" on the *Johnny 99* album, and it's another good choice for him. It tells of a fiddler named Coleman Bonner who plays his fiddle while contemplating his family leaving Kentucky and moving to Texas. Coleman prefers to stay in Kentucky rather than move away. The arrangement on this track is overly elaborate, and Cash has to struggle against a wall of sound. A simpler arrangement might have helped Cash interpret this song better. Bobby Bare had also released it as a single in 1982, and took it to number 18 on the country chart.

For his 1987 debut album for Mercury Records, *Johnny Cash Is Coming to Town,* Cash included two of Clark's finest compositions. "Let Him Roll," a captivating story-song about a wino who is "years old before his time" and who used to be an elevator man in a cheap hotel. The song has a twist ending, as we learn very matter-of-factly that he died, and the one woman he ever loved, Alice, a whore in Dallas, somehow made it to his funeral. Guy Clark had a style of writing unlike anyone else. His sense of character and detail is impeccable. Clark and Bobby Bare had previously recorded this song. Cash relates the story with great authority, as June,

Helen, and Anita Carter add angelic background vocals to this track.

In 1985 all four Highwaymen joined forces on "Desperados Waiting for a Train," one of Clark's finest compositions. The song tells about a young boy who worships an older gentleman who's like a father to him. Clark wrote this semi-autobiographical song about an oil-drilling drifter named Jack Prigg, whom Clark has referred to as his grandmother's boyfriend. The tobacco-chewing old man befriended Clark and left a lasting impression on him. Kris sings the first verse, which introduces the young man who plays "Red River Valley" for the old man while he sits in the kitchen and cries. Waylon sings the second verse, which describes the older man as a "drifter and a driller of oil wells and an old school man of the world." He had let the younger man drive his truck when he was too drunk to as he'd wink and give him money for the girls. Willie picks up the third verse, about how the older man would take him with him to a bar called the Green Frog Café. And Johnny handles the final verse, in which the old man is pushing eighty, with brown tobacco stains all down his chin. The younger man had always idolized him and it's hard to see him now looking like an old man. In the end, the younger man is present when the train, a metaphor for death, arrives to separate the two desperados. The song was originally recorded by Clark for his *Old No. 1* album, as well as by Jerry

Jeff Walker and David Allan Coe. This second single from the *Highwayman* album made it to number 15 on the country chart.

John Prine and Steve Goodman

If ever there was an artist who could match Cash's ability to transition effortlessly from a song of utter conviction to an off-center observation on the minutiae of life it is John Prine. Prine was born and raised in Illinois, and worked as a mailman, writing and performing songs in Chicago before being discovered by Kris Kristofferson. Kristofferson helped him land a recording contract with Atlantic Records, and produced Prine's first, self-titled album in 1971. The album was filled with future Prine classics, like "Sam Stone," "Paradise," "Hello in There," "Angel from Montgomery," and "Donald and Lydia," some of which Cash would cover in years to come.

The first Prine song Cash released was "The Twentieth Century Is Almost Over," from the *Rockabilly Blues* album. It is a satirical gem of a song Prine wrote with Steve Goodman. No one can fashion a lyrical phrase like Prine, and he has proven himself to be one of popular music's most original and innovative singer-songwriters. This whimsical meditation on the closing of the twentieth century is full of Prine and Goodman's clever wordplay and offbeat metaphors. Choice lyrics include: "Does anyone remember the Great Depression, I read all about in the True Confession."

The chorus has everyone joining in to make this a full-blown sing-along. Cash would record the song again in five years on the *Highwayman* album as a duet with Willie Nelson.

In 1982 Cash released Prine's "Paradise" on *The Adventures of Johnny Cash*. He had recorded the song earlier with a just a guitar and vocal, in a version that would appear on the *Personal File* album in 2006. "Paradise" recalls the disappearance of a small western Kentucky town that the singer fondly remembers. In its own way, it's a standout protest song about how progress, this time in the guise of Mr. Peabody's coal train, can ultimately destroy an entire way of life. John Denver originally covered the song on his album *Rocky Mountain High* and helped bring great attention to Prine. Denver's rendition is near perfect, as is Prine's own recording of the song. Cash gives it all he's got and even slightly alters the name of where the abandoned old prison stood. In the original lyric it's "Adrie's Hill," but Cash changes it to "Adrian's Hill." He also pluralizes "coal company," implying that more than one came and stripped all the land. But little flourishes like that only serve to make this a very good performance of a great song.

On *Rainbow,* Cash covered "Unwed Fathers," an insightful John Prine and Bobby Braddock ballad about the plight of unwed mothers and the unwed fathers, "who can't be bothered, they run like water through a mountain stream." It's a stark piece of social commentary that finds the young pregnant girl in the song leaving her family in shame and taking a Greyhound bus to go off and have her baby. We are told that from teenage lover to unwed mother, she's had to face it alone, while the teenage father of her baby can't be bothered to involve himself. Prine had originally recorded the song, and Tammy Wynette released it as a single in 1983, as did country singer Gail Davies in 1985.

Kristofferson not only introduced Cash to Prine, but he also introduced him to the songs of a young man named Steve Goodman. Like Prine, Goodman grew up in Illinois, and played in clubs in and around Chicago. It was there that Goodman met Prine, who came to view Goodman as a mentor. In 1971 Goodman opened for Kristofferson, who was so impressed with him that he introduced him to Paul Anka, who was equally impressed and brought Goodman to New York to record some demos. Goodman landed a recording contract with Buddah Records, and began writing songs like "The City of New Orleans," and "You Never Even Called Me by My Name," which became a country jukebox favorite as recorded by David Allan Coe. The song also contains one of the most memorable verses ever heard in a country song: "I was drunk the day my Mom got out of prison, and I went to pick her up in the rain / But before I could get to the station in my pickup truck, she got run over by a damned old train."

Cash believed that "The City of New Orleans" was the one that got away. He regretted not record-ing the song when Kristofferson originally brought it to him. Johnny knew it could have been a certified hit for him. In his autobiography, Cash explains his theory for his sagging record sales during the seventies and letting this song slip by him, "My own version of my music's success or failure is a little different from that prevalent in 'the industry.' For instance, one of the main reasons my record sales dropped off so dramatically in the early '70s is that making secular records simply wasn't my first priority; that's when I turned down recording 'City Of New Orleans' because I was too busy working on *Gospel Road*" (Cash, *Autobiography*, 263). It's also interesting to note that earlier in his autobiography, Cash had referred to this song and his regret about not recording it in a different context. He writes, "Marshall and Luther limited me, it's true, especially in later years. Songs would come along that I'd want to record, but I didn't because I couldn't figure out the chords myself, and neither could anyone else in the studio. 'City Of New Orleans' by Steve Goodman was one of those. Kris Kristofferson sent it to me before anyone else got a shot at it, and if I'd taken the time and made the effort to learn it, I might just have had myself a major hit" (Cash, *Autobiography*, 103). Well, both theories might hold truth, but there's no denying that this was the perfect Cash song. Goodman wrote the song in 1970 while taking a trip with his wife to meet her grandmother in Mattoon, Illinois. The train they were riding on was called the City of

New Orleans. Goodman was inspired by the scenery and included the song on his self-titled debut album in 1971. The song is a picturesque train ride through the heart of America, and Cash's performance of the song is perfection. John Denver was the first artist to cover the song on his 1971 album *Aerie*, although he insisted on rewriting a verse and taking a cowriter credit. Then in 1972 Arlo Guthrie recorded Goodman's original version and enjoyed the biggest hit of his career. In 1984 Willie Nelson took the song to the top of the country chart. Had Johnny released this song as a single, even after Guthrie's version, it might have been a giant country hit for him.

Ian Tyson, Gordon Lightfoot, and Neil Young

If "The City of New Orleans" was the song that got away from Cash, then Ian Tyson's "Red Velvet" is the song Cash would not let go of. Cash was one of the first artists to record the songs of the talented Canadian folk singer-songwriter who, as part of the duo Ian & Sylvia with then-wife Sylvia Fricker, would enjoy a successful recording career during the sixties before branching out on his own in the seventies. Tyson influenced other great songwriters of the time, such as Gordon Lightfoot and Neil Young.

During the sessions for *From Sea to Shining Sea* Cash recorded "Red Velvet," which was released as the B-side of "The Wind Changes." It's a truly inspired piece of writing from Tyson, and a song Cash was immediately drawn to. Cash once remarked that he usually had good ears for picking a hit song, and he thought this song would be a huge hit for him. Ultimately it wasn't, but it should have been. It's a beautiful, descriptive western-themed story with poetic lyrics. It tells about a girl who comes down on a day coach to be with her boyfriend, told very well and nicely sung.

Cash's 2006 album *American V: A Hundred Highways* includes his cover of Tyson's "Four Strong Winds," one of the grandest modern folk songs of the times. It was originally recorded by Ian & Sylvia. Bobby Bare and Neil Young also released outstanding covers of the song. Cash takes the coming-of-age saga one step further and presents it as a fond recollection of lost love and faded youth. It's a profound lyric bolstered by Cash's impassioned singing, "Four strong winds that blow lonely, seven seas that run high, all these things that won't change come what may / Well, our good times are all gone, and I'm bound for moving on, I'll look for you if I'm ever back this way."

Cash was also one of the first artists to record the songs of Gordon Lightfoot. The Ontario-born Lightfoot began his career writing and recording folk ballads such as "Early Morning Rain," "Ribbon of Darkness," and the historical "Canadian Railroad Trilogy." During the seventies he became one of the premier singer-songwriters of his generation, with hits like "If You Could Read My Mind," "Sundown," and the epic sea saga, "The Wreck of the Edmund Fitzgerald."

In 1966 Cash turned in a fine rendition of the Lightfoot classic "For Lovin' Me." Early on, Lightfoot's songs were recorded by artists such as Marty Robbins and Peter, Paul and Mary, who reached number 30 on the pop chart with their version of "For Lovin' Me" in 1965. One year later Waylon Jennings had a country hit with it, taking it to number 9. Cash's cover is right on the mark, as he once again takes on the persona of the rambling man who never promised he would stick around forever. He turns the tables on his lover and blames her for becoming too attached to him. He kisses her off with the biting line, "I've got a hundred more like you, so don't be blue, I'll have a thousand before I'm through."

Forty years after "For Lovin' Me," Cash included his cover of Lightfoot's "If You Could Read My Mind" on *American V: A Hundred Highways.* This was Lightfoot's first hit to reach number 5 on the pop chart, in 1970. One can't help but compare Lightfoot's young, vibrant vocal with Cash's tired, world-weary cover. When Cash sings, "you know that ghost is me," we have to ultimately view the hero as a youthful reflection of Cash's aged balladeer. And he does express the notion that "heroes often fail." The song becomes in Cash's hands a brave coming to terms with love lost and life lived.

Neil Young was another Canadian singer-songwriter Cash admired, and Young had long acknowledged Cash as an inspiration on his music and career. In 1993 Cash recorded a duet version of "The Little Drummer Boy" with Young for a projected Neil Young Christmas album that never materialized. Young updated the musical arrangement and made it a more solemn production than Cash's original recording. "The Little Drummer Boy" was Johnny's only charting Christmas single and, after all these years, he still owns it. Originally known as "Carol of the Drum," it was written by classical music composer and teacher Katherine Kennicott Davis in 1941. Johnny's version made it to number 24 on the country chart in 1959 and number 63 pop, one year after the Harry Simeone Chorale took it to number 13 pop. The song has become a seasonal standard, and though many artists have recorded it, it's Cash's version that's usually played on the radio and issued on yearly Christmas compilation albums. The story of the poor little drummer boy being summoned by the Magi to play for the newborn baby Jesus is an enduring one, and Johnny's recording of this song is among the finest.

Cash included Young's "Pocahontas" on the *Unearthed* box set. Young first recorded the surrealistic story-song, revolving around the brutal treatment of Native Americans, on his album *Rust Never Sleeps.* Rick Rubin brought the song to Cash, who at first was apprehensive about recording it.

He shouldn't have worried; he conveys the dream-like lyrics convincingly, and the thought of Cash meeting up with Pocahontas and Marlon Brando, as the last verse suggests, is priceless.

Also included on *Unearthed* is Cash's cover of Young's "Heart of Gold." Cash delivers a fine vocal, and when he sings "It keeps me searching for a heart of gold and I'm getting old," you believe it. The Red Hot Chili Peppers add tasteful background accompaniment.

Bruce Springsteen

After the lackluster response Cash received for *The Adventures of Johnny Cash*, he decided to reteam with Brian Ahern, who was responsible for his last major hit, "(Ghost) Riders in the Sky," and his *Silver* album. But this time there was tension between Cash and Ahern. Cash was suffering from lack of interest as Ahern had, in Johnny's words, "played producer" with him, "dominating the choice of songs and stealing his emotional investment in the whole affair" (Streissguth, *Johnny Cash: The Biography*, 214). The *Johnny 99* album was recorded in California, now out of Cash's comfort zone, and what emerged was a darker album that contains some great songs, but lacks the emotional impact of a first-rate Cash collection. Three singles were released from the album, but only two charted, and poorly at that. The third single, "Johnny 99" was by far the best of the three and one of the best songs on the album. This was the first time that Cash had recorded songs by Bruce Springsteen, who, like Cash, revered Woody Guthrie and embraced the folk idiom while recording some of the greatest rock albums of the twentieth century. Springsteen counted Cash among his musical influences, and Springsteen's songs gave Cash some exceptional new material to cover.

Both of the Springsteen songs Cash chose to record were from the critically acclaimed acoustic album *Nebraska*. The stark, haunting songs from that album painted a dismal picture of the shattering of the American dream, with an array of individuals who experience dark and devastating life occurrences with no hope of redemption in sight. "Highway Patrolman" is the searing story of a cop named Joe Roberts who feels responsible for his younger brother, Frankie, a Vietnam War veteran who comes home and finds himself in trouble after having a fight with a young man in a roadhouse. The original glow of hope is dashed as he recalls, "Me and Frankie laughing and drinking, nothing feels better than blood on blood / taking turns dancing with Maria, while the band played 'The Night of the Johnstown Flood' / I catch him when he's straying like any brother should, a man turns his back on his family, he ain't no good." Joe married Maria, and Frankie came back from war a troubled man. This is the kind of song that really challenged Cash to imbue it with its own stamp of believability. As Joe Roberts, he has to go against his better judgment and let his brother flee across the border to Canada. "Highway Patrolman" is like a movie in itself, and Cash performs it brilliantly as the world-weary cop who struggles to do the right thing by his conscience and by the law.

Columbia Records waited to release "Johnny 99" as the third single from the album. Unfortunately, by that time the support for this album had waned, and the song never charted. It's another Springsteen original, and by far one of the two best songs on the album, along with "Highway Patrolman." Cash had found material worthy of him in Springsteen's catalog, and one wishes that he had taken the opportunity to record an entire album of Springsteen songs. For "Johnny 99" Cash takes on the persona of a laid-off autoworker from Mahwah, New Jersey. The man is so desperate that he shoots and kills a night clerk while drunk. As a result he's remanded to prison for a life sentence, but asks to be executed rather than face ninety-nine years in a cell. Cash gives it all he's got, and the result is an outstanding performance of a graphic story-song that has us hooked from beginning to end.

In November 2000, Cash contributed his cover of Bruce Springsteen's "I'm on Fire" for the all-star album *Badlands: A Tribute to Bruce Springsteen's Nebraska*. Cash turns in a first-rate performance of the scathing ballad, which fellow Highwaymen member Waylon Jennings had also recorded. This was a bonus track on the tribute album, since the song "I'm on Fire" was not included on Springsteen's *Nebraska* album, but rather appeared on *Born in the U.S.A.*

"Further on (up the Road)" is one of the newer songs on *American V: A Hundred Highways*, and the last Springsteen song Cash would record. Springsteen had originally released it on his critically acclaimed post-9/11 album *The Rising* in 2002. That was one year before Cash's death. When Cash sings "got on my dead man's suit," we shudder a bit. Springsteen could not have written a more prophetic song for Cash to cover. But the remarkable thing about it is that, despite the graveyard imagery that permeates the lyric, there is a sense of hope as Cash sings, "One sunny morning we'll rise I know, And I'll meet you further on up the road."

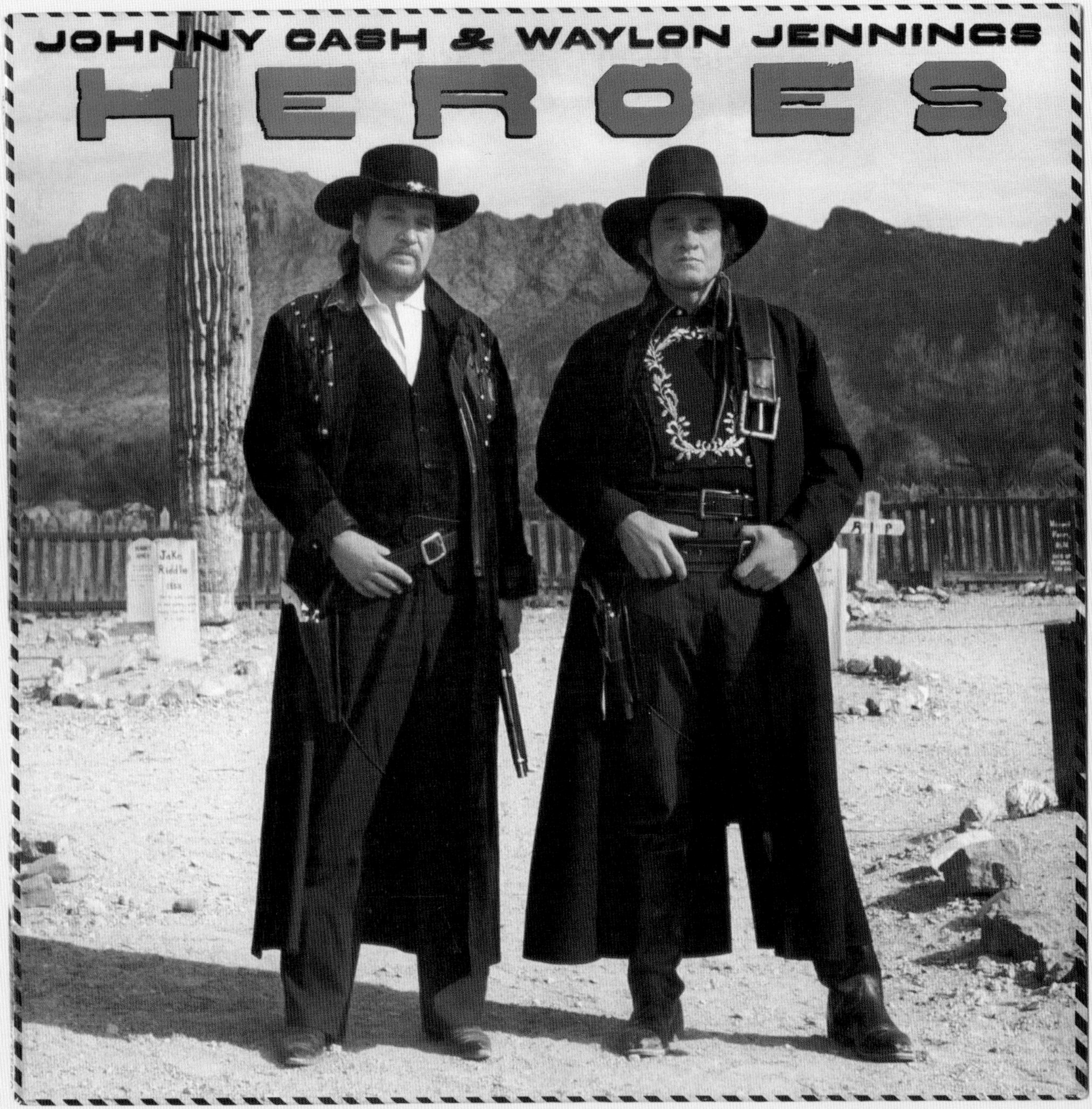
JOHNNY CASH & WAYLON JENNINGS
HEROES

Chapter 9

HEROES

HANK WILLIAMS, BOB DYLAN, AND OTHER MUSICAL INFLUENCES

*A study of the singers and songwriters who influenced
Johnny Cash's life and music*

From early childhood, Cash forged a strong bond with the music he heard on the radio in Dyess. He loved all kinds of music: the country sounds of the Carter Family and the Louvin Brothers, the gospel style of Sister Rosetta Tharpe, and the pop sounds of stars like the McGuire Sisters and Dean Martin. But it was country music that helped shape his future and served as a paradigm for all that he would accomplish. During the Sun years he was able to record some of his favorite Hank Williams songs, along with pop hits of the day like "Sugartime." By the time he moved over to Columbia he was able to indulge himself further by recording more cov-ers of songs from his musical heroes. Cash was not finished with Hank Williams, either. Hank's shadow loomed large, and his legacy would both haunt and inspire Cash during his entire career. At Sun he had recorded "I Can't Help It (if I'm Still in Love with You)," "You Win Again," "Hey Good Lookin'," "I Could Never Be Ashamed of You," and "Cold, Cold Heart." For his 1960 country cover-song album *Now, There Was a Song!*, Cash chose to include "I'm So Lonesome I Could Cry," Hank's most mournful and devastating ballad. Cash certainly delivers on this confessional masterpiece. We feel the sheer terror right from the opening line, "Hear that lonesome whippoorwill, he sounds too

« Heroes. *Courtesy of Sony Music Entertainment.*

blue to fly." Cash so admired and emulated Hank's simple, yet profound, way with words and always sought similar poetry in his own songs.

For his 1962 album *The Sound of Johnny Cash*, Cash wrote "Sing It Pretty, Sue." The song has an interesting history and owes a great deal to his earlier hit "Ballad of a Teenage Queen." In this song, like its predecessor, a girl gives up all she and her lover had between them to pursue a glamorous career, this time as a singer. Unlike "Ballad of a Teenage Queen," this song examines what happens when the fame-seeking former flame does not return. He's content to watch her on TV and drop her a card every now and then to tell her he's still listening. This song might have been influenced by Cash's reported romance with Billie Jean Horton, the widow of both Hank Williams and Johnny Horton. After Horton's tragic death, Cash helped console Billie Jean, and may have fallen in love with her in the process. She wanted a career in music, however, and turned down his marriage proposal.

Cash's most obvious tribute to Hank would be the song "The Night Hank Williams Came to Town" from the album *Johnny Cash Is Coming to Town*. Country disc jockey and songwriter Charlie Williams cowrote "The Night Hank Williams Came to Town" with songwriter Bobby Braddock. Williams had written Cash's early favorite "I Got Stripes" and Braddock wrote or cowrote numerous classics including George Jones's "He Stopped Loving Her Today." This nostalgic retrospective about a young man's excitement at seeing the great Hank Williams coming to his town is filled with era-specific imagery and vivid description. From the opening line that informs us that Harry Truman was president and a Coca-Cola and hamburger cost thirty cents, we know that we're in for an enjoyable ride through recent American history. We are completely drawn into the excitement of the moment, as the crowd anticipation builds and builds for the arrival of Hank Williams to perform in their small town. Cash was greatly inspired by Williams, and although Williams's short but storied career ended two years before Cash's had begun, they both remain, arguably, the greatest icons in country music history. During one of his low points, Cash said that if he had died at twenty-nine like Williams did, he would have been revered in the same way Hank was. Well, Cash thankfully lived long enough to enjoy a major career resurgence, and today he is viewed as one of the great figures in any genre of popular music. Interestingly, an earlier Stoney Edwards tribute song from 1973 called "The Night the Ernest Tubb Show Came to Town" may have inspired songwriters Williams and Braddock to change the title to "The Night Hank Williams Came to Town." Furthermore, the song was originally released by T.C. Brown under the title, "The Night Porter Wagoner Came to Town." In that version Richard Nixon was president and Coke and Pepsi sold for fifteen cents. Charlie

Williams does the announcer voice at the end of the song, and Waylon Jennings takes the lead on the third verse. Unfortunately, the song made it to only number 43 on the country chart.

George Jones

On his third Columbia album, *Songs of Our Soil*, Cash adapted and arranged "I Want to Go Home," more commonly referred to as "Sloop John B." He changes the word sloop to ship in the first line, singing, "We sailed on the ship John B., my grandfather and me, around Nassau town we did roam." They drink and fight and he feels so homesick, not "broke-up," as in the popular Beach Boys' rendition of the song. Otherwise, the lyric is quite similar and the theme of wanting to return home must have appealed to the touring and traveling Cash. The song originated in the West Indies in 1927, and Alan Lomax made a field recording of it in Nassau in 1935 under the title "The John B. Sails." Artists such as Cisco Houston, the Weavers, the Kingston Trio, and Jimmie "Honeycomb" Rodgers recorded it, by various titles. The Beach Boys may have been influenced enough by Cash's recording to release their own version in 1966. While Cash's rendition was never released as a single, the Beach Boys' "Sloop John B" reached number 3 on the pop chart.

Cash was so anxious to pay homage to his musical influences that in December 1960, he released *Now, There Was a Song!* Cash's fifth Columbia release was a concept album of sorts since all the

tracks are country songs Cash recorded by other artists he admired. In his autobiography, Cash explains that this album "is also unique because it was recorded at only one session and no master required more than three takes to complete" (Cash, *Autobiography*, 409).

George Jones and Darrell Edwards wrote "Seasons of My Heart." It was one of two George Jones songs Cash wanted to include on this album. Cash greatly admired Jones, who was a major country music star by this time. They became lifelong friends and, in fact, Cash helped George out on many occasions. "Seasons of My Heart" was originally released as the B-side of George's first hit single, "Why Baby Why" in 1955, and then it became a Top 10 hit for Jimmy C. Newman in 1958. Cash's cover reached number 10 on the country chart, and deservedly so. It's a beautiful ballad that Cash infuses with deep intimacy. The narrator's loved one is leaving and he knows that it will bring him sorrow, where "his tears like autumn leaves will fall." Still, he clings to the hope that spring will bring a new tomorrow and they can be together again. While garnering praise as one of the greatest vocalists in country music history, George Jones remains underrecognized for his songwriting talent. This is one of his finest compositions and one of Cash's most profoundly moving vocal performances. "Just One More" is the second George Jones song Cash includes on this album. This one charted for George in 1956, reaching number 3 on the country chart. It's a drinking song wherein the singer yearns to drown away the memory of his lost love. He'll have another drink of wine, and if she's still on his mind then "one drink, just one more, and then another." Jones's battle with the bottle was well known, and this song makes no excuses for drinking or for drinking to forget. That's what country music was all about.

Longtime Bob Wills & His Texas Playboys lead vocalist Tommy Duncan wrote "Time Changes Everything," a western swing classic about trying to heal after a failed love affair. Roy Rogers took the song to number 4 on the country chart, which was called the "Hillbilly" chart in 1941. The song has also been recorded by artists such as Ray Price, Merle Haggard, and George Jones. Cash turns the tempo down a notch and takes the song in a more country direction. Cash takes on another Bob Wills favorite in "My Shoes Keep Walking Back to You." It was cowritten by Wills and recorded by a wide array of pop and country artists. It reached number 45 on the pop chart by Guy Mitchell, while Ray Price's version remained at number 1 on the country chart for four weeks in 1957. Even though the singer pretends he doesn't miss his love, when the day is through he misses her most of all, lamenting, "my lips keep calling for you, and my shoes keep walking back to you." It's pure country heartache as performed by Cash.

Canadian country star Hank Snow had originally recorded Erwin King's "Why Do You Punish Me." Snow, nicknamed "The Singing Ranger" was one of Cash's all-time favorite artists. Cash had already recorded his song "Two Timin' Woman" while at Sun. Through the years Cash would cover other Snow songs on various albums. In this yearning ballad the narrator tries to share the blame with a lover who is punishing him. He is stuck in love's prison and wonders, "Is love a crime, if so I'll spend a lifetime loving serving time." During the seventies, Cash covered "Miller's Cave," a number 9 hit for Snow in 1960. Jack Clement penned the classic that also reached number 4 for Bobby Bare four years later. This perennial story-song is a country standard and Cash's cover stands up nicely alongside Snow's and Bare's versions.

"I Will Miss You When You Go" is a hurting song written by the legendary Ernest Tubb. Johnny easily conveys the sense of pain and anguish when he sings, "I will miss you when you go, much more than you'll ever know, but I'll have a memory to keep you near." She will remain in his heart although he admits it won't be the same. There's a sense of true regret and resignation as he foreshadows how sad he will be when she leaves. Still in all, he magnanimously wishes her all the best when she departs. Cash had earlier covered Tubb's "Goodnight Irene," "I Love You Because," and "Remember Me (I'm the One Who Loves You)," recorded while at Sun.

The late fifties and early sixties saw a newfound interest in folk music. Folk songs were a way for the younger generation to voice their fears and concerns regarding what was happening in the country at the time. Cash saw this burgeoning fervor among the young, who were embracing artists like Pete Seeger and the Weavers, the Kingston Trio, Peter, Paul and Mary, Joan Baez and a young man from Hibbing, Minnesota named Robert Zimmerman, who landed in New York City and would ultimately change the course of popular music as Bob Dylan.

Cash had already saluted the Weavers when he recorded "Goodnight Irene" while at Sun, and Seeger, with his rendition of "If I Had a Hammer." As mentioned earlier, his devotion to the Kingston Trio led him to record songs he'd discovered on their albums such as "Remember the Alamo," "I Want to Go Home," and "Jackson." In 1964, on the Carter Family album *Keep on the Sunny Side,* Cash included the song "Lonesome Valley." Pop songwriters Leiber and Stoller collaborated with country songwriter Billy Edd Wheeler on "The Reverend Mr. Black / Lonesome Valley (Medley)," a moralistic story-song that was first recorded by the Kingston Trio in 1962. The Trio took it to number 8 on the pop charts. Cash covered it on *The Baron* album. The song combines the saga of the God-fearing, soft-spoken Reverend Mr. Black with a chorus of the classic folk song "Lonesome Valley," which was recorded by Woody Guthrie, among many others. Cash's honest and authoritative delivery makes this a perfect song for him. It's a mystery why it only made it to number 71 on the country chart.

Woody Guthrie and Bob Dylan

Woody Guthrie was born on July 14, 1912, in Okemah, Oklahoma. As a child, he fell in love with the western ballads and Indian songs his father taught him. In 1931 Woody left Oklahoma for Texas, where he made his first attempt at a musical career. The Great Depression made it hard for Guthrie to support his family. The 1935 dust storms forced thousands of desperate farmers and unemployed workers to leave Oklahoma, Kansas, Tennessee, and Georgia to head west in search of work and a better life. Woody was among these uprooted and disenfranchised individuals who hitchhiked their way across the country on Route 66, searching for any means to support their families. Guthrie arrived in California in 1937, and eventually was hired to perform his songs on the radio in Los Angeles. And those songs—"I Ain't Got No Home," "Pretty Boy Floyd," "Goin' Down the Road Feelin' Bad," "Talking Dust Bowl Blues," and "Hard Travelin'"—made him one of the most revered and respected artists of his time. John Steinbeck published *The Grapes of Wrath* in 1939, about the Joad family, from Oklahoma, traveling to the supposed promised land of California. Guthrie wrote his song "Tom Joad," after seeing the 1940 film of *The Grapes of Wrath* starring Henry Fonda. He spoke out for the poor, the hungry, the laborer looking for work, and all individuals who felt abandoned by their own country. Guthrie recorded the classic *Dust Bowl Ballads* album for RCA, and ultimately found his way to New York City where he made friends with artists of the day like Lead Belly, Burl Ives, and Cisco Houston. Guthrie and Seeger were part of the Almanac Singers, who promoted union organizing and fighting for human rights and peace through their songs of protest.

Guthrie's greatest song might be "This Land Is Your Land," which he wrote in response to Irving Berlin's sentimental and sweet "God Bless America." Guthrie loved his country, but believed strongly that it belonged to everyone, and that not everyone in America was treated equally. Cash recorded a brilliant rendition of "This Land Is Your Land," included on the 2008 *Johnny Cash's America* album. The Woody Guthrie classic couldn't have found a better voice than Cash's. This is a folk song for the ages, and Cash delivers it with the respect and empathy it so richly deserves. And the circle certainly remained unbroken because Guthrie had long been a fan of the Carter Family, and now Cash had recorded Guthrie's most renowned composition.

In 1975 Cash recorded five songs with the Earl Scruggs Revue. One of those tracks was Bob Dylan's "Song to Woody," where Johnny duets with Earl Scruggs along with John Dawson, Skip Battin, and David Nelson of the New Riders of the Purple Sage. Dylan wrote the song as a tribute to his greatest musical influence Woody Guthrie. The song allows Cash to salute two legends in song. Even though

Dylan appeared on the scene after Cash, his influence on Cash is enormous.

The friendship of Cash and Dylan cannot be overemphasized. These two iconic individuals found a common ground in the songs they wrote and recorded. Dylan's songs spurred Cash on. He intrinsically knew that Dylan was reshaping popular music, by infusing it with elements of folk, rock, country, and blues. He embraced Dylan's promise immediately, and anxiously awaited Dylan's albums so that he could comb through them and find songs that fit his own unique style. In fact, Cash acknowledged *The Freewheelin' Bob Dylan* as one of his favorite albums of all time. And the admiration was mutual; Dylan was as much a fan of Cash's, having recorded "Big River," "Belshazzar" and "Folsom Prison Blues" for the Basement Tapes sessions with the Band in 1967, just a few years before joining Cash in Nashville to appear on his television series and record duets together.

Cash and Dylan's friendship would grow over the years. In 1964, when Dylan was criticized for using electric guitars and moving away from politically themed acoustic music, or what he termed "finger pointin' songs," Cash wrote an editorial for the March 1964 issue of the folk-based *Broadside* magazine wholeheartedly defending Dylan's right to record whatever type of music he wanted. Cash boldly admonished Dylan's critics to "Shut Up! . . . And let him sing!" Dylan never forgot Cash's brave defense. On February 6, 2015, during Dylan's acceptance speech as the MusiCares Person of the Year, he recalled, "Johnny Cash recorded some of my songs early on, too, up in about '63, when he was all skin and bones. He traveled long, he traveled hard, but he was a hero of mine. I heard many of his songs growing up. I knew them better than I knew my own. 'Big River,' 'I Walk the Line,' 'How High's the Water, Mama?' I wrote 'It's Alright Ma (I'm Only Bleeding)' with that song reverberating inside my head. I still ask, 'How high is the water, mama?' Johnny was an intense character. And he saw that people were putting me down playing electric music, and he posted letters to magazines scolding people, telling them to shut up and let him sing. In Johnny Cash's world — hardcore Southern drama — that kind of thing didn't exist. Nobody told anybody what to sing or what not to sing. They just didn't do that kind of thing. I'm always going to thank him for that. Johnny Cash was a giant of a man, the man in black. And I'll always cherish the friendship we had until the day there is no more days."

Cash and Dylan first met at the Newport Folk Festival in Newport, Rhode Island, on July 26, 1964. Johnny played the historic festival the same year that Dylan, Joan Baez, Peter, Paul and Mary, and Judy Collins took the stage. Cash always considered himself as much a folk artist as he was country. Folk icon Pete Seeger introduced Cash as a songwriter and singer, and this became one of his most important showcases, bringing him a new, younger audience. Two highlights of Cash's set included his performance of his then-current single "The Ballad of Ira Hayes," and Dylan's "Don't Think Twice, It's All Right." Cash talked about how honored he was to be performing a Bob Dylan song as he introduced Dylan from the stage. He called Dylan "the best songwriter of the age since Pete Seeger." He even gave Dylan his guitar to show his appreciation. Five years later, in 1969, Cash would introduce Kris Kristofferson from the Newport stage, gaining Kris a wider audience and paving the way for his own future stardom. At Newport in 1964, Cash performed "Big River," "Folsom Prison Blues," "I Still Miss Someone," "Rock Island Line," "Don't Think Twice, It's All Right," "I Walk the Line," "The Ballad of Ira Hayes" and "Keep on the Sunny Side."

Dylan's influence can clearly be heard on "Understand Your Man," an ornery, chauvinistic song that proved to be one of Johnny's biggest hits of all, remaining at number 1 on the country chart for six weeks in 1964. With Johnny's marriage to Vivian falling apart, this song could be interpreted as being about the dissolution of their marriage. In the song, the singer feels misunderstood and accuses his partner of failing to appreciate what his job entails and why he has to be away so much. He's leaving her and won't even turn his head to say goodbye. He's tired of her bad-mouthing and finally decides to assert himself and just leave. There's no sign of the victim persona Cash portrayed earlier. He reaffirms, "I'll be as gone as a wild goose in winter, then you'll understand your man." He even continues to reprimand her as the song fades, taunting her to "meditate on it."

One can't help but feel Dylan's influence on the melody of this song, which clearly recalls "Don't Think Twice, It's All Right." Nearly forty years later Cash rerecorded the song for the *Unearthed* box set. The big production of the original hit single was replaced with a simple guitar-strummed background as Cash sings his self-described "kiss my butt goodbye, I'm leavin' song!"

In 1965 Cash would record his own cover of the Dylan folk standard "Don't Think Twice" for his *Orange Blossom Special* album. That album included three Dylan songs. In the song, the singer tells his girl that he'll be leaving her but not to think twice about it. It's a song about perpetual freedom and moving on. Still, he wishes it could have been different and they could have stayed together, reasoning "I'm a-thinkin' and a-wonderin', walkin' down the road, I once loved a woman, a child I'm told, I gave her my heart but she wanted my soul, don't think twice, it's all right."

Cash turns Dylan's ballad of separation "It Ain't Me, Babe," into a hit country song with June Carter on harmony vocals. The singer lists the reasons why he is wrong for his woman because she's looking for someone never to part, someone to die for her and more. The writing is extraordinary in its profound simplicity and one of Cash's most spirited vocals on the *Orange Blossom Special* album. A full-page ad in *Billboard* magazine for this song read, "A new song from Bob Dylan on a new single sung by Johnny Cash." The song made it to number 4 on the country chart in 1964, and number 58 pop, one year before the folk-rock group the Turtles took their version to number 8 on the pop chart.

"Mama, You've Been on My Mind" is the third Dylan song Cash recorded for the *Orange Blossom Special* album, and it was the first time anyone had recorded this song. The theme of the song is similar to "Don't Think Twice." The singer informs his lover that when she wakes up he won't be lying next to her, although he won't forget her and she will still be on his mind. Again, the restless sense of freedom finds the singer at the crossroads of love and life. He refuses to be tied down, but he will not forget her. Cash plays loose with the meter of the song, and the result is a freewheeling song of escape.

In February 1969, Cash recorded a historic session with Bob Dylan that was never released. In April, Dylan released his critically acclaimed *Nashville Skyline* album. He had gone to Nashville to record a country-influenced album. While Dylan was in the process of recording his album, Johnny stopped by to see him. The two friends and labelmates decided to record some duets together. During those sessions, recorded at Columbia Studios, Nashville on February 17 and 18, 1969, and referred to as the "Dylan/Cash" or "Nashville Sunset" sessions, they recorded the following songs: "One Too Many Mornings," "Don't Think Twice, It's All Right," "I Still Miss Someone," "Matchbox," "That's All Right Mama," "Mystery Train," "Big River," "I Walk the Line," "Guess Things Happen That Way," "Blue Yodel #1 and #5," "Ring of Fire," "You Are My Sunshine," "Good Old Mountain Dew," "Careless Love," "Just a Closer Walk with Thee," "Five Feet High and Rising," and "Wanted Man." The only song released from these sessions was their duet of Dylan's "Girl from the North Country," which had previously appeared as a solo performance on Dylan's classic *The Freewheelin' Bob Dylan*. The song is a lovely folk-infused ballad with echoes of "Scarborough Fair." One verse was omitted from the original Dylan recording. The song shows the warmth and camaraderie between the two music giants and, even though they stumble over a line in the lyric, the song remains among Cash's greatest duet performances. Bob Johnston produced the sessions and Cash wrote the award-winning liner notes for Dylan's *Nashville Skyline* album. On June 7, Dylan would appear on the debut episode of *The Johnny Cash Show*.

Cash and Dylan's friendship lasted nearly forty years, and both inspired each other to push the limits of their respective genres and create some of the greatest music of the twentieth century. Like Cash, Dylan loved all kinds of music, and would not be restrained by recording the same type of material repeatedly. Dylan would constantly reinvent himself, while writing and recording folk, rock, blues, and even gospel songs. Dylan has acknowledged his love for big band and pop music, most recently with the release of the 2015 *Shadows in the Night* album, with covers of songs by Frankie Laine, Perry Como, and Frank Sinatra. While covering pop standards may appear out of character for one of the greatest songwriters of his generation, it should not be surprising. Dylan shared this deep love of all musical affinities with Cash.

As previously mentioned, Cash had long loved the tender pop ballad "Memories Are Made of This," which was originally recorded by crooner Dean Martin. Martin's recording remained at number 1 on the pop chart for five weeks in 1955. Cash succeeds in making this song his own, just as he had done years before with the McGuire Sisters' "Sugartime." He recalls in the liner notes to *Unchained*, "When I only had one or two records out, I sang whatever was popular or whatever else I liked. . . . One of the songs I loved was Dean Martin's 'Memories Are Made of This.'" Cash's version has an intimacy Martin's lacked because there are no background singers chiming in and also because Cash does not croon the lyrics, he just recites them with honesty. And, in truth, every song Cash interprets has his own unique stamp on it. No one had ever sung a song like Cash before, and it's unlikely anyone will again. While his own compositions convey his lyrical passion, the songs he chose to cover by other artists reveal his love for country, pop, folk and gospel music.

Chapter 10

HIGHWAYMAN

JACK CLEMENT, WAYLON JENNINGS, WILLIE NELSON, AND OTHER COLLABORATIONS

The fruit of Johnny Cash's musical friendships,
pairings, and partnerships

At the close of 1956, when Sun Records' Sam Philips turned Cash over to his studio engineer, Jack Clement, a creative friendship was born that would last throughout Cash's entire life and career. Whenever Cash needed inspiration he would call up Clement, and the two would indulge all of their musical whims and fantasies. From "Ballad of a Teenage Queen" and "Guess Things Happen That Way," to some of Cash's most interesting recordings for Columbia and Mercury Records, Clement was by his side at the studio console recording everything they did together. Clement's Cowboy Arms Hotel

and Recording Spa in Nashville was Cash's refuge whenever he wanted to escape the trappings of celebrity and return to the comfort of friends and cohorts. Clement was born on April 5, 1931, in Memphis, Tennessee. He attended Memphis State University, and learned to play the steel guitar. In 1956 he joined Sun Records, where he worked with Cash, Roy Orbison, Carl Perkins, and ultimately discovered Jerry Lee Lewis. During his career he produced artists such as Charley Pride, Ray Stevens, and Waylon Jennings. In 1971 he co-founded J-M-I Records with Allen Reynolds, who produced the first albums by Don Williams

Highwayman 2. *Courtesy of Sony Music Entertainment.*

for the label. Artists ranging from Elvis and Tom Jones to Jim Reeves and Hank Snow have recorded Clement's songs. He even produced the 1975 cult classic horror movie *Dear Dead Delilah,* starring Agnes Moorehead.

A Sense of Humor

Aside from some early singles on Sun, Clement only released two albums in his lifetime, the critically acclaimed *All I Want to Do in Life* in 1978, and *Guess Things Happen That Way* in 2004. As mentioned, Clement was instrumental in recording Cash during the Sun years and was also responsible for production work on Cash's first Christmas album and "Ring of Fire." In May 1966, Cash released the album *Everybody Loves a Nut,* and it went a long way to showcase Cash's sense of humor. Although his songs had a penchant for being more serious or thought provoking, this album reveals Cash as a lighthearted master of songs with sly, clever twists and turns. It wasn't quite a full-fledged novelty album, although some of the songs certainly qualify as novelty tunes. The songs all have a point of view, and Cash takes advantage of using humor to entertain and educate his listeners. Even though Don Law and Frank Jones are listed as producers, Jack Clement had a lot to do with the song selection and production of the album. *Everybody Loves a Nut* made it to number 5 on the country album chart and number 88 on the pop album chart.

The album opens with Clement's "Everybody Loves a Nut," and it's clear that he is the driving force behind this collection. Clement always had an ability to creatively find new ways to express his skewed view of life in song. The album's title song depicts a series of vignettes explaining how endearing some folks who might be considered crazy can be. Throughout history we are told, quirky people have made their mark by being labeled nuts and weirdos. There's the hermit named Fred who kept a dead horse in his cave, the Colombian man named Frank who kept a tiger in his tank, and Christopher Columbus who believed the world wasn't flat. Cash slyly makes his point, and this seemingly nonsensical song seems less nonsensical after all. The song made it to number 17 on the country chart and number 96 pop.

Clement also wrote "The One on the Right Is on the Left," and if ever there was a method to Cash and Clement's madness, this song proves it. In the guise of a harmless folk song we are presented with a pointed political satire about entertainers who express their political beliefs through their music. The self-righteous folk group in the song is perceived as a talented band until they infuse politics into their lyrics, which ultimately leads to their downfall. While they appeared to be a well-tuned singing group, they are at complete odds politically behind the scenes until they have a brawl during a performance. The lyric is witty and quite funny. This was a great change-of-pace single for

Cash that became a big hit, reaching number 2 on the country chart and number 46 pop.

Clement teamed with a young Allen Reynolds to write "Take Me Home." Reynolds would go on to become a first-rate songwriter, publisher, and producer for artists such as Waylon Jennings, Crystal Gayle, and Garth Brooks. Reynolds remembers writing this song with Jack fairly early in his career, while he was writing and singing songs in Texas.[1] "Take Me Home" is a humorous travelogue of the many places the singer has been across the country, exclaiming, "I've seen New York City and Washington, seen Montreal and Saskatchewan, and Rhode Island." But now the singer just wants to go back home. Ultimately, it's a highly unusual catalog of all the many things the singer misses while being away from home.

Another notable song on *Everybody Loves a Nut* is "A Cup of Coffee," a quirky talking dialogue that was written by Ramblin' Jack Elliott, another musical influence on Cash. According to Michael Streissguth in his book, *Johnny Cash: The Biography*, while Elliott and Cash were driving together, Elliott sang Cash a verse of this song. Cash liked it and thought it was funny, so Elliott finished writing it during their drive. Then when Cash decided to record it, he called Elliott up and told him to come to Nashville and sing it with him. In the song, Cash drops by to visit Ramblin' Jack and is served a cup of coffee which has been spiked with whiskey. Ramblin' Jack yodels along as Cash proceeds to get drunker and drunker on the whiskey he's being served. Cash begins slurring and babbling until he ultimately winds up having to stay over at Ramblin' Jack's. It's quite amusing and all in good fun.

"Boa Constrictor" is another song written by Shel Silverstein. It has a similarly frantic feel to Cash's earlier recording of Silverstein's "25 Minutes to Go." In this song, the singer is being swallowed by a boa constrictor and counting down the body parts the snake is consuming along the way. It was also famously covered by the folk trio Peter, Paul and Mary. Cash's version was released as the third single from this album and made it to number 39 on the country chart. The snake's burp at the end is priceless.

Clement wrote 1978's "Gone Girl" and he had always wanted Cash to perform it. It features an offbeat lyric describing in quirky detail the woman who has left him and become a "gone girl." It's pure Clement with whimsical words and an accordion melody. Cash gives it all he's got and even hums his way through the final verse. It deserved a better fate than it received. Clement had recorded the song himself earlier that year for his album, *All I Want to Do in Life.* "Gone Girl" was a number 23 charting country single for Tompall & The Glaser Brothers in 1970. Cash's cover made it to only number 44.

"I Will Rock and Roll with You" is a nostalgic rockabilly nod to Cash and Clement's early days at Sun Records. The song explains how it all began for Cash and recognizes many of the performers he worked with at the time and how he's still willing to rock and roll for the one he loves. At the end of the song, during the fade-out, he ad-libs "somebody call Sam . . . let me speak to Jack Clement." And although the song is less rock and roll than country, it's nice to hear Cash fondly acknowledging his rockabilly roots. "I Will Rock and Roll with You" proved to be a minor hit from this album, making it to number 21 on the country chart. Cash puts his heart and soul into this up-tempo rockabilly charmer.

Right away one can sense that Jack Clement had a hand in selecting the song "No Expectations" for Cash. There's no reason this song should work for Cash, but it does, and very well indeed. Cash succeeds in making this Rolling Stones song his own, and that's not an easy feat. Cash is not intimidated by the rollicking arrangement as he takes control of this Jagger and Richards classic. And Clement brought Cash "It'll Be Her," a very good song by Billy Ray Reynolds that had previously been recorded by Waylon Jennings. The song features top-notch musicians and a convincing vocal by Cash, and the results should have been spectacular. Instead, the arrangement is plodding and busy, and the song suffers from being too dirge-like. "It'll Be Her" also holds the dubious distinction of being Cash's lowest-charting single of all, only making it to number 89 on the country chart.

The Return of Jack Clement

In 1982, with Columbia Records caring less and less about what he was doing, Cash decided to reteam with Clement for *The Adventures of Johnny Cash,* an album of music the way he wanted to do it. Clement had been an integral part of much of Johnny's recordings over the years, and whenever Cash was feeling frustrated with the reception his records were receiving and record label politics, he always retrenched and returned to Jack.[2] The result was a strong album of new material along with well-chosen cover songs. It received critical acclaim and was named *Country Music Magazine*'s album of the year. But unfortunately, Columbia did not expend much money on promoting this project and the singles that were released fared poorly. Once again, a Johnny Cash album failed to make the country or pop chart.

The Adventures of Johnny Cash opens with a rousing cover of Billy Joe Shaver's "Georgia on a Fast Train." The arrangement is loose and raw. Gone are the over-produced flourishes of past albums, replaced here with a less-polished sound. From the cathartic opening yodel, it's as if Cash has been set free to do the songs he wants to do and not what outside producers and record executives tell him he should do. It's as good a rendition of this song as any, but surprisingly it only debuted on the country chart at number 55.

Songwriter extraordinaires Bob McDill and Allen Reynolds teamed up to cowrite "We Must Believe in Magic," a beautiful ballad that Jack Clement always loved. McDill, who had just recently enjoyed a number 2 country hit with Don Williams's "Good Ole Boys Like Me," and Allen Reynolds, whose songs "Take Me Home" and "My Ship Will Sail" Cash had already recorded, collaborated on this whimsical piece of sound advice to hold on to our ability to always believe in magic and the guiding hand. The metaphorical ship bound for Alpha Centauri is filled with a crew of "dreamers and poets and clowns." And that's essentially how Cash and Clement viewed themselves. They were the dreamers who believed in the music and, ultimately, had the universe at their command. Reynolds recalls that the song was about Jack and the label they started together, J-M-I Records. When he and McDill first wrote it they called it "The Company Song." And the magic appears to have worked because J-M-I achieved success when they released the first two Don Williams albums. It's a noteworthy song and one that was recorded by many artists, including Crystal Gayle. Clement himself released a single of the song, which was included on his album *All I Want to Do in Life.* Cash's single made it to only number 84 on the country chart, two notches higher than Clement's original version.

The Mercury Years

Johnny Cash Is Coming to Town was released on April 13, 1987. It marked Cash's first album for Mercury Records after a contentious release from Columbia, and it reteamed him with Clement. Cash's contract with Columbia had expired shortly after the release of *Rainbow,* his last album for the label. There was still hope of negotiating a new contract, but Cash felt that Columbia was not promoting his albums properly and had lost faith in him as a record seller. He also wanted a bigger up-front payment in keeping with what the newer, younger artists were receiving. By summer, Rick Blackburn, a marketing man, and then head of Columbia's Nashville division since 1985, had decided to drop Cash from the label. The story took on a life of its own, as irate fans and Music City insiders were genuinely angered that Johnny Cash had been fired from Columbia Records, the label his albums and singles helped sustain through tough times during the sixties.

During the early to mid-eighties Mercury Records had been home to artists such as Kathy Mattea, Tom T. Hall, and the Statler Brothers. In 1986, Dick Asher, President and CEO of Mercury/Polygram hired Steve Popovich, a true visionary and music lover, as Senior Vice President of Mercury/

Polygram Nashville. Popovich had an impressive resume, having been appointed the first Vice President for Promotion at Columbia Records by Clive Davis in 1972. Then in 1977 he founded Cleveland International Records where he discovered Meat Loaf and released his multi-platinum selling album *Bat Out of Hell*. Popovich truly loved country music and had known and revered Cash during his tenure at Columbia. When he learned that Columbia was about to drop Cash, he made it one of his first tasks at Mercury to sign Johnny Cash to the label. He convinced Cash that he genuinely believed in him. On August 21, 1986, Cash signed on to Mercury Records, where he would record and release five highly undervalued albums between 1986 and 1993.

Steve Popovich wanted Cash to create the album that he wanted, and not what some label executive dictated to him. Cash writes in his autobiography, "I found a deal I liked at Mercury/Polygram with Steve Popovich, a good man, and with his blessing I teamed up with Jack Clement again. So I was very happy for a little while. We all were" (Cash, *Autobiography*, 342). Steve Popovich was a brilliant but very humble man who knew he had helped initiate something special. While much credit has been given to Cash's major career comeback in 1994, it should be noted that *Johnny Cash Is Coming to Town* is a first-rate album that deserved to have found a wider audience. Esteemed country music

journalist John Lomax III wrote the liner notes for this album. Despite the publicity surrounding the album's release, of its four singles, two charted poorly ("The Night Hank Williams Came to Town and "W. Lee O' Daniel (and the Light Crust Dough Boys)"), and two—"Sixteen Tons" and "Let Him Roll"—never even made the singles chart. The album only made it to number 36 on the country album chart. Still, it was Cash's best solo ranking in over five years.[3]

We can feel Cash's newfound enthusiasm as he opens the album with "The Big Light," an energized rendition of an Elvis Costello composition. Cash had met Costello in 1979 through Costello's producer Nick Lowe, who was married at the time to June's daughter Carlene. "Oddly, 'The Big Light' came to Cash not through Costello nor even Lowe. Rather, a Michigan radioman that was emceeing a Cash show in Grand Rapids pointed the singer to Costello's new album *King of America* and its befitting 'The Big Light.' Indeed, the song melded completely with Cash's booming baritone and the big, roaring sound Clement built around it" (Streissguth, *Johnny Cash: The Autobiography*, 229). Cash seems to be animated and enjoying himself on this song about waking up with a major hangover after carousing the night before.

It certainly took Cash awhile to get around to recording the country classic "Sixteen Tons" written by his friend Merle Travis. Of course, Cash had covered many of Travis's songs over the years, but this was Travis's biggest song. It was a number 1 country and pop hit for Tennessee Ernie Ford in 1955. Cash turns in an impressive performance of this coal-mining saga about the misery and hardship of spending your life working in a coal mine.

Songwriter Allen Reynolds calls "My Ship Will Sail" a gift.[4] It's another standout ballad that Cash always believed in. This is the third version of a song Cash first recorded with the Earl Scruggs Revue, and a few years later with the Carter Family. Reynolds had written what some consider to be one of Waylon Jennings's greatest songs, "Dreaming My Dreams With You." "My Ship Will Sail" is an inspirational gem that features the Carter sisters and assorted guest vocalists on the chorus, and a rich, textured vocal from Cash on this perfect finale to Cash's first album for Mercury Records.

In 1988, after his debut album for Mercury and *Classic Cash,* a collection of new recordings of earlier greatest hits, Cash chose to do an album of duets with musical friends and family. Once again produced by Clement, *Water from the Wells of Home* brought together a prestigious group of performers to join Johnny on ten new tracks, including a rerecording of one of his classic hits with his daughter, Rosanne, and the Everly Brothers. The result was a good album that failed to catch fire. It made it to only number 48 on the country album chart, despite its all-star cast. Two singles were released from the album and only one made it into the country Top 25.

Highlights include a new version of Clement's "Ballad of a Teenage Queen." It's a more subdued rendition than the original. Cash takes the first verse setting up the story of the teenage queen and the boy she loved who worked at the candy store. Rosanne and the Everlys join him on the chorus, before Rosanne takes the lead on the revised second verse. Johnny shares the third verse with Rosanne, and the Everly Brothers take the lead on the fourth verse. And Johnny gets to finish the story in the final verse with the happy ending of the teenage queen returning home to the boy next door. It's a welcome new cover of a classic that Cash seldom performed. Rosanne recalls, "the Everlys weren't there — they had already recorded their part. Dad and I went to Jack Clement's Cowboy Arms studio to do it. It was fun" (Rosanne Cash interview). This was the second single released from the album after "That Old Wheel," and it made it to only number 45 on the country chart.

Cash teamed up with the angelic Emmylou Harris and country pioneer Roy Acuff on Acuff's classic ballad "As Long as I Live." Acuff charted his first pop hits in 1938 with "The Great Speckled Bird" and "Wabash Cannonball," his signature song. It was also the year he joined the Grand Ole Opry and became a fixture there. In 1942 he formed Acuff-Rose Music with Fred Rose, and it quickly became the most important publishing company in country music. "As Long as I Live" is a tender song of eternal devotion that benefits from Cash and Harris's beautifully blended vocals. Waylon Jennings and Jessi Colter join them on the chorus.

Cash had previously recorded the song "Jordan," a lovely gospel duet with Emmylou Harris that appeared on her critically acclaimed 1980 bluegrass-infused album *Roses in the Snow*. Brian Ahern, who was married to Harris at the time, produced this track. It's a tender though urgent plea for us to take Jesus as our savior as we prepare to cross over the Jordan River. Cash and Emmylou's voices blend beautifully, and Ricky Skaggs adds some soaring high harmonies. All in all, this is a magnificent collaboration. Interestingly, in his autobiography Cash listed *Roses in the Snow* among the albums he would need if he were stranded on a desert island.

An All-Star Album

For *Water from the Wells of Home* Tom T. Hall wrote "The Last of the Drifters," a song that very nicely fits him and Cash. These two old friends are in many respects the last of a certain breed of entertainers. The song lists many milestones from their lives that have passed them by and disappeared. Hall's lyrics are always sharp and filled with vivid imagery. He ties together diverse observations such as being a "World War baby holding mama's hand . . . Chuck Berry's music and poverty and wealth." There's a reason Tom T. Hall is regarded as one of country music's greatest songwriters, and this song is a prime example.

The late Tulsa Oklahoma swamp-rock singer-songwriter J. J. Cale, composer of Eric Clapton's hits "After Midnight" and "Cocaine," wrote "Call Me the Breeze," a bluesy tune that Cash and John Carter Cash duet on together. Cash lets John Carter take the lead on this up-tempo rocker. It's the least country track on this album. Southern rockers Lynyrd Skynyrd and country star Bobby Bare had previously covered this song.

Cash and Hank Williams Jr., a country legend in his own right, join forces on songwriter Jennifer Pierce's "That Old Wheel," a philosophical duet that finds the two old friends just rolling along through life like "that old wheel." Their voices blend together perfectly, and there's good reason this song became a minor hit single, making it to number 21 on the country chart. The song is filled with sage advice about standing strong and overcoming life's obstacles. And to those who injure us, know that "they will sow as they reap . . . and that old wheel will roll around again."

Cash wrote "A Croft in Clachan (The Ballad of Rob MacDunn)," performed here as a duet with Glen Campbell. Campbell's songs topped the country and pop charts during the sixties and seventies, and his television variety series, *The Glen Campbell Goodtime Hour*, ran from 1969 to 1972, roughly the same period that Cash's series aired. Both had guest-starred on each other's show, and they remained friends through the years. Cash sings the first verse about the warring Campbells and MacDonalds who unite to fight for Scottish independence. There's a picturesque sense of time and place as the battle rages in Glasgow and Edinburgh, and the clans join together to evict the English from their land. The scene shifts to the tiny town in Clachan and a mother who sews a coat for Rob MacDunn, her sixteen-year-old son, as he prepares to leave for battle. Campbell takes the second verse describing the boy's joining the fight as he marches into battle with bagpipes playing in the background. The song has a happy ending, as Rob MacDunn returns home to his mother and girlfriend.

The song "New Moon over Jamaica" came about when Cash invited Paul McCartney, who was a neighbor of his in Jamaica, and Tom T. Hall to have dinner with him and June at their home at Cinnamon Hill. The three men wrote this song during that visit, and then Cash went to England to record it with the former Beatle at his studio in West Sussex. McCartney produced the session; later, he added harmonies by June Carter, Linda McCartney, and Tom T. Hall. Cash recalled, "We were at my house right after New Year having one of our all-night singin's and guitar pulls on the front porch. We'd been singing for about six hours and the moon started setting and Tom T. Hall had this idea for a song called 'New Moon over Jamaica.' We wrote the song together" (Turner,

184). McCartney and Hall started writing the song together and Cash came in and joined them for the chorus and he wrote the third verse. It's a lovely, lilting ballad about watching a new moon rise as it reminds the singer that he is still living with an old memory. Cash sings the first part of the song with McCartney on harmony, before McCartney takes the last verse. As with Cash's earlier pairings with artists like Ray Charles, it's nice to hear him collaborating with a music icon from a different genre of music.

"Water from the Wells of Home," is a duet Cash wrote and performed with John Carter. Both sing soothingly about wishing they could drink again the waters from the wells of home. About this song, Cash writes, "The spiritual well is so deep and unfathomable, but some beautiful water flows out of it. That's partly what John Carter and I had in mind when we wrote 'Water from the Wells of Home.' The song wasn't just literal (though it was that too)" (Cash, *Autobiography,* 305). The song benefits from an unusually sparse arrangement courtesy of Jack Clement and makes a nice finish to another worthwhile Cash collection.

Mercury Descending

In March 1991 Mercury released *The Mystery of Life.* This was Cash's last original album for the label. The enthusiasm that Mercury had originally expressed upon signing Cash in 1987 had dissipated by 1991. The label had gone through a regime change, and there was little interest in promoting a new Cash project. Cash insisted on working once again with Jack Clement, and the result was an album of music he was proud of. However, he equated it to singing in an empty hall and recalled, "There was no publicity. They only pressed five hundred copies of my last Mercury album *The Meaning of Life* [sic]" (Cash, *Autobiography*, 342). That may not have been an accurate number, but there was no doubt that Mercury had lost interest in Cash. The album included some very good songs, but because of lack of promotion it only reached number 70 on the country album chart. On March 11, 1991, Cash's mother died at the age of eighty-six. Cash dearly loved his mother, and her death affected him greatly. *The Mystery of Life* was released that same month. Cash's career and personal life were at an all-time low at this point.

Highlights of the album include a new cover of "The Greatest Cowboy of Them All" that benefits from Clement's fuller arrangement, featuring Anita Carter's pristine background vocal. It was a good song when he first recorded it on *A Believer Sings the Truth*, and it holds up very nicely. As noted earlier, Jesus is the greatest cowboy, and the western analogy makes this one of Cash's most clever lyrics.

Radio personality and songwriter Joe Nixon, who also composed Kenny Rogers's "Mother Country Music," wrote the title song. "The Mystery of Life" is another truck driving song with a chorus that

begins, "When I was young I had a Gene Autry gun but I never had a Lionel train." Interestingly, Cash had been a spokesperson for Lionel Trains years before. The song is a well-written trucker's waltz, using vivid imagery to tell the story of the well-read truck driver who ponders the meaning of life.

Cash revisits one of his earliest Sun recordings with an updated version of "Hey Porter." Jack Clement's energized production gives this cover a fresh, new feel that works well. And Cash wrote the humorous "Beans for Breakfast" for Clement, about a guy who's a mess since his woman took off. Cash recalled, "I wrote that song as a joke, just for fun. I wrote it for Jack Clement when we were in the middle of a session. I wrote it and took it in saying, 'I've got a great new song, I'll sing it for you.' I thought it was the worst song I ever wrote and I still may have. June thought it was the worst thing I'd ever written but of course Jack wanted to record it" (Miller, 241). And it is a quirky, off-center song to say the least. Cash's dramatic and exaggerated performance of the silly lyric ("Beans for breakfast once again . . . I'm a hungry, nasty lonesome man") actually makes the song somewhat interesting.

Cash collaborates again with good friend Tom T. Hall on "I'll Go Somewhere and Sing My Songs Again," a new ballad by Hall that has the singers talking about going back to a simpler time. They fish together, discuss philosophy, and quietly ponder their livelihoods. As mentioned, Cash had previously recorded "A Letter from Home," on

Ballads of the True West, which was cowritten by Mother Maybelle Carter and Hall's journalist wife Dixie Dean. Cash also recorded "Troublesome Waters," also written by Mother Maybelle, her husband, Ezra "Pop" Carter, and Dean.

Cash closes out *The Mystery of Life* with "Angel and the Badman," another song he wrote that borrows a western motif, and the title of a 1947 John Wayne movie. It's about an outlaw who rides into town and meets a girl unlike any he's ever known. She doesn't care about what he's done and he tries to settle down with her, but his old habits eventually take control of him, and he returns to his wild ways. But he sees her angel face before him, and he ultimately rides away a better man than when he first rode in.

Two Old Desperados

Waylon Arnold Jennings and Johnny Cash shared a deep friendship that lasted from the mid-sixties to the end of their lives. They were both immensely talented and creative musical renegades who knew what they wanted to do. Jennings was born on June 15, 1937, in Littlefield, Texas. Like Cash, he spent time working in the cotton fields of Littlefield before moving on to Lubbock, Texas, in 1954. And, also like Cash, he fell in love with music and learned to play the guitar and write songs early on. While working at a radio station in Lubbock, Jennings befriended a skinny young man with thick-rimmed glasses named Buddy Holly.

Holly believed that Jennings had talent and produced his first single, the Cajun "Jole Blon." In 1958 Jennings became the bass player in Holly's band, the Crickets. Just when things seemed to be moving along nicely for Jennings, tragedy struck. After a show in Iowa, Holly booked a plane to take himself, Jennings, and band member guitarist Tommy Allsup to Minnesota in order to avoid a long bus ride. However, Jennings kindly gave up his seat to an ailing J. P. Richardson, known as the Big Bopper, who was fighting the flu. Allsup lost his seat to a coin toss with Ritchie Valens. On February 3, 1959, Holly, Richardson, and Valens died when their plane crashed, immortalized by Don McLean in "American Pie" as "the day the music died."

Waylon Jennings moved to Phoenix, Arizona, formed his band, the Waylors, and began performing in clubs in the area. In 1963 he signed with A&M Records, and released a number of unsuccessful singles. In 1964, country star Bobby Bare heard Jennings on the radio, and went to see him perform in Phoenix. He liked what he heard, and called Chet Atkins to sign Jennings to RCA Records. During this time, Jennings had befriended another up-and-coming singer-songwriter named Willie Nelson. When Jennings asked Nelson his advice, Nelson told him to stay in Phoenix. Fortunately, Jennings didn't listen and moved to Nashville and signed with RCA. In 1965 Jennings made the country Top 20 with his single "Stop the World (and Let Me Off)." In 1966 he reached the Top 20 again with the heartbreaking ballad "Anita, You're Dreaming," quite possibly addressed to Anita Carter, with whom he would record the hit duet "I Got You" in 1968.

When Jennings moved to Nashville, he and Cash shared an apartment together for a year and a half. They were both managed by the same booking agency, and frequently performed dates together. Jennings was separated from his second wife, Cash's career was at a low point, and both were taking pills and acting recklessly. Jennings recorded some of Cash's songs during this time including "You Beat All I Ever Saw," and "I Tremble for You." Cash returned the favor by recording some of Jennings's compositions, such as "The Singing Star's Queen" on the *Everybody Loves a Nut* album. Jennings cowrote the song using the pseudonym Jackson King. Waylon's name is referenced throughout the song and, in fact, Waylon recorded his own version of the song under the title "John's Back in Town," using Johnny as the country star in the narrative. The singing star's queen of the title is Waylon's woman, who comes on to the singer while Waylon is away performing. They're together while Waylon is away, as the singer implores listeners to keep buying Waylon's records and going to his shows so that he can keep on smoking his cigars, driving his limousines, and staying with his queen. The song is a good-natured bit of fun between friends, with a slight commentary on what really transpires in the music industry.

Like Cash, Jennings had a vision for his music and refused to be restricted by what Nashville producers wanted him to record. In 1972 he released the album *Ladies Love Outlaws*, creating a persona that would ultimately bring him superstardom. In 1973 he released the album *Honky Tonk Heroes,* wherein he asserted his control as producer. Waylon was one of the first artists in Nashville to gain control of his own musical output. In 1976 the album *Wanted! The Outlaws*, featuring Jennings, his wife Jessi Colter, Willie Nelson, and Tompall Glaser became the first country album to be certified platinum by the RIAA. And the hits kept coming. Waylon charted ten number 1 hits during the seventies, including the classic ballad "Amanda," which was written by legendary songwriter Bob McDill.

In 1979 Cash and Jennings reached number 2 on the country chart with their duet of McDill's "I Wish I Was Crazy Again." It's a sincere slice-of-life saga about two "old desperados" who meet by chance and start reminiscing about the good times they shared together. And while one friend wishes to stay in the tavern and keep remembering, the other informs him that he can't because his wife is home waiting for him, but admits that sometimes at night when he hears the wind blow, he wishes he was crazy again. This is the perfect duet for the two former roommates who always loved each other. In his autobiography Jennings recalls, "I sent that song of Bob McDill's to John Cash once when he had gone straight and I was still messed up. We wound up recording it as a duet, which seems fitting" (W. Jennings, 372). Cash and Jennings produced the track, and the sound is grittier and more energized than the other songs on Cash's *I Would Like to See You Again* album.

Cash enjoyed his biggest hit since "One Piece at a Time" in 1976 with "There Ain't No Good Chain Gang" in 1978, another duet with Waylon. Also produced by Cash and Jennings, the song benefits from a less polished production and a more freewheeling arrangement. The two old friends volley back and forth on this story of having to write home while working on a chain gang. It's truly a unique take on prison life and an extremely well-written song. It was cowritten by Hal Bynum ("Papa Was a Good Man") and Dave Kirby ("What Have You Got Planned Tonight, Diana"), and it brought Cash one of his biggest hits of the seventies, reaching number 2 on the country chart.

Willie Hugh Nelson was born on April 29, 1933, in Abbott, Texas. He was just one year younger than Cash. Like Cash, Nelson was a child of the Great Depression. He was raised by his grandparents and wrote his first song at the age of seven. Also like Cash, music was his escape from the struggles of life in a small town. Just like Cash, he joined the Air Force in 1950; he was discharged shortly after and enrolled in Baylor University, but left to pursue a career in music. Nelson played in honky tonks throughout Texas, and in 1956 he

wrote and sold the song "Family Bible." That same year, he also recorded Leon Payne's "Lumberjack," four years before Cash released his version. In 1960 Willie moved to Nashville and became a successful songwriter while striving to be recognized as an artist. He wrote classic hits like "Crazy" for Patsy Cline, "Night Life" for Ray Price, and "Funny How Time Slips Away" for Faron Young. It wasn't until he took control of his own music, as Waylon had before him, and recorded the sparsely arranged *Red Headed Stranger* album that fame finally found him. Columbia Records initially did not want to release the stirring cowboy saga because it was one long story with songs interspersed and very minimal production. Willie's instincts proved right, and the album earned critical acclaim and sold a million copies.

One year later, Waylon included Willie on *Wanted! The Outlaws*, and his star began to rise. By the mid-eighties, Willie Nelson had become a bona fide superstar, enjoying a string of country hits that had begun in 1975 with "Blue Eyes Crying in the Rain" (from the *Red Headed Stranger*), and including "Good Hearted Woman," "Mammas Don't Let Your Babies Grow Up to Be Cowboys," and "Just to Satisfy You," his number 1 duets with Waylon. Willie had even crossed over to the pop chart with the Top 20 hit "On the Road Again," and his Top 5 pop hits "Always on My Mind," and "To All the Girls I've Loved Before," a duet with Julio Iglesias. Also by this time Willie had recorded

The Johnny Cash Show with Waylon Jennings. *Courtesy of Sony Music Entertainment.*

duets with almost everyone in Nashville, including old friends and colleagues like Roger Miller, Faron Young, Webb Pierce, Leon Russell, and Ray Price. One person Willie had not recorded with yet was Johnny Cash. By 1985 Willie's star was shining brightly, while Cash's record sales had slipped, his albums were no longer charting, and his record label had all but given up on him.

Highwaymen

The *Highwayman* album was originally planned to be a duet album for Cash and Nelson, but it

Performing in concert with Waylon Jennings. *Courtesy of Sony Music Entertainment*

ultimately became a collaboration between four music icons. With the addition of Waylon Jennings and Kris Kristofferson, a country supergroup was created. It all started when Johnny invited Willie, Waylon, and Kris to join him in Montreux, Switzerland, in November 1984 to film a Christmas special. Joining the group was producer Chips Moman, who was handling the sound recording for the special. Moman produced Elvis's critically acclaimed Memphis recording sessions in 1968 and

had recently been working with Willie on his solo projects. The original idea was for the two of them to get together and record a duet album. Willie had recorded duet albums with almost everyone in Nashville, and this would have been a good time for the gold- and platinum-selling Nelson to help bolster Cash's weak record sales. Moman, for his part, had already produced some of Waylon Jennings's most highly regarded albums such as *Ol' Waylon*, which included the Waylon and Willie hit "Luckenbach, Texas." Cash and Moman didn't really know each other at the time, but Moman had approached Nashville Columbia Records head Rick Blackburn to produce the Cash–Nelson duet album. Back in Nashville, the duet sessions were proving to be less than dynamic, when Moman recalled the chemistry between the four music legends that he had witnessed in Montreux. The end result was a number 1, platinum country album that also made it to number 92 on the pop album chart. *Highwayman* spawned two singles, with the title song making it all the way to number 1 and winning the Grammy Award for Best Country Song. Cash and Willie are featured on every song on the album, while Waylon joins them on six tracks and Kris on five.

"Highwayman" is a picturesque Jimmy Webb composition that proved to be the perfect song for these four music legends to record together. Webb is regarded as one of the greatest songwriters in popular music having written standards like "MacArthur Park," and a string of Glen Campbell hits, including, "By the Time I Get to Phoenix," "Wichita Lineman," and "Galveston." In fact, Campbell had originally recorded "Highwayman" in 1979 as the title song of an album. Campbell wanted to release the song as a single, but Capital Records refused his request. Enter Marty Stuart, who was introduced to the song by Carl Jackson, Campbell's banjo player, as a good song for Cash to record. Stuart listened to the song and agreed,

encouraging Cash to take the first verse. Instead, Willie opens the song and Cash closes, with Kris and Waylon taking the second and third verses respectively. The song is a spiritual tale of eternal life through reincarnation. Willie is the highwayman who robbed coaches and killed soldiers only to be hung in the spring of '25, yet claiming that he is still alive. Kris is the sailor who dies at sea, but insists that he is living still. Waylon is the dam builder who falls into the wet concrete and perishes, but tells us he'll always be around. Johnny is the future starship rider, who could be the spiritual rebirth of any of the others and who says, "perhaps I may become a highwayman again."

In 1986, Columbia released *Heroes,* a duet collaboration between Cash and Waylon Jennings. In his autobiography, Jennings said "Looking at John was like catching a reflection of myself; driven, restless, searching for acceptance. We liked to get wild, but we were funny, and we didn't get mean. We used to egg each other on. It's a worn-out word, but we were soul-mates, and our lives would continue to run parallel through all the changes the years would bring" (W. Jennings, 111). They had recorded two duets together up to this time and the *Highwayman* album. In May 1985, Johnny's guitar player Bob Wootton had to miss some shows and Johnny asked Waylon who he might recommend for a temporary fill-in. Waylon graciously offered to play himself, and the two old friends finally had the opportunity to spend some quality time together. That's when the idea for a duet album came up. It had been a long time coming, but the final product was an above-average album filled with very good songs, including one Cash cowrite and a reworking of the Dylan ballad "One Too Many Mornings," which Cash had recorded previously. The album was produced by Chips Moman and made it to number 13 on the country chart. *Heroes* was Cash and Jennings's only duet album, and it was Johnny's last album for Columbia Records, excluding *Highwayman 2*, greatest hits compilations, and reissue product.

Cash and Jennings both had a fascination with cowboys and cowboy movies. They even dressed up as cowboys for the *Heroes* album cover. "Heroes," a Chips Moman cowrite, finds them paying tribute to their childhood cowboy heroes. Interestingly, Waylon recorded a different song with the same title about the same thing on his 1982 duet album *WWII* with Willie Nelson. Even more interestingly, that song was also written by Chips Moman and Bobby Emmons.

On *Water from the Wells of Home,* Johnny and Waylon duet on "Sweeter Than the Flowers," a country heartbreaker that was originally the B-side of Roy Acuff's 1948 cover of "Tennessee Waltz." It was cowritten by Ervin T. Rouse, who had also written "Orange Blossom Special." The song is about the passing of the narrators' mother, the rose of his heart. It's a pure country tearjerker

as the family gathers together after their mother has passed away. The song is similar in theme and sentiment to Cash's earlier ballad "Don't Step on Mother's Roses." Emmylou Harris and Jessi Colter add ethereal harmonies that make this one of the most impressive songs on this album.

In December 1988, Cash was admitted to Baptist Hospital in Nashville where he underwent double bypass open-heart surgery. Ironically, Cash's old friend Waylon was in the same hospital with him, having himself just undergone triple bypass surgery. Both performers recovered and, one year later, reteamed with Willie and Kris. Despite his recent health crisis, Johnny's vocals sound as strong as ever. *Highwayman 2* was released in February 1990, once again produced by Chips Moman. Unfortunately, it failed to produce a sizeable hit single, but did manage to make it to number 4 on the country album chart and to number 79 pop.

Highlights include the Kristofferson songs "Anthem 84" and "Living Legend," Cash's "Songs That Make a Difference," and "Silver Stallion." Singer-songwriter Lee Clayton, who had written Waylon Jennings's 1972 album cut "Ladies Love Outlaws," wrote "Silver Stallion." The album *Ladies Love Outlaws* made it to number 11 on the country chart and helped kick-start the "Outlaw" movement in country music. "Silver Stallion" is an enigmatic ballad about stealing a silver stallion, finding a woman, and riding off together. The surreal lyric has sexual overtones, and the song has an ethereal, moody feel to it. It's a very good song, though it lacks the energy and impact of a song like "Highwayman." "Silver Stallion" made it to number 25 on the country chart.

The Highway Never Ends

Riding on the wave of his career resurgence and critically acclaimed *American Recordings* album, Cash reunited with his fellow Highwaymen one last time in 1995 to tour behind their new album *The Road Goes on Forever*. The album was originally released on Liberty Records and then reissued in 2005 with bonus tracks on EMI-Capitol. It was produced by Don Was, who originally was a member of the pop group Was (Not Was), and had produced albums for a who's who of pop, rock, and country artists such as Bob Dylan, Carly Simon, The B-52s, Bonnie Raitt, Elton John, as well as Waylon Jennings, Willie Nelson, and Kris Kristofferson. Was brought a grittier sound and sparser arrangements to the group, and the resulting album has a looser, less polished feel to it. But despite the critical accolades and the tour to promote it, the album only made it to number 42 on the country album chart.

For this album each of the four members of the group contributed song suggestions, and "The Devil's Right Hand" and "Live Forever" were songs Cash had brought to the table for one of his ses-sions with Rick Rubin in 1993. "The Devil's Right Hand" is a gutsy saga about a gun, called the devil's right hand, written by country-Americana singer-songwriter Steve Earle. Earle is undoubtedly one of the most important artists to have emerged from Nashville during the 1980s. Earle enjoyed early success with his brilliant album *Guitar Town*, before moving in a more rock-oriented direction with another magnificent album *Copperhead Road*. Earle has since released a string of critically acclaimed albums, authored several books, and appeared in movies and on television series. "The Devil's Right Hand" was one of Earle's early record-ings for Epic Records. Cash takes the first verse of the song describing how he saw his first pistol in the general store when he was just thirteen, think-ing it's the finest thing he'd ever seen. Nelson sings the second verse where the boy asks if he can have one when he grows up only to have his mother drop a dozen eggs in shock at his request. His angered mother informs him that the pistol is the devil's right hand. Kristofferson comes in for the third verse after the boy has grown up and gotten his first gun, where the youth learns that the pistol can get you into trouble but it can't get you out. Then Jennings explains in the fourth verse that the young man now has a Colt .45. Next we learn that the man has gotten into a card game fight and shot a man down, before being taken and tried, pro-fessing his innocence by claiming that "nothing touched the trigger but the devil's right hand." It's a riveting song that benefits from a first-rate performance by all four Highwaymen.

Billy Joe Shaver cowrote "Live Forever," an inspirational ballad, with his late son Eddy Shaver. Nelson opens with the first verse followed by Kristofferson explaining how the spiritual plan is to live forever through the works and good deeds we do. There's a "Highwayman" theme that permeates the song, but rather on a more spiritual plain. It is in the afterlife where the soul will live eternally after we cross that river. It's a well-written plea to fathers and mothers to raise their children right so that they will find eternal life.

Kristofferson's friend and longtime band member Stephen Bruton cowrote "It Is What It Is," which was selected as the first single and video from this album. This is a rocking song about the contradictory nature of the singers' personas. And they make no apologies for their bad behavior, asserting, "I am what I am 'cause I ain't what I used to be." It's all about the artists listing their darker predilections but in a musically infectious way. The camaraderie these four superstars share is most prevalent on this freewheeling track. Bruton also wrote "Waiting for a Long Time," an up-tempo tune about the narrator waiting a long time for true love. The chorus is catchy and the energized arrangement gives the group the chance to interact together as they rapidly exchange lines and verses.

Cash takes a solo turn on "Death and Hell," a striking story-song he wrote with his son John Carter. From the first line we are hooked, and curious to learn more about the woman the singer is describing in vivid detail. The lovely, wealthy woman entrances the singer and when he makes his desires known she offers him some wisdom of her own. The hook is that "death and hell are never full and neither are the eyes of men, cats can fly from nine stories high and pigs can see the wind." But there's a price to pay for the wisdom of the flesh and the singer awakens to visions of Jesus Christ and Pontius Pilate just above his head. This enigmatic story-song could just as easily have fit onto Cash's *American Recordings* album.

In his informative coffee table book, *House of Cash,* John Carter explained that the inspiration for "Death and Hell" came as he and his father were traveling on the bus between shows during a series of one-night gigs. He recalls that "Dad read in the newspaper a very unusual scientific study: It had been determined that when a cat fell from a window three to nine stories high, it would die upon landing because its body was tense and the cat felt the full impact of the fall. However, if the cat fell out of a window more than nine stories high, it had enough time to stretch out and relax its limbs and torso, which helped it survive. We laughed about this all day. Dad had also read somewhere that according to an old wives' tale, pigs can see the wind. Inspired by these two unique bits of information, we developed the chorus for the song 'Death and Hell.' The main story came from our imaginations" (Cash, *House of Cash*, 103).

Texas singer-songwriter Robert Earl Keen wrote the closing track "The Road Goes On Forever." Keen is a major star in the Lone Star State and artists such as George Strait, Lyle Lovett, and the Dixie Chicks have covered his songs. He had originally recorded his version of this song for his 1989 album *West Textures*. "The Road Goes on Forever" is a breezy story-song about a waitress named Sherry who meets a pot-dealing loner named Sonny and the trouble they ultimately get into together. It's a detailed, mini-movie of a song that has a twist ending that validates the hook line, "The road goes on forever and the party never ends."

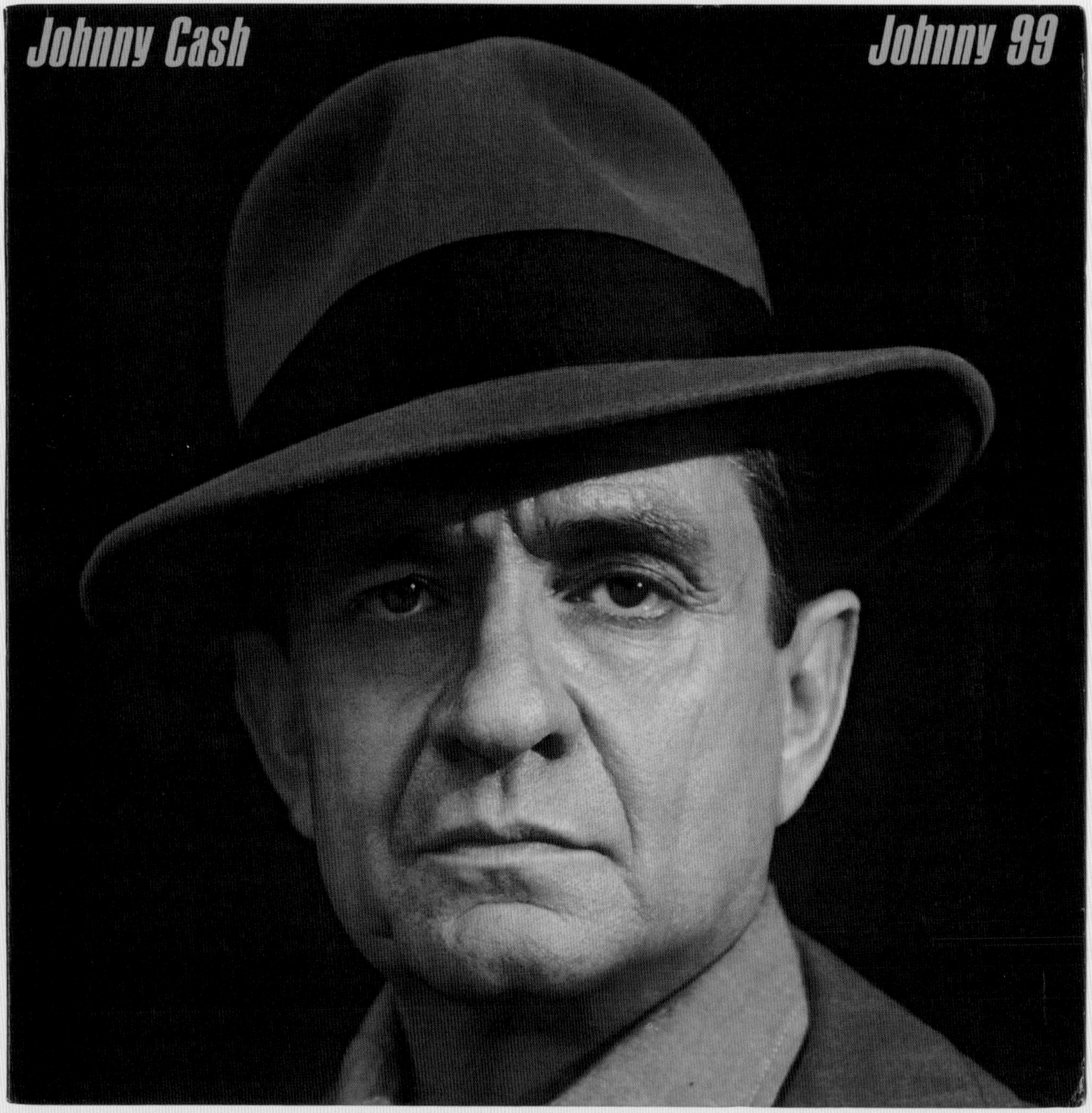
Johnny Cash
Johnny 99

Chapter 11

DELIA'S GONE

THE MURDER BALLADS

Johnny Cash's intriguing songs of murder and death

The country and folk music that Cash grew up listening to in rural Arkansas had its roots in the Appalachian Mountains. The songs were brought to America from England, Scotland, and Ireland, firmly planted in the oral tradition, handed down from generation to generation, spoken and sung, and ultimately embellished with banjo and fiddle lines. The songs travelled far and wide throughout the South, as they were altered and adapted to fit the sound and style of the region they were performed in. Many of A. P. Carter's songs were adapted from these mountain ballads. The songs were drenched in the harsh realities of life that the settlers faced, as well as a means of escape for brief moments where the music could help carry them away from their despair.

Murder ballads were a part of the fabric of these early folk tunes. Nothing stirred the emotions more than songs about death and dying. They were haunting sagas and moving vignettes that captivated their audience with depictions of violent acts of desperation. Mostly, they were shocking and indelible. Cash knew these songs well and recorded his own adaptations of these ballads throughout his career. Ironically, when Cash moved to American Recordings one of the first songs he recorded was a murder ballad, and a cover of a song he had recorded more than thirty years before. In fact, one of his biggest hits was entrenched in this tradition, as the narrator in "Folsom Prison Blues" is incarcerated for murdering a man just to watch him die.

« Johnny 99. *Courtesy of Sony Music Entertainment.*

Cash also sang of murder in the previously discussed "Mister Garfield," about the president who was shot by Charles Guiteau and died two and half months later. In "Orleans Parish Prison," the narrator's green-eyed son "shot a man down with a sawed off gun." The argument for his freedom is that he's sorry for what he's done, which is more than can be said for the narrator in "Kate," who kills Kate and blames her for his ending up in prison. The tragic young Billy Joe in "Don't Take Your Guns to Town," who truly seems to regret not heeding his mother's warning before being shot, shows remorse. We are told that the boy meant no harm, but got into a bad situation that took his life. The same can't be said for the amped-up narrator in "Cocaine Blues," who gets up early one morning, takes a shot of cocaine and shoots his woman down because she was cheating on him.

In Cash's account of historical figure John Wesley Hardin, we learn that Hardin was killed after serving his time in prison. But in the more whimsical "Austin Prison," the outlaw narrator is imprisoned for murdering a woman he may not have killed. He's found guilty and sentenced to die, but in a rare happenstance the jailer helps him escape. There certainly is a sense of ambiguity since we don't know for sure if he did or did not kill anyone. But we know that he got away. Even more ironic is "Joe Bean," who murdered twenty people in Arkansas, but is being hanged for the one murder he did not commit. And in "The Wall," the prisoner sets himself up for his own death when he tries to climb the impenetrable wall and gets shot in the process.

In "When It's Springtime in Alaska," we learn that when the narrator takes a shine to saloon singer Lil, he is murdered by her soon-to-be husband Big Ed. It was simply flirting that took the narrator down in "Alaska," whereas mockery is the reason for murder in Harlan Howard's "The Sound of Laughter." The narrator's girl leaves him after he's spent all his money on her, and she mocks him with laughter as she goes. He shoots her with his .44, and the sound of her laughter keeps ringing in his ear. The singer regrets not leaving her rather than killing her, but he'll take responsibility as he goes even crazier in prison. The song has an Edgar Allan Poe feel to it, and it would have certainly felt out of place on the generally humorous *Everybody Loves a Nut* LP.

One of the oldest murder ballads Cash recorded was "The Banks of the Ohio," a nineteenth-century murder ballad whose author is unknown. Many performers have arranged and recorded their own versions of this dark, haunting tale of unfathomable tragedy. The narrator murders his girl because she will not agree to marry him. Her rejection spurs the narrator to kill her by plunging a knife into her breast. She even begs him crying "Oh, Willie don't murder me." But her pleas go unheard as he stabs her and drags her "by her golden curls" down to the riverside where he throws her into the water to drown. Cash admits in the liner notes to *Unearthed* that "Banks of the Ohio" was always June's favorite Carter Family song. He acknowledges that it wasn't his favorite, but he certainly gives it all he's got. He had originally recorded the song years earlier with Mother Maybelle, June, Helen, and Anita for the 1964 Carter Family album *Keep on the Sunny Side.*

Cash also revisited and reimagined other murder ballads over the years. The previously discussed "The Long Black Veil" was reinterpreted, switching verse placement from the original, when Cash covered it on *Unearthed.* And a similar revamping took place with "Delia's Gone," which was adapted by Karl Silbersdorf and Dick Toops, and originally included on *The Sound of Johnny Cash.* The murder of a fourteen-year-old African-American girl, named Delia Green, on Christmas Eve 1900 in Savannah, Georgia, by her fifteen-year-old lover, Moses "Cooney" Houston, is thought to be the inspiration for this folk song. One theory is that he killed her because she called him a son of a bitch. Houston was arrested for Delia's murder, and served twelve years of his life sentence before being paroled in 1913. In Cash's 1962 version we are not given a reason or motive for why the narrator would want to kill Delia. Many artists have recorded the song, including Pete Seeger, the Kingston Trio, and Bob Dylan. Pat Boone reached number 66 on the pop chart with his version in 1960, and Waylon Jennings took it to number 37 on the country chart in 1969. But Cash's fascination with the song led him to record it twice in 1962 and then again, in an updated version, in 1994.

The 1994 cover of "Delia's Gone" was promoted as the first single from the *American Recordings* album, and Cash filmed a video for it featuring model Kate Moss as the violently murdered Delia. Right from the start we hear a more guilt-ridden, world-weary Cash relating the story of killing his darling Delia and being haunted by her ghostly memory. He alters the lyrics from the original recording, and in the second verse he informs us that he met Delia in Memphis, found her in her parlor and tied her to her chair. We get a more graphic description of the events that took place before and after he murdered her. In this version we are told that "she was low down and triflin', she was cold and mean, the kind of evil make me want to grab my sub-machine," giving the narrator ample reason to plan her demise. Cash also adds a final verse warning us that, "if your woman's devilish, you can let her run, or you can bring her down and do her like Delia got done." The narrator is almost desperately trying to justify the reason for his actions and convince us, and himself, that he just did what had to be done. Who would have thought that a murder ballad would become one of the two most defining songs from Cash's prolific tenure at American Recordings?

John R. Cash

Featuring:
The Lady Came From Baltimore
My Old Kentucky Home
(Turpentine And Dandelion Wine)
The Night They Drove
Old Dixie Down
Reason To Believe
Hard Times Comin'
Lonesome To The Bone
Clean Your Own Tables
Jesus Was Our Saviour
(Cotton Was Our King)
Cocaine Carolina
Smokey Factory Blues

Chapter 12

COMMITTED TO PARKVIEW

DRUG USE AND ABUSE

*A survey of songs influenced
by Johnny Cash's lifelong addictions*

The pressures of touring, and the entrapments of fame led Cash to begin taking amphetamines during the late 1950s. That's when it all started for Cash, and his drug use has been well documented. Cash admits in his autobiography, "I took my first amphetamine, a little white Benzedrine tablet scored with a cross, in 1957, when I was on tour with Faron Young and Ferlin Husky, and I loved it" (Cash, *Autobiography,* 191). And so began his "journey into addiction." Cash used the amphetamines to keep him going, as the touring and his marriage to Vivian began to take their tolls on him. He would then take barbiturates to bring him down from his high and help him sleep. It was a vicious cycle he had fallen into, and one that he would relapse back into for most of his life. But Cash did not back away from recordings songs that had drug inferences. The previously discussed "Transfusion Blues," which morphed into "Cocaine Blues," is a prime example of a song that warned listeners of the perils of drug addiction.

As mentioned, in 1967 Cash was arrested for public drunkenness in LaFayette, Georgia, and by the fall of that year, Cash was spiraling out of control on amphetamines. His appearance had

« John R. Cash. *Courtesy of Sony Music Entertainment.*

drastically changed, as can be seen from the cover photo of the *Carryin' On* album and on the following *From Sea To Shining Sea*. He was gaunt, drawn, and skeletal looking. The once robust giant of a man had succumbed to his demons and was wasting away right before everyone's eyes. It was during this time that he supposedly drove out alone to a cave in Tennessee with the intent of killing himself. Devastated by the breakup of his marriage to Vivian and the direction his life had taken, he planned to crawl into the cave and end it all. What happened next has been recounted many times and in many different ways. Cash drove out to Nickajack Cave, which was located by the Tennessee River just north of Chattanooga. The cave took its name from the Nickajack tribe, who were slaughtered by Andrew Jackson during the Civil War. The cave was so large that Confederate soldiers hid in it during the Battle of Lookout Mountain. Being a Civil War enthusiast, Cash knew of the cave and often traveled to it to search for Civil War and Indian artifacts. This time he came to the cave to crawl in so far that he would not be able to find his way out. But just when his flashlight gave out and it appeared that all hope was lost and that he would not emerge from the cave alive, Cash felt a divine intervention. He crawled through the darkness toward the cave's opening on his hands and knees, believing that God had given him a second chance to remedy his life and change his self-destructive ways.

The story of Nickajack Cave has been questioned by Marshall Grant and Robert Hilburn, and many believe that the episode did not unfold as Cash has related it, or never happened at all. And Cash certainly did continue to fight drug addiction long after the events described. One interesting side note is that Cash did find inspiration there to write a song. "The Whirl and the Suck" is a quirky yet fascinating story of perseverance that tells of the ten good men with salty hands that are needed to navigate the whirl and the suck. In the liner notes to *From Sea to Shining Sea,* Cash explains, "The Whirl and the Suck was a real spot near Chattanooga. Until the 1930's, when a dam was built there making the Tennessee River deeper and the water wider, there was a sharp, narrow bend with high cliffs above. In the bend, there were whirlpools and suckholes, and the water was swift and deep. A small boat, raft or canoe didn't' have a chance." Cash goes on to explain that he wrote the song while a half a mile inside Nickajack Cave, and the result is a well-written, first person observational story-song.

It was also during the mid- to late sixties that Cash rented an apartment in Nashville with Waylon Jennings, as the two old friends comically tried to hide their drugs from each other. But thanks to June's intervention, Cash cleaned up, and by the end of the sixties he was drug free and at his musical peak. The years he spent on his television series were joyful ones, and the birth of his son, John Carter, kept him happy and away from the temptations of pills and other drugs for a while. The seventies started out strong for Cash, but by the end of the decade Cash enjoyed fewer and fewer hits, and his solo albums were performing poorly. The late seventies and early eighties found Cash relapsing into drug use, and by the mid-eighties Columbia Records dropped him from the label.

In 1975, outlaw and renegade David Allan Coe wrote "Cocaine Carolina," which was included on Cash's *John R. Cash* album. Cash had taken a liking to the then up-and-coming singer-songwriter. Coe came to Nashville with a story about serving time in prison and finally being afforded the opportunity to write and record his own songs. Cash invited him to join him on this extended metaphor that juxtaposes girls' names with drugs. He wonders how he got hooked on Cocaine Carolina, and wonders if he should go back to Sandy Skag ("skag" being a slang term for heroin) because "she don't love me for my money, she just wants my body, honey." It's an infectious tune that benefits from a lighter production touch than heard on the rest of the album. The wordplay is clever and Cash's performance feels more engaged on this offbeat song than on many others on the album. Just try not singing along with this one!

Cash wrote and recorded "Committed to Parkview" for his album *One Piece at a Time*. Cash provides an insider's look in "Committed to Parkview," a vivid account of what goes on in a rehabilitation facility. It's a dark portrait of what someone must endure in order to be free of his addiction and become whole again. It was also a brave song for Cash to write, since he had fought addictions himself through the years. One can't help but see Cash's firsthand knowledge of the subject matter given the intricate details he shares about being committed to the facility: "They wake me about six-thirty, just before the mornin' meal. While they're takin' my blood pressure, they ask me how I feel. And I always say, 'Fantastic. There ain't nothin' wrong with me.' And then they give me my injection. And I go right back to sleep."

Nine years later, Cash would record "Committed to Parkview" as a duet with Willie Nelson on the *Highwayman* album. It's well written and carefully handles the very dark subject matter. Cash opens the song telling about the man who sits staring at the floor, thinking he's Hank Williams as he sings through the door, and the girl who talks about her songs and the star that she should be. Willie sings the second verse about a girl who's coming down on Thorazine, and a superstar's ex-drummer trying to kick Benzedrine. Cash and Willie both sing the third verse that tells about a girl who screams loud enough to wake the dead and a failed writer and singer who's brought in after attempting suicide. Both share the final verse where they explain the daily rituals of being in such a place and how "they are taking good care of me while committed to Parkview."

While producing Porter Wagoner's final album, *Wagonmaster*, in 2007, Marty Stuart remembered that Cash had pitched him this song years earlier to give to Porter Wagoner. Wagoner had previously recorded a song called, "The Rubber Room," which followed a similar theme about being in a mental institution. Wagoner did end up recording "Committed to Parkview," according to Cash's wishes.

In November 1990, Cash spent two weeks in a rehab facility in Nashville for drugs and alcohol, proving this was an ongoing struggle for him. Interestingly, the 2014 album *Out Among the Stars* included the ultimate drug saga, "I Drove Her Out of My Mind," recorded in 1984 for the aborted Billy Sherrill produced follow-up album to *The Baron*. Gary Gentry and Hillman Hall wrote "I Drove Her Out of My Mind." Gentry had penned David Allan Coe's Hank Williams ghost story "The Ride," as well as Cash's "Chicken in Black." Hall was the brother of Tom T. Hall, and had written the Johnny Rodriguez hit "Pass Me By." This song is about a dejected madman who tries to drown his woman's memory in drugs before devising a plan to buy a Cadillac and take her for one last ride . . . off a cliff.

Its dark and twisted subject matter is set against a lively melody. But the cutting lyric notes, "So I turned to ups and downers, and everything between," but he is still unable to get her off his mind. It depicts the ultimate addiction as the narrator devises a drug-induced scheme to do away with the object of his torment once and for all. And the narrator has decided he must perish too, leaving behind a suicide note explaining that only death could ultimately drive her out of his mind. Cash is able to pull off a song like this one, and it makes for one, excuse the expression, enjoyable ride.

So from "Transfusion Blues," to "I Drove Her Out of My Mind," Cash was always drawn to songs about the perils of drug abuse. He certainly knew the danger, and felt compelled to find various means, such as humor, insight, and metaphor, to address his own personal experiences fighting drug addiction, a lifelong battle he never really won.

Chapter 13

ONE PIECE AT A TIME

THE GREAT STORY-SONGS

*The sad, seriocomic and just plain silly
story-songs that Johnny Cash loved to sing*

t can honestly be said that Johnny Cash did a lot to promote the story-song paradigm in country music. From his earliest Sun recordings of "Ballad of a Teenage Queen" and "Give My Love to Rose," to "The Ballad of Ira Hayes" and "A Boy Named Sue," Cash embraced the idiom and intrinsically knew that it was a powerful means for him to connect with his audience. Of course Cash did not invent the genre. Woody Guthrie sang about "Pretty Boy Floyd" and "The Philadelphia Lawyer" long before Cash emerged on the scene. The Carter Family and Roy Acuff sang about "The Wabash Cannonball," and even Hank Williams was able to bring the story of the wooden Indian "Kaw-Liga" to life in 1953. But for some reason, Johnny Cash has become identified with the long list of story-songs he recorded over the years. Maybe it was his professorial stance or his unique ability to communicate the ballads about the everyman, that made Cash's name synonymous with the story-song. In fact, when Shelby Singleton acquired Sun Records from Sam Phillips in 1969, the first thing he did was release a series of repackaged Cash compilations focusing on this type of song. The reissued titles included *The Singing Storyteller* and *Story Songs of Trains and Rivers*. And, of course, "A Boy Named Sue," cemented Cash's reputation as the proverbial purveyor of tall tales and sagas in song.

The narrative genre served Cash well. "Ballad of a Teenage Queen" was his longest-charting single, "A Boy Named Sue" was his highest-charting pop

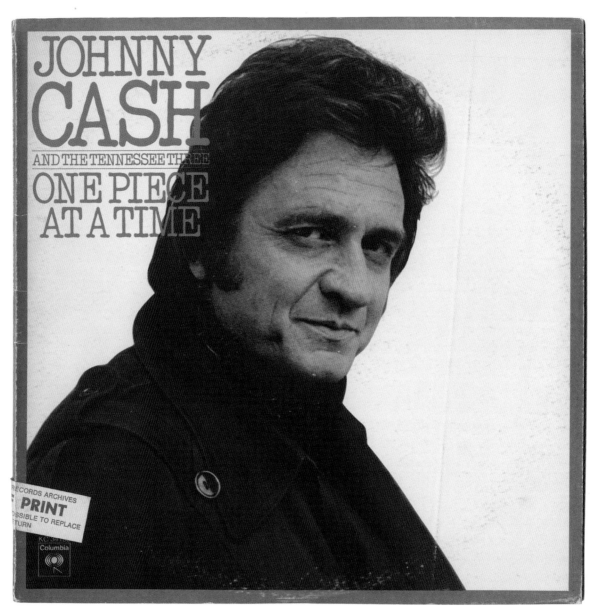

One Piece At A Time. *Courtesy of Sony Music Entertainment.*

single, and in 1976 when Cash had hit an all-time low on the pop and country charts, it was a story-song that brought him back to number 1. "One Piece at a Time" was the song that Johnny Cash needed to revitalize his career at the time. Don Davis, the producer of the *One Piece at a Time* album, was responsible for introducing the song to Cash. It's a clever, funny narrative about a fellow who leaves Kentucky to go work in a Detroit car factory. He determines to build his dream "psychobilly Cadillac" by sneaking it out of the factory one part a day over several years. It's the kind of song Cash excelled at and radio and record buyers agreed that this was the quintessential Johnny Cash song.

Songwriter Wayne Kemp had already written the George Jones classic "The Love Bug" and would go on to cowrite the heart-rending Ricky Van Shelton hit "I'll Leave This World Loving You." Kemp wanted to record the song himself, but Davis persuaded him to let Cash have it. Davis recalls he found Kemp in a honky tonk in Texas and explained to him that Cash might want to do the song. "Kemp laughed and said, 'You know I was told this tale about this plane mechanic who made off with enough material, a little bit at a time, to build a helicopter. I thought it was a funny story, true or not, and wrote 'One Piece at a Time,' substituting the Caddy for the 'copter. Sure, go ahead, give it to Cash" (D. Davis, 108). Davis and Kemp had found the perfect artist for this novelty story-song. Cash also filmed one of the first country music videos to help promote this song. This was Johnny's first number 1 country hit since "Flesh and Blood" in 1970, and, at number 29, his biggest pop hit since "A Boy Named Sue" in 1969.

Three years would pass before Cash would once again have a hit on the country chart, and that was "(Ghost) Riders in the Sky." Cash turns in a splendid cover of the classic western-gothic story-song written in 1948 by Stan Jones. Artists such as Bing Crosby, Peggy Lee, Vaughn Monroe, Burl Ives, Frankie Laine, and Marty Robbins had previously recorded the song as "Riders in the Sky," and sometimes subtitled "A Cowboy Legend." The song feels tailor-made for Cash, who helped introduce it to a new generation. The song was included on Cash's *Silver* album, and Brian Ahern's production and arrangement was right on the mark. The song made it to number 2 on the country chart, Cash's best ranking since his duet with Waylon on "There Ain't No Good Chain Gang." Southern-rock band the Outlaws reached number 31 on the pop chart with the song in 1981.

The Nashville Sound

Two years later, after another drought on the singles chart, Cash returned with the saga of "The Baron." In April 1981, Columbia released *The Baron*. Johnny had finally gotten around to working with legendary Nashville producer Billy Sherrill. Ironically, in 1962 Sherrill was hired by Sam Phillips to run the Nashville studios of Sun Records. The following year Sherrill moved over to Epic Records as a staff producer and would ultimately end up working with and shaping the sound and styles of artists like Tammy Wynette, George Jones, Charlie Rich, and Johnny Paycheck. As a songwriter, Sherrill cowrote with Wynette her classic "Stand By Your Man." As producer he was responsible for helping create the "Nashville Sound." The "Nashville Sound" was a more polished, sweetened style of country music that removed some of the twang and infused the songs with layered strings and fuller orchestration. That may be precisely why Cash avoided collaborating with Sherrill. Cash always held to his country roots, and making pop-sounding records was never his passion. But the reality was that Cash was not selling as many records as he had been, and his songs were either charting poorly or missing the charts completely. The songs selected for this album were quite good, and Cash and Sherrill seemed to meet in the middle as far as production. While the songs are more fleshed out musically, they are not as overwrought as the arrangements on an album such as *John R. Cash*.

Cash recalls in his second autobiography, "Periodically, someone took the initiative and suggested something new or different to turn the situation around, but nothing ever worked. *The Baron*, my 1981 album with Billy Sherrill producing, was like that. Billy is legendary in the country music business for creating the slick 'Countrypolitan' sound of the late 1960s and early 1970s and producing

strings of hits for George Jones, Tammy Wynette, Charlie Rich, Tanya Tucker, and others. But by the time I got to him and he got to me, we were both pretty cynical" (Cash, *Autobiography*, 339). The album made it to number 24 and one of its three singles, the title track, made it to number 10 on the country chart and spawned a TV movie, *The Baron and the Kid*, starring Johnny and June. Cash, however, did not write any original songs for this album.

Billy Sherrill and songwriters Paul Richey and Jerry Lee Taylor wrote "The Baron," an imagery-filled story-song about an aging pool hustler and the young man who challenges him to a duel. The Baron puts up his fancy pool stick and the young man, Billy Joe, offers up his mother's wedding ring if he loses. Needless to say, there is a major reveal at the end, showing the baron to be Billy's Joe's father, that made the song perfect for a music video and ultimately a made-for-TV movie. The song brought Cash back into the country Top 10, but it would prove to be his last solo single to do so.

Cash's follow-up single was also a story-song. Country songwriters Dave Kirby ("What Have You Got Planned Tonight, Diana") and Curly Putman ("Green, Green Grass of Home") collaborated on "Mobile Bay," a descriptive ballad concerning the thoughts and dreams of a group of winos who are freezing and gathered around a garbage-can fire in Chicago sharing stories about better times and warmer places. The lyric is poetic, with lines like,

"Mobile Bay, magnolia blossoms, cool summer nights, warm rolling sea." Cash's delivery is on the mark, and maybe a more acoustic arrangement might have made this the hit it deserved to be. Sadly, it only made it to number 60 on the country chart.

Cash's next single, "The Reverend Mr. Black," was also a story-song, as was its B-side, "Chattanooga City Limit Sign." "Chattanooga City Limit Sign" is a silly, humorous song that plays out like a cartoon with Cash taking on the role of a hitchhiker heading to Chattanooga, Tennessee. He's picked up by a car full of young people who proceed to test his endurance by drinking and driving fast around the winding roads leading up to the Chattanooga city limit sign. Cash is in on the joke and delivers a hilarious performance as we brace ourselves for one crazy trip. As the B-side of "The Reverend Mr. Black," it made it to number 71 on the country chart.

After the disappointing performance of that single, Cash collaborated with singer-songwriter Thom Bresh, the son of Merle Travis, on "The General Lee" for the soundtrack album of the popular television series *The Dukes of Hazzard*. Waylon Jennings had written the show's theme song and enjoyed a number 1 hit with it in 1980. Cash made it to number 26 on the country chart in 1982 with this record celebrating the famous red Dodge Charger that the Duke boys drove. The single was released on Scotti Bros. Records.

Chicken in Black

And it was a double-sided story-song that closed out Cash's tenure with Columbia Records. In June 1984, "Chicken in Black" was released. It was Johnny's last charting solo single for Columbia Records and arguably the worst song he ever recorded. Songwriter Gary Gentry wrote the song "Chicken in Black" which was originally titled "Brain Transfusion." "Chicken in Black" tells the convoluted story of Johnny Cash having his brain replaced with that of a bank robber, and then having his brain implanted in a chicken, hence, the "Chicken in Black." While not even remotely funny, the song was forced upon Cash by producer Billy Sherrill who thought it could be a humorous hit in the vein of "A Boy Named Sue." The difference was that Shel Silverstein's satirical "Sue" was truly a clever and funny song. "Chicken in Black," on the other hand, seemed a like a desperate attempt at humor and served only to embarrass Cash. Maybe because of its bizarre story line, the song reached number 45 on the country chart, but remains the low-point in Cash's body of recordings. A music video was filmed for the single that featured a cameo by Roy Acuff, and Cash dressed in a chicken suit. In his Autobiography, Cash states that, "Looking back on 'Chicken In Black,' it's no wonder to me that it took a while to get another decent record deal. People were probably afraid to bank on an artist who'd make a mockery of himself like that" (Cash, *Autobiography*, 341).

"Battle of Nashville," also produced by Sherrill, was the B-side to "Chicken in Black," and a much better song in every way possible. First, it was one of the rare new songs written by Cash, and secondly it uses a fading romance as a metaphor for Cash's ongoing battles with the record executives in Nashville who were trying to tell him what he should or shouldn't record. The irony is that this song in which Cash admits that his heart is no longer in it, is actually one of the most insightful songs he'd written or recorded in quite a while. Both "Chicken in Black" and "Battle of Nashville" were intended for an album called *In Living Color* that was never released.

The only other song in Cash's catalog that might battle "Chicken in Black" for most polarizing single is Cash's "Smiling Bill McCall," a brutal song about a popular radio performer and deejay named Bill McCall. McCall sounded so good on the radio that boys wanted to be like him, and girls dreamed about him, imagining him to be handsome and over six feet tall. The song tells us that in reality Bill McCall was really vain, bald-headed, and four feet tall. The song is believed to be a slap at 4 Star Records owner Bill McCall, a ruthless businessman in Nashville with no music background who claimed composer credits on songs he did not write. McCall's behavior must have infuriated Cash, who had no tolerance for such discrimina-

tion. The song was released as a single and reached number 13 on the country chart as the B-side of Cash's "Seasons of My Heart" single in 1960.

The Moral of the Story

As a writer, Johnny Cash was strongly drawn to the story-song genre. We've already seen how he could adapt an old folk song like "Frankie and Johnny" and make it his own, and there were many others. "Hank and Joe and Me" is a banner story-song written by Cash. It's about three prospectors searching for gold in the desert. For days and days they fight the heat until the narrator falls, weak and thirsty for water. Hank tells Joe the narrator's dying for water. Hank wants to leave the narrator to die in the desert alone because he can't stand to hear him cry for water. Somehow the narrator manages to survive the night and wakes up the next day with buzzards flying overhead, knowing Hank and Joe are dead. It's the price you pay. The moral of the story is that if you leave your friend to die alone, fate will catch up with you and you just may perish first. The ultimate irony is that the dying narrator finds that he'd been lying on a bed of gold nuggets all the while. Overall, this is a very imaginative saga simply told and nicely sung. The song was included on Cash's *Songs of Our Soil* album.

"Hank and Joe and Me" is reminiscent of "Lost on the Desert" from *The Sound of Johnny Cash*. "Lost on the Desert" was composed by Dallas Frazier —

who wrote the Oak Ridge Boys' "Elvira," Jack Greene's "There Goes My Everything," and Charley Pride's "All I Have to Offer You (is Me)"—and Buddy Mize, who wrote songs for Marty Robbins, George Jones, and Buck Owens, among many others. The song has a Marty Robbins flavor to it, as Cash returns to the theme of being lost on the desert. This song has a more sinister feel, as the narrator is an escaped convict who had hidden his money in the desert before being jailed. Now he's running back to get it. The devil becomes a hallucinatory figure that follows the narrator as he stumbles and falls along his way.

There were other fine story-songs on the *Songs of Our Soil* album. Billy Mize was a songwriter, recording artist and television host from Bakersfield, California. Among his credits are the hit "Who Will Buy the Wine" for Charlie Walker and songs recorded by Dean Martin. "Clementine" was a story-song he wrote with his brother Buddy. It plays upon the popular folk ballad "Oh My Darling, Clementine" adding a story about Clementine's love for a man named Cody, who was going to town for one last night out with his friends before returning to marry his beloved Clementine. No one really knows what happened, but speculation was that Cody took up with a dancehall girl called named Nan and provoked the jealousy of her lover. A shot rang out and Cody is found dying, calling out to Clementine. The song's theme is similar to "Don't Take Your Guns to Town." But instead of heeding his mother's advice, in this song he should have avoided the lures of the town.

Cash's "The Man on the Hill" is a chilling plea from a poor young boy to his father wondering how they will survive the hard times. Plowing time is over and the fields are all bare, but the father promises to beg for more money from the man on the hill. They have very little, but they hope that with the help of the boss who lives well up on the hill they might get by. By the final verse there is little hope as the focus shifts from the wealthy boss on the hill to the "Man" in the sky. The sheer futility is revealed in scathing lines like, "But who's gonna pay the dying bills, if we all should die." Well, they leave that to the Man in the sky, knowing at least they will have a home in heaven.

"The Caretaker" is a melodramatic ballad written by Cash. Old John, the "caretaker" of the song's title, lives in the cemetery. And while he tends to the grounds, he also sees through the people's grief, "their greed and hate and jealousy." He witnesses those who come for the funeral, bury their dead, and then go away. Now that he is old, he ponders his own mortality, wondering, "Who's gonna cry when Old John dies?" It's both sad and haunting at the same time, as we watch someone who is old and tired getting ready to face his own mortality.

"Don't Step on Mother's Roses" is one of the most haunting tracks on *Songs of Our Soil*. It recounts how a family is called back to their old home on the farm when the mother passes away. The singer watches his father's reaction when someone accidentally steps on one of the roses his mother had planted. It is a tender moment that makes this song all the more impressive. The song states a harsh truth; she is gone and will no longer tend her earthly garden. The lyrics never leave your mind, "'Don't step on mother's roses,' father cried, 'She planted them the day she was my bride.'" He takes comfort knowing they will bloom again each year and he will see her face in every rose. This is Cash at his best, and one of his truly most overlooked songs.

The tick-tock sound of a clock opens "My Grandfather's Clock," which Cash adapted from Henry Clay Work's 1876 song. The story is a familiar one about the narrator's grandfather's beloved clock that "stopped short, never to go again, when the old man died." Once again, Cash finds a way to make an old favorite new again. We can see the parallel of the grandfather's love for his old clock and the narrator's love for his grandfather. And this song was truly a "song of the soil" for Cash, as he recalled singing it with his sister Reba while they picked cotton as children in Dyess.

Johnny wrote the semi-autobiographical "Tennessee Flat-Top Box" while he was living it. He *was* "the little dark-haired boy who played the Tennessee Flat-Top box." Though Cash didn't play the guitar very much when he was younger, it was while he was in the military that he became a competent guitarist. The single reached number 11 on the country chart in 1962, and twenty-five years later in 1987, daughter Rosanne Cash would take the song all the way to number 1. Interestingly, Rosanne did not even know her father had written the song when she recorded it. It truly is a notable song performed equally well by father and daughter.

The Folk Influence

To appreciate Cash's affection for the story-song, one only has to look further into Cash's musical influences, specifically the folk idiom. The Irish and Scottish folk songs Cash studied were largely songs with moralistic tales of strength and struggle. It is also clear that Cash used and adapted those folk songs for his own compositions. "The Ballad of Barbara" is a prime example. In *Country Music, U.S.A.,* Bill C. Malone writes, "If it is possible in this modern era for one to be of folk origin, than Johnny Cash definitely meets the requirements. Not only was his family socially and economically representative of those elements who had traditionally comprised the southern folk population, it was also a group in which the singing of gospel and folk tunes was almost second nature" (259). A prime example of Cash's folk influence is revealed in his own recordings and adaptations of classic Irish story-songs.

Johnny opens his excellent rendition of "Danny Boy" from 1965's *Orange Blossom Special* album with a spoken introduction. An Englishman named Frederic Weatherly wrote the song more than a century ago. He wrote lyrics to the melody of the old Irish standard "Londonderry Air." Cash begins "Danny Boy" with a spoken introduction recalling his father Ray Cash, courting his mother, Miss Carrie Rivers, whom he married when she was sixteen. Cash recounts a story his father told him about an Irish immigrant he worked with on the Cotton Belt railroad line who talked about going back home to Dublin. That immigrant told him the story of a young boy named Daniel McKinny, who worked in the fields, when his darling Rosalie came running and crying to him to tell him that "there's a bloody war a-raging and I've come to tell you that and they're a-wanting you to fight." She pleads with him to go and fight for Ireland, but to come back to her where she'll be waiting. Cash affects an Irish brogue as he recalls what he believes to be the basis for this enduring folk ballad. The song is usually sung in the first person, but Cash sings about "Danny Boy" in the second person, stating, "But if you fall as all the flowers are falling / And if you're dead, as dead you well may be / I'll come and find the place where you are lying / And kneel and say an ave there for thee." His performance is memorable, making this an essential recording of the iconic story-song.

Cash includes two other Irish-influenced standards on his acoustic album *Personal File*. He describes Thomas P. Westendorf's "I'll Take You Home Again Kathleen" as a song he's loved since he was a child. This one stands up well alongside Cash's earlier cover of "Danny Boy." This was specifically the kind of song that influenced early country music. "Kathleen" dates back to 1875, and despite the fact that it was written by an American composer from Indiana for his wife, Jennie, it has become an Irish standard. Artists from Bing Crosby to Elvis to Willie Nelson have recorded it over the years. Cash first performed it on his television show in 1971 and, fortunately for us, recorded it a few years later. "Galway Bay" is the second Irish standard Cash includes here. He performs this lovely ballad with deep yearning. And we see just how much this song influenced him to write "Forty Shades of Green," his own picturesque reminiscence of the Emerald Isle.

Cash had visited Ireland and felt at home there. "Forty Shades of Green" is his love song to the Emerald Isle, and, over the years, it has become a favorite among Irish singers the world over. It almost feels like an old Irish folk ballad, as Cash name-checks cities, towns and rivers throughout the country. The singer yearns to be back in the land of his dreams. From the opening line "I close my eyes and picture the emerald of the sea," we are drawn into the poetry of love for the girl he met in Tipperary Town, and the land he fell in love with. As he was traveling through the country he had a road map in his lap and picked out all the names of the places, rhymed them and started singing it.

"Shamrock Doesn't Grow in California" was recorded in 1962 and never released. Cash wrote the song one year after writing and recording "Forty Shades of Green." While both songs share a similar theme of Irish romance, this one describes a letter the dejected singer receives from his sweetheart in Dublin filled with shamrock seeds. "The leaf of all the chiefs," as he calls it, just doesn't have a chance to flourish in California. It's a good song, but "Forty Shades" is the stronger track by far.

Stories from the Seventies

During the seventies, Cash recorded many story-songs with varying degrees of success. His album *Any Old Wind That Blows* included two exemplary story-songs. Before "Take This Job and Shove It," there was "Oney." Songwriter Jerry Chesnut, who had written songs for Elvis, George Jones, and Loretta Lynn, among many others, wrote this one about a working man who finally gets revenge on his boss. It's a story-song with a message, as Cash takes on the persona of the retiring employee who has been badgered and harassed by his boss, Oney, for so many years. All that time he's been saving up all his frustration to give Oney what he deserves, a right hand full of knuckles, "'cause today I show old Oney who's the boss." Cash performs the song as if he truly empathized with the retiree, and we all cheer him on as he finally gets to give it to Oney. This was the first single released from the album and the most successful. It made it all the way to number 2 on the country chart.

In the mid-1970s, Cash bought a home in Jamaica. The house at Cinnamon Hill was an escape for Cash where he would take his family to vacation. In his autobiography, Cash says that he felt like he belonged there. The beauty of the land and the stories surrounding Rose Hall, an old sugar cane plantation, also enraptured him. Cash was inspired to write "The Ballad of Annie Palmer" after hearing a local legend about an English-born woman who came to Jamaica from Haiti named Annie Palmer. She became the mistress of Rose Hall plantation, and was also known as the "white witch of Rose Hall." Annie Palmer was believed to have practiced voodoo and badly mistreated many of the five thousand slaves on the plantation. She also was believed to have murdered three husbands before she herself was murdered by one of the slaves. Cash authoritatively recounts the saga in another first-rate original composition.

In 1975 Cash covered "The Lady Came from Baltimore" on his *John R. Cash* album. He appears to put more into his performance of this song than most of the others on the album. It paid off for him; the song was the most successful single he'd released in over three years, making it to number 14 on the country chart. It's a very good Tim Hardin song, and Cash had certainly enjoyed great success with his earlier Hardin cover of "If I Were a Carpenter." "The Lady Came from Baltimore" finds him taking on the persona of a man who marries a wealthy woman with the intent to rob her, but instead falls in love with her. As with "If I Were a Carpenter," Bobby Darin had released the original single of this song in 1967 where it made it to number 62 on the pop chart.

Also in 1975, Cash recorded *The Johnny Cash Children's Album.* It included a few unique story-songs. Cash wrote the song "Tiger Whitehead" with Nat Winston, a psychiatrist who was the Tennessee State Commissioner of Mental Health. Winston helped counsel Cash for his amphetamine abuse. He also played the banjo and wrote songs. "Tiger Whitehead" is a very good story-song, although the subject matter might be too intense for younger children. It's about Tiger Whitehead hunting and killing bears for their hides. We're told that he killed ninety-nine bears before he died. Dark subject matter aside, this is one of the best songs on the album. *Personal File* includes Cash's original acoustic demo of "Tiger Whitehead." In the spoken introduction Cash says the song is based on the true story of Tiger Whitehead who was born in 1819 and died in 1905. His wife Sally Garland lived to be ninety-seven years old. Dr. Nat Winston had taken Cash to the cemetery where Tiger Whitehead was buried and that gave Cash the inspiration to write this song.

"Old Shep," the Red Foley standard, feels like it was written expressly for Cash. It is undoubtedly the finest performance on the children's album. If you ever loved a dog you can hardly listen to this one without tearing up. Elvis recorded a nice cover of this ballad, but Cash, with only a guitar for accompaniment, manages to hit you right in the heart with his rendition. Cash closes the original album with "The Timber Man," a story-song about a timber man who lived in the forest and cut down trees so that we could build houses and make furniture. Once again, it's just Cash and his guitar delivering a winning acoustic performance.

Songs Covered by Cash

Cash was also drawn to story-songs that were the hits of the day, but he would only record them if he felt he had something to add to them. "The Night They Drove Old Dixie Down" was a natural for Cash to cover on the *John R. Cash* album. And he really does turn in a credible performance of this southern-rock classic. This is the memorable story of Virgil Cane and his struggle to get through the Civil War during the winter of 1865. Cash certainly would have benefited from a less orchestrated arrangement, but a great song is a great song, and Cash delivers the lyric with honest conviction. Written by Robbie Robertson and sung by Levon Helm, the song was released by the Band as the B-side of their single "Up on Cripple

Creek" in 1969. Folk icon Joan Baez had the hit with the song, taking it to number 3 on the pop chart in 1971. While she altered some of the lyrics, Cash holds true to the Band's original version.

On 1990's *Boom Chicka Boom* Cash turned in a moving cover of the Harry Chapin classic "Cat's in the Cradle." The song follows the circle of life as the father in the song explains how he's always too busy working to pay much attention to his young son, who proclaims that he wants to be just like his father. Ultimately, the boy grows up and has a job that keeps him busy, with no time to spend with his aging father. Cash's vocal is on the mark, although too far back in the mix. The arrangement somehow distracts from the poignant song lyrics. This was a good song choice for Cash, but it might have benefited from a less syncopated background. Harry Chapin's original recording made it to number 1 on the pop chart in 1974. Cash's single failed to chart.

The Gambler and The Diplomat

Kenny Rogers released his version of "The Gambler" as a single just one month before the release of *Gone Girl* in December 1978. That precluded Cash from releasing his version and, in retrospect, although he turns in a fine performance of the song, Kenny Rogers truly nailed it. Cash delivers a more inspirational rendition of the song, almost as if he were a preacher rather than the rider on the train gaining the gambler's wisdom.

He changes the opening lines from Rogers' familiar "On a warm summer's evening," to "About twenty years ago," making it more of distant recollection than an immediate response song. Larry Butler produced both versions, so the arrangements are quite similar. The difference is in the matter-of-fact delivery Rogers affords the song that more readily draws the listener in. Rogers' gambler is more world-weary and tired. These are certainly two viable ways of interpreting the lyrics of the great story-song. Interestingly, it was Bobby Bare who was the first artist to release "The Gambler." It was included on his criminally neglected album *Bare,* which was released earlier that same year.

Gone Girl also included "The Diplomat," an impressive story-song by Roger Bowling, and another one that got away from Cash. Cash included it as an album track, but it certainly warranted wider exposure. It would have been the perfect single for Cash. "The Diplomat" is an epic love story that revolves around an old man's love for his train, the Diplomat, and Margaret, his beloved wife. The opening description of the old man, retired for twenty years, slowly brushing a silver strand of hair from his wrinkled brow is striking. Cash imbues the poetic lyric with tenderness and honesty. It's more like a movie than a song and would have made a fine film at that. There's a twist at the end that pays off and solidifies this as the best song on this album, and one of the best in Cash's entire catalog of recordings.

Cash's story-songs remain among his most beloved and enduring recordings. In 2001 Sony Special Products released the album *A Boy Named Sue and Other Story Songs,* to further capitalize on Cash's "singing storyteller" identity. Along with the classic title song, the album included such standout tracks as "One Piece at a Time," "Oney," "Boa Constrictor" and "Look at Them Beans." It also included "Smiling Bill McCall" and "Chicken in Black" for good measure. Cash began his short tenure at Mercury Records with "The Night Hank Williams Came to Town," and his later years at American Recordings with "Delia's Gone." In fact, story-songs factored prominently into every phase of Cash's career, and his legacy as the "singing storyteller" remains intact.

Chapter 14

YOU WILD COLORADO

DEEP CUTS AND BURIED TREASURES

*A selection of less familiar album tracks that were
among Johnny Cash's personal favorites*

Everyone has a favorite Johnny Cash song, though it's probably one of a dozen or so that they are familiar with. The fact of the matter is that Cash recorded hundreds of other noteworthy songs that for one reason or another never had the chance to seep into listeners' consciousness. Of course, record-label politics resulted in certain songs being chosen as singles and promoted, or not promoted, based on the status of Cash's relationship with his record label at the time. Cash did have the freedom to record songs he believed in for his albums, but they may have lacked commercial appeal. Some

of those records got lost, due again to what Cash considered lack of support from the record companies. There were also singles that never made it onto an album and that got lost along the way, and single B-sides that benefited the singer and the songwriters, but sometimes got left off the album. So, call them buried treasures, or deep cuts, some deserve a second listen because many of them are as valuable as Cash's more familiar recordings.

Sometimes time and distance changed Cash's perspective of a song. For his first Columbia single, Cash wrote and recorded the song "All Over Again," a song of love and devotion with the singer

« The Fabulous Johnny Cash.
Courtesy of Sony Music Entertainment.

proclaiming, "Every time I look at you I fall in love all over again." It was the perfect transition single, sounding as if it might have been a Sun release, and yet there was something very fresh and new about it.[1] The single reached number 4 on the country chart and made it to number 38 pop. Interestingly, it was never included on an album at the time of its release in 1958, and yet Cash never forgot about it. He also favored the single's B-side, "What Do I Care." "What Do I Care" represents a strong piece of philosophical wisdom from Cash. "What do I care if I never have much money, and sometimes my table looks a little bare / Anything that I may miss is made up for each time we kiss, you love me and I love you so what do I care." It's an inspired ballad and Johnny's future protégés the Statler Brothers would record a fine version of the song for their 1974 Mercury Records album *Carry Me Back*.

Cash's first Columbia LP, *The Fabulous Johnny Cash*, included two such buried treasures. The opening track, "Run Softly, Blue River," is a lovely pastoral ballad about the singer's devotion to his loved one who dreams of tomorrow when she'll be his wife, as they both dream along to the calm, soothing sounds of the blue river. It's sweet, tender, and reveals a side of Johnny we had not yet seen. The gospel quartet the Jordanaires, who often performed with Elvis, back up Johnny brilliantly. This might be one of the most underrated gems in the Cash catalog, both as a singer and as a songwriter.

"The Troubadour" is another outstanding performance by Cash. The theme is one that Cash would return to time and again over the years, the plight of the singer who travels from town to town singing from the heart. It examines the loneliness of the heartbroken singer yearning for a loved one. He's adored by his devoted fans but all alone in his misery because the object of his love is out there in the crowd, "and her heart aches most of all." This simple, stark ballad was written by legendary country songwriter Cindy Walker, who wrote such classic songs as "Cherokee Maiden," a hit for both Bob Wills and Merle Haggard, "You Don't Know Me," recorded by artists including Eddy Arnold, Elvis Presley, and Mickey Gilley, and "Dream Baby (How Long Must I Dream)" for Roy Orbison.

Ten years later, Cash released the similarly themed ballad "The Folk Singer." It was issued as the B-side of "Folsom Prison Blues." Cash wrote this with songwriter Charles E. Daniels (not to be confused with southern rock legend Charlie Daniels). It's a stark story about an ill-fated, once popular folk singer, and allegedly based on the career of singer-songwriter Tommy Roe. It's an honest account of the roller coaster ride of fame. One minute the multitudes are screaming your name, and the next the streets are empty and nobody knows who you are. Artists such as Burl Ives and Glen Campbell later recorded "The Folk Singer." Cash's unforgettable version certainly deserved a better fate than to be relegated to the B-side of a single.

Cash also selected 1962's "A Little at a Time" as one of his personal favorites. It was the B-side of "In the Jailhouse Now," and although it was recorded at the same sessions for *The Sound of Johnny Cash,* it was not included on the album. The singer here pleads with his lover to leave him a little at a time so that the pain won't be so overwhelming. The song was cowritten by Cash and his friend Gordon Terry, an Alabama-born songwriter, fiddler, and member of the Country Music Hall of Fame. Terry traveled and performed with Cash periodically, and remained part of Cash's show for a time.

"I'd Still Be There" was included on *Ring of Fire: The Best of Johnny Cash.* Johnny wrote the song with Johnny Horton. Cash and Horton had spent time together fishing and even toured together. Horton tragically died in a horrific car crash on November 5, 1960. This lilting ballad of regret is about a man who lost his love because he selfishly took her for granted. He would give anything if she would just return to him. He pleads with her to reconsider and take him back, reasoning, "If I only knew you loved me too, I'd still be there." Cash explained that he wrote the song after Johnny Horton hypnotized him. He recalled that, "Once I was in that state, Johnny would start opening up my memory to me. That's how I was able to complete the writing of 'I'd Still Be There,' the song

I heard Webb Pierce singing in a dream" (Cash, *Autobiography,* 142).

"Girl in Saskatoon" is another exceptional collaboration between Cash and Horton. It's unfortunate that it did not find a wider audience. It was originally released as a single in 1960, but failed to chart. It's a breezy retro ballad wherein the singer follows the girl he's in love with all the way to Saskatoon, Canada, where he ultimately finds her and weds her. And, despite the cold temperatures, he "found eternal spring with the girl in Saskatoon." An interesting side note is that while performing in Saskatoon in 1961, Cash selected a girl from the audience named Alexandra Wiwcharuk to sing the song to. She was a local beauty queen who dreamed of becoming a stewardess. Tragically, a few months later, the young woman was found murdered on the banks of the Saskatchewan River. The story goes that once Cash heard this news he never sang the song again.

"You Wild Colorado" is one of only two songs Cash wrote for the album *Orange Blossom Special,* and it's a hidden treasure. The Colorado River is a metaphor for the woman the singer loves. Just like his love, the river flows on with no chance of returning. There's a veiled notion of suicide as the singer voices his wish to become part of the river's flow, although his love of life restrains him from doing so. He reasons, "You're as wild as my woman, you wild Colorado." This is the only time Cash recorded this track, but it deserves a place among his finest compositions. It is yet another song he selected as being among his personal favorites for *The Legendary Johnny Cash.*

Peter La Farge wrote "She Came from the Mountains" for Cash's *Happiness Is You* album. It's a haunting ballad that could have fit nicely into many of Johnny's concept albums. It's a highlight of this collection and one of the stronger story-songs. It tells of a girl whom the narrator meets in the Rocky Mountains, at the foot of Pike's Peak. He falls in love with her and asks her to go back with him to his Iowa home. Despite her grandmother's warnings for her not to go, she leaves with him. Although they are initially happy, she gets homesick and goes back to the mountains. It's a beautifully written ballad, and Cash delivers it well. The Statler Brothers and the Carter Family add stunning background harmony to make this one of Cash's most inspired performances.

The 1968 album *From Sea to Shining Sea* included "Call Daddy from the Mine," a harrowing saga about the daughter of a miner who has a frightening premonition that something bad is going to happen to her father. It's one of the strongest tracks on the album and ranks right up there with the best Merle Travis mining ballads. In the liner notes, Cash admits that he wrote this song ten years before and forgot about it. After playing it for June, she encouraged him to record it for this album. We are drawn into the story about the little girl whose words echoed so loudly that her father somehow heard them and crawled to a fresh air pocket and survived the mining disaster.

Cash and Roy Orbison collaborated on "See Ruby Fall," from Cash's *Hello, I'm Johnny Cash* album, after seeing a billboard in Tennessee that read "See Ruby Falls." Ruby Falls is a waterfall in Chattanooga, Tennessee. They took that hook and turned it into a song of frustration, as you watch someone you love drift further and further away from you. The narrator admits that he knew someday Ruby would leave him for a more exciting life than the one he could provide for her. She certainly did, as he explains that she can now be found under the red light downtown. It's a brutally frank song without a happy ending for the singer. It was released as the B-side of "Blistered."

The 1971 recording "Orphan of the Road," from the *Man in Black* album, epitomizes the deep album cut. In Cash's catalog of story-songs there is probably none more profound and poetic than "Orphan of the Road," written by songwriter Dick Feller. Feller had written many songs including "Biff, the Friendly Purple Bear." His recording of "Biff" reached number 22 on the country chart, and it was also was covered by Mac Davis. Another Feller composition, "Some Days Are Diamonds (Some Days Are Stone)," was a Top 10 country hit for John Denver. "Orphan of the Road" tells the heart-wrenching tale of a rodeo performer who had a brief relationship with a "fiery carny queen." The result was a child who was born "the too late son of something that was gone." The boy is left to grow up on his own, ultimately becoming a hobo riding the rails. The self-described "black sheep child that grew up wild from the seed the four-winds sowed, unwanted son of ice and fire, an orphan of the road." The lyric is memorable and the story has a bittersweet ending. This is the kind of song that Cash was drawn to when given the freedom to choose the songs he wanted to record, without interference from producers or record label executives.

A Heartfelt Ballad

"Any Old Wind That Blows" is a lovely, lilting ballad about letting someone go and hoping they might return someday. The singer explains with frustration and resignation, "She's a butterfly in mid-July who just can't wait to try her brand new wings, on brand new things. And she needs no rhyme or reason when she goes. Her mind is on what lies beyond that wall of blue horizon, I suppose, and heaven knows, she'll go sailing off on any old wind that blows." The lyric is poetic and the message is heartbreaking. Dick Feller, who had already supplied Cash with "Orphan of the Road," wrote the song. But whereas "Orphan" was a bit too stark, this one, helped along by a breezy banjo accompa-

niment, proved to be a successful single for Cash, making it to number 3 on the country chart. It would also be his last Top 10 single for three years.[2]

The *Any Old Wind That Blows* album also included Cash's "Kentucky Straight." After a brief spoken introduction, the singer compares his wife to a fine Kentucky bourbon. It's a tender love song about appreciating and enjoying the simple things in life and having the company of someone to share those simple pleasures with: "Cause I'm happy here with my Kentucky straight." This is another song that lets us see how astute a lyricist Cash was.

The album *Johnny Cash and His Woman* included four exemplary solo Cash tracks: the aforementioned "Matthew 24 (Is Knocking at the Door)," and "The City of New Orleans," as well as "Saturday Night in Hickman County" and "Tony." "Saturday Night in Hickman County" is a spirited solo performance by Cash. We learn that Hickman is a place for moonshine, packed bars, and loud music. And parked down by the Piney River in the "backseat of a Chevy is your next door neighbor's daughter." Cash is the reporter in song serving up this stark, observational narrative.

Thanks to Merle

Cash takes on the persona of a homesteader in Dave Kirby's "What Have You Got Planned Tonight Diana," a song originally recorded by Merle Haggard. The narrator is cutting his way through the ponderosa pines in Alaska, in order to build a cabin for himself, his wife and their children. There is no happy ending, as they go on to endure assorted hardships and tragedy over the years. It's a heartbreaking ballad of enduring love and devotion. Interestingly, Cash takes some liberties with the song's lyrics, when compared to Haggard's recording. Cash's version mentions the "older son Jim and the babies in the cradle." Haggard sings of "Jim and the baby in the cradle." In the Cash version the kids grow up and go off to see the world as he remembers how much he loved Diana and how much she loved him; it's ambiguous how it ends. In Haggard's version we learn that it's been almost two years since Diana's been gone and the singer's time on earth is almost over as he readies himself to meet Diana in heaven. Cash chose a less tragic ending to the song, while Haggard pulled no punches. Either way, it's a great song and a great performance by Cash.

"Diana" was included on *Look at Them Beans*. That album also featured "I Never Met a Man Like You Before," Johnny's first recording of a song by his daughter Rosanne Cash. Rosanne wrote the song when she was just eighteen years old. It's a stunning first-person narrative of faith in a father figure, and a powerful indication of the deeply personal songs Rosanne would go on to write. One year later, for the *One Piece at a Time* album, Cash recorded "Love Has Lost Again," another ballad

penned by Rosanne. It's a sad lament about the end of a love affair. After assessing the situation the singer rationalizes that there doesn't have to be a reason for a relationship to end, and the only truth that he is certain of is that love has lost again. Also on the album, Cash wrote "Mountain Lady," a nostalgic ode to an Appalachian woman who raised her children in the hills only to have them grow up and go off on their own. It's a simple song with striking imagery as the narrator wonders, "Did you ever get a rug to cover the cracks where my diaper drug on your wooden floor?" We can envision the mother tenderly rocking her baby in her homemade rocking chair. This is country balladry at its best.

The 1978 song "I Would Like to See You Again" is a thoughtful, nostalgic ballad that brought Cash back into the country Top 20, making it all the way to number 12. Songwriters Larry T. Atwood and Charlie Craig also wrote the Billie Jo Spears and Del Reeves duet "On the Rebound." And Charlie Craig would go on to cowrite the Alan Jackson hit "Wanted" with Jackson. Kenny Rogers had originally recorded "I Would Like to See You Again" in 1976 for his Larry Butler–produced album *Love Lifted Me*. Don Williams would also cover the song. "I Would Like to See You Again" is the kind of ballad the more mature Cash could handle with charm and ease. It's a tender reminiscence about missing someone and wishing you could see them one more time. The lyric is packed with penetrating imagery and Cash's performance leaves us misty-eyed for that someone special from our past.

Cash also recorded many standout songs during his tenure at Mercury Records during the late eighties and early nineties, and many of them have been discussed in previous chapters. While it's easy for some to feel that they understand Cash from watching a movie about his life and knowing a select sampling of his recorded works, the truth is that there is so much more to the man than what may be perceived on the surface.

Chapter 15

I'VE BEEN EVERYWHERE

TRAVELIN' CASH

Johnny Cash's songs about ramblers, hobos,
and people that are always on the move

Johnny Cash has always incorporated an element of freedom and escape into his songs. Many are frantic and present narrators and characters who are always on the move. They are wanderers, searchers, and hobos who are trying to find their place within the fabric of the American dream. Cash's protagonists and antagonists are frequently running away from something while trying to find something better. And they travel by train, truck, cars, boats, and planes, always assessing and contemplating where they would rather be. One of Cash's earliest train songs was "Hey Porter," with the narrator riding the rails and longing to return to the comforts of home. Trains factored mightily into Cash's early

repertoire, and they inspired him to write songs about locomotives for the rest of his career. Cash is often identified as a purveyor of train songs, a subject he savored throughout his recording career. From Sun selections like "Rock Island Line" and "Blue Train" to Columbia classics like "Orange Blossom Special" and "Wreck of the Old 97," and up to American Recordings' "Down There by the Train" and "Let the Train Whistle Blow," Cash continued to nurture and develop the theme of the train as a symbol of personal freedom and American progress.

On his first Columbia album, *The Fabulous Johnny Cash,* he included "One More Ride," which he arranged and adapted from a song by Bob Nolan

« America. *Courtesy of Sony Music Entertainment.*

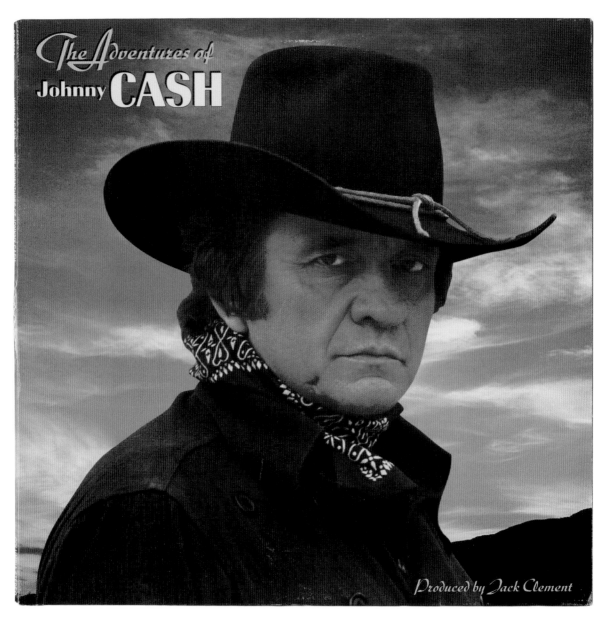

The Adventures of Johnny Cash. *Courtesy of Sony Music Entertainment*

of the Sons of the Pioneers. The percolating rhythm of the record is a good fit for Cash. The narrator in the song relishes his freedom as he travels all over the country without a single tie to bind him to anything or anyone. The train is his means of escape to go "where there ain't no snow a-fallin'." It's a picturesque narrative about a man who chose to leave home and ramble around the country without a care in the world. Cash changes the harmony-laden Sons version and gives it a faster pace and more urgent feel. The song was originally recorded for Sun Records in 1956 in an incomplete version but never released. Cash revived it and rerecorded it for his Columbia debut two years later.

In 1963 Cash released the previously mentioned "Casey Jones." And in 1964 he first recorded "The Wabash Cannonball" on *Keep on the Sunny Side: The Carter Family with Special Guest Johnny Cash.* "The Wabash Cannonball" is an old folk song about a fictional train, believed to have been written by J. A. Roff in 1882. A. P. Carter re-arranged the song, and the original Carter Family recorded it in 1929. In 1936 Roy Acuff recorded it in an arrangement that ultimately became his theme song. Anita Carter opens this version with her beautiful, crystalline voice taking the lead all the way through, with Johnny barely audible on the track. In 1966 Cash took "The Wabash Cannonball" for a memorable ride on the *Happiness Is You* album. Though the train in the title may be fictitious, Cash's performance is dynamic and very real.

In 1964 Cash recorded "Engine 143," a slow, sparse, subdued acoustic version of the A. P. Carter train song about the FFV (Flying Fast Virginian) railroad train, the "fastest on the line." The narrator tells of an engineer named George, whose mother warns him to be careful running the train while trying to make up for lost time. The engine bursts into flames after it crashes into the rocks. George is injured and his father, a doctor, tries to save him, but George wants to die for the engine he loves, Engine 143. It's a sad, dirge-like tale that might have slowed down the pace of the *Orange Blossom Special* album had it been included. It remained unreleased in the United States until it was included as a bonus track on the 2002 Legacy CD reissue of *Orange Blossom Special*. In August 2004, a new version of Cash singing "Engine 143" was included on the John Carter Cash–produced all-star *The Unbroken Circle: The Musical Heritage of the Carter Family.* According to John Carter, this was Cash's last completed vocal before his death. But his voice seems to build up strength just as the train does, before breaking for the tragic ending.

A Thing about Trains

Cash didn't take long to usher in the seventies with a train song, albeit a different kind. "Southwind," from Cash's critically acclaimed *Hello, I'm Johnny Cash* album is a self-penned sequel of sorts to Cash's classic "Big River." This time, it's the South

Wind, a passenger train operated jointly by the Pennsylvania Railroad, the Louisville and Nashville Railroad, the Atlantic Coastline Railroad, and the Florida East Coast Railway, which ran from 1940 through the 1970s. The wind replaces the river as the metaphorical means of escape and freedom for the woman the narrator sorely misses. It's a breezy song of pining for someone who has decided to leave. As with the narrator in "Big River," the singer wants to follow her and track her down, although he knows that she is gone, and that the south wind will "take her fast and take her far, 'cause that's the way she always likes to go."

Jack Clement's "I've Got a Thing About Trains," also from *Hello, I'm Johnny Cash*, is a first-rate ballad that mourns the passing of the passenger train. And who better than Johnny to put across that point? He sings it with a mixture of nostalgia and anger as he laments the cost of progress and wishes he could still go for a train ride. We feel the singer's frustration as he wonders what he will say when his son asks him what it was like to ride a train. The same holds true for Cash's cover of "The City of New Orleans," as the singer admonishes the passengers to please refrain because "the train's got the disappearing railroad blues."

Train nostalgia is once again the subject of Cash's "Destination Victoria Station" from the *Strawberry Cake* album. England's Victoria Station was the place that soldiers would leave from to go off to war and then return to in order to meet with their loved ones under the clock above the station. Cash explains that he wrote a love song based around this historic train station. In the song the narrator is hoping that his girl will come back to him as he waits for her under the clock. That same year Cash wrote "Daughter of a Railroad Man" for the *One Piece at a Time* album. It combines two themes Cash is quite comfortable with: fading love and trains. This time the central figure is the daughter of a railroad man who breaks hearts. Cash compares her physically to a train that's "long and sleek and made for movin'." It's a clever metaphor and a good Cash song overall.

In 1977 Cash paid tribute to his father in the aforementioned "Ridin' on the Cotton Belt," the train his father rode from town to town, looking for work during the Great Depression. For the *Silver* album in 1979, Cash recorded "The L&N Don't Stop Here Anymore," by American folk musician Jean Ritchie. Cash counted the semi-autobiographical ballad among his favorites. The Kentucky-born Ritchie spent her career writing and recording songs about the Appalachian mountain country. She played the dulcimer and was affectionately known as "The Mother of Folk." The song tells of a boy born and raised in the mouth of the Hazard hollow, whose father encouraged him to go to school and not become a miner like him. It's a true-to-life, firsthand account of the consequences of growing up in coal country.

The album *The Adventures of Johnny Cash* included "Ain't Gonna Hobo No More." Songwriter Don Devaney, who had also written "Someone Loves You Honey," recorded by Brenda Lee and a number 1 hit for Charley Pride in 1978, wrote the churning train song that details the last ride of a hobo who has long ridden the rails and is bidding all of his hobo friends goodbye. He's ready to settle down now and quit riding the Canadian Railroad boxcars.

Cash's love affair with train songs continued throughout his later recordings. For his *American Recordings* album he included his own "Let the Train Whistle Blow." It's an impressionistic ballad about a man waiting at the train station and not caring if his woman shows up or not. Cash seems to find a sense of comfort in using the train as a metaphor for passing time and in this song he warns the gossipers and liars that he will see them in the fire, as the familiar train whistle blows for him to get on board and escape without any regrets. The younger Cash was anxious and agitated waiting for his disappearing lover in "Train of Love," while the mature Cash of "Let the Train Whistle Blow" is ambivalent at best.

Cash included a mournful version of Hank Williams's tragic ballad "On the Evening Train," on 2006's *American V: A Hundred Highways*. We find the grieving narrator at the train station watching porters place his wife's casket on the train. Adding even more hurt is the image of his child crying beside him. The singer turns to walk away from the depot as he imagines his wife calling to him to take care of their baby. It's about as sad a scenario as one can perceive, and somehow Hank Williams had a way of making the most devastating of life's occurrences seem tolerable. Cash makes this little-known Hank Williams lament his own and it stands out as one of the most revelatory songs on this album.

On the same album, Cash wrote the opening track, "Like the 309." Cash, suffering from asthma, struggles to sing the line, "It should be awhile before I see Doctor Death, so it would sure be nice if I could get my breath." Cash defiantly explains that, "I'm not the crying nor the whining kind, 'til I hear the whistle of the 309." The train as metaphor for death is nothing new for Cash, but what is new is how close to the impending train Cash is in this riveting ballad. After a difficult first verse, Cash seems to gain his strength back as the song progresses, as if the power of the music had reinvigorated him. This would be Cash's last train song, and the last song Cash would record for an American Recordings album.

No Easy Run

Cash's "Come Along and Ride This Train" medley from *The Johnny Cash* Show album salutes the truck driver, whom Cash labels "the modern mover of America."

The Johnny Cash Show. *Courtesy of Sony Music Entertainment.*

The medley opens with "Six Days on the Road" a quintessential truck-driving ballad that reached number 2 on the country chart for Dave Dudley in 1963. It's followed by Dudley and Tom T. Hall's "There Ain't No Easy Run," an up-tempo ballad that references all the various trucking companies that were operating at the time as the singer explains to the trucker that "there ain't no easy run," especially since he's missing his woman back home. The song reached number 10 on the country chart for Dudley in 1968, as Cash was able to introduce it to an even wider audience through

television. And the medley concludes with Merle Travis's "Sailor on a Concrete Sea" a tribute to the truck driver who keeps our country moving along.

In 1974 Cash included the truck-driving song "All I Do Is Drive" on his *Ragged Old Flag* album. The singer questions an old truck driver about his job and what it means to him. The truck driver explains that all he does is drive in order to make a living. Cash seems fascinated by the truck driver's lifestyle and wants to learn all he can learn about it. In 2015 "All I Do Is Drive" was featured in Apple's iPhone 6 commercial.

Motorcycles and motorcycle riders also fascinated Cash because of their distinct sense of freedom and abandon. Johnny's self-penned "Rollin' Free" from the *Little Fauss and Big Halsy* soundtrack is a good example of this. The breezy ballad sets the tone for the film's theme about two motorcycle riders who drift freely across the country without being tied down to anything or anyone. It's a driving song about enjoying the freedom of experiencing "just the sun and the wind and the road and me." The narrator doesn't want any chains to tie him down and to live his life as he chooses.

Carl Perkins wrote "Ballad of Little Fauss and Big Halsy," and it was nominated for a Golden Globe Award for Best Original Song in 1971. Cash performs it with carefree abandon and captures the sense of freedom the two motorcycle racers embody. The original movie poster for the film claimed, "Little Fauss and Big Halsy — not your father's heroes." And Cash seems, as usual, to relish the fact that he's singing about two antiheroes who do not conform to society's rules.

Cash also recorded a few songs about boats as a means of escape. Initially, in "Port of Lonely Hearts," the narrator is dejectedly waiting for his ship to come in, preferably with a girl on board. He's determined to wait as long as it takes for love to arrive so he can leave the port of lonely hearts with the one he loves. "Fast Boat to Sydney," from *Carryin' On with Johnny Cash & June Carter,* is a charming little ballad written by June's sisters Helen and Anita Carter. The song is about an admitted "cheat and liar" who threatens to leave his woman behind and go as far away as he can on a fast boat to Sydney, Australia. But despite his wandering ways, she still loves him.

Wayfaring and Wandering

The motif of the free-spirited, wandering, wayfaring drifter always appealed to Cash. The notion of traveling from place to place was something Cash found enticing. Perhaps because he had grown up poor in Arkansas, Cash was drawn to songs about escape and travel.

"Bad News" depicts a different kind of drifter, one who has a bad reputation and is known as bad news everywhere he goes. He laughs maniacally as he recounts the failed attempts to slow him down or hang him, but the rebel in him just taunts authority and continues to laugh in the face of those who chase after him. It's a unique take, and a nice play on Johnny's original outlaw reputation. John D. Loudermilk wrote this song, which sounds tailor-made for Cash. It's fun to listen to him grunt and carry on as he recounts all he has to do to stay free of those who want to capture him. The song made it to number 8 on the country chart and served as a change of pace follow-up to his somber single, "The Ballad of Ira Hayes."

"Sing a Traveling Song," from *Hello, I'm Johnny Cash,* is an exceptional song with a story of its own. It's about a man who cannot settle down and live a calm life, but rather continually has to keep moving on. Johnny and June's nephew, Kenneth Jones, the son of June's sister Helen, wrote it. He was a promising young singer and songwriter who had signed a deal with Monument Records in Nashville before being killed in a car accident when he was sixteen. This song, which he wrote when he was fourteen, hints at what might have been and it's certainly a worthy addition to this fine album. Anita Carter's angelic harmony adds so much to the incisive lyric. Johnny thought so much of the song that he performed it live at Madison Square Garden and programmed it as the B-side of "What Is Truth."

The entirety of Cash's concept album *The Rambler* was based on the idea of the rambler searching from coast to coast for something he couldn't find. After we hear the closing of the car door and the revving of the engine, the song "Hit the Road and Go" begins and we learn that the singer is disillusioned with his life. With a road-map by his side, he decides to pull up stakes, hit the road and go. Cash informs us that when love is gone it's time to go as he recounts the first part of the rambler's travels, with his only companion being a car radio.

Cash closes out his award-winning album *Unchained* with a cover of "I've Been Everywhere," Hank Snow's number 1 country hit from 1962. Cash succeeds in stealing this song right out from under one of his musical heroes and making his record-ing the definitive version. If there were any justice in the universe this would have been a number 1 hit for Cash as well. He takes us for a musical travel-ogue through all of North America. Cash appears to have no problem handling the machine-gun-like rattling of place names. And through his American Recordings work, Cash seemed even more drawn to the notion of the drifting way of life. Surprisingly, it was Rick Rubin who brought Dolly Parton's "I'm a Drifter" for Cash to record. It was included on *Unearthed,* as Cash slows down Dolly's original tempo and enlists Tom Petty and the Heartbreakers for backup. It's a sad song about being alone, feeling lost and empty and perpetu-ally wandering down roads in order to feel alive and a part of something.

Folk singer Tom Paxton originally wrote and recorded "Can't Help but Wonder Where I'm Bound" in 1964 for his album *Ramblin' Boy.* Cash's version of the song was included on his post-humous 2006 release *American VI: Ain't No Grave.* As a folk ballad this is a rambling tale of a drifter wondering where he will eventually wind up. But in Cash's hands it becomes a treatise about the inevitable destination of our souls once our earthly journey is over. It's a panoramic journey through Cash's life as he recalls all the good and bad people he's met along the way, while he ponders his arrival at his ultimate destination.

On *American III: Solitary Man,* Cash covered a classic. Many artists have performed and recorded the folk song "Wayfaring Stranger" over the years, including Burl Ives, who recorded it in 1944 for his album *Wayfaring Stranger.* Cash may have heard this version on the radio, as a young boy in Dyess. Emmylou Harris even made it to number 7 on the country chart in 1980 with her sublime rendition. The song dates back to the nineteenth century and describes one person's journey through life and finding his ultimate reward. John Carter's former wife Laura suggested this song, and Cash turns in a performance that makes us believe that he is all but ready to cross over Jordan and finally make it to his heavenly home.

Chapter 16

THE MAN COMES AROUND

THE AMERICAN RECORDINGS

Johnny Cash's renewed relevance and musical
revival in collaboration with Rick Rubin

I n early 1993 Cash was disillusioned with the music industry and was all but ready to give it all up. He did not want to deal with record companies any longer and felt that he was no longer able to sell records. He believed that he was better off just working the road in smaller venues and touring with close friends and family, performing for people who really wanted to see him. And just when he had resigned himself to this new reality, a thirty-year-old record producer named Rick Rubin contacted Johnny's manager Lou Robin asking about the possibility of meeting with Cash. Rubin had watched Cash perform at Bob Dylan's Thirtieth Anniversary Celebration at Madison Square Garden, and he was greatly impressed with what he saw. Rubin was drawn to Cash's outlaw persona and viewed him as the perpetual outsider who was no longer embraced by the country-music establishment but would be an icon to a younger generation. Cash agreed to meet with Rubin backstage after a show in Los Angeles.

Rick Rubin expressed his interest in having Cash record for his label, American Recordings, and told Cash he wanted to hear the music Cash hoped to record. Rubin was a highly regarded producer of hip-hop, metal, punk, and hard rock artists such as the Red Hot Chili Peppers, the Beastie Boys, Aerosmith, and AC/DC. Rubin was familiar with Cash's catalog of music and believed he could work well with him by just letting him do what he wanted. Cash, for his part, was wary at first and quite disillusioned from past dealings with producers and record label executives. He was not sure he could trust Rubin. He was convinced that Rubin would eventually lose interest and forget about him. However, Rubin did not give up on Cash and was finally able to convince him that he truly wanted to work with Cash on Cash's own terms.

Cash had been yearning for this type of musical freedom for some time, and Rubin told Cash that he would only have to come to Rubin's house with his guitar and play his songs for him in his living room. Rubin explained that Cash could play the songs he loved with no interference, and that Rubin would begin the recording process once Cash felt comfortable. This was a long held desire of Cash's: to simply record an album with just a guitar and vocal and let the songs speak for themselves. What was also inspiring for Cash was that he was being courted by a new alternative audience that began when he recorded "The Wanderer" with U2. This was specifically the audience Rubin wanted to attract for Cash. Country radio had lost interest in him, and country fans were no longer buying his records.

Rubin knew that there was a younger generation of music lovers who truly identified with Cash's cool, rebellious persona, and would want to hear any new music he released, as long as it was not over-produced, sweetened, or robbed of its purity. The result of this union was the rebirth of Johnny Cash. Rubin guided Cash through some of the most important music of his life and helped him bravely face his own mortality as no other artist had ever done before. One cannot overestimate the magnitude of Cash's American Recordings, and as Cash himself noted in his autobiography, "Rick really did succeed in what he set out to do: he got the honest, unadulterated essence of Johnny Cash, whatever that is" (Cash, *Autobiography*, 346).

An Acoustic Album

American Recordings was released in April 1994, and it was the first album Rubin produced for his new label American Recordings, which was formerly called Def American. Cash had wanted to record an acoustic album like this one for over thirty years. He recalled talking with Marty Robbins about just such a project thirty years earlier and that he suggested it to Columbia right after that. The executives at Columbia thought it was a bad idea, as did Mercury Records executives when he approached them years later. He recalls in his autobiography that he even had a name picked out for the album: *Late and Alone*. Cash was elated when Rick Rubin suggested this very concept for him, although Cash was wary about whether a younger audience would be interested in his music. The new album featured just Johnny and his guitar, no bells, no whistles, and no complicated arrangements. Cash recalled, "It was a great experience. I took my music all the way back to the heart, and recorded about a hundred songs. Then we listened to it all, marked out the songs that had the late-and-alone, intimate feeling we were looking for, and went to work getting them right" (Cash, *Autobiography*, 346). And get it right they did.

American Recordings brought Cash back in a big way. Free of all the misconceptions of what others thought he should be, Cash had succeeded with the help of Rubin in reinventing himself and his music the way he wanted, as a modern-day Woody Guthrie with just his guitar and voice. Cash included a six-page foldout facsimile of notepad pages with extensive liner notes describing his childhood on the Delta and the songs he first heard on the radio. He tells about when he bought his first guitar while serving in the Air Force in Germany, and the formation of his first group, the Barbarians. The decidedly folk-flavored album made it to number 23 on the country album chart and number 110 pop. This was Cash's highest-charting country album since *The Baron* in 1981, and his best pop showing since *A Johnny Cash Portrait: His Greatest Hits, Volume II* in 1971. *American Recordings* also earned Cash the 1995 Grammy Award for Best Contemporary Folk Album. This was Cash's first Grammy since 1971, when he and June won for Best Country Performance by a Duo or Group for "If I Were a Carpenter."

The album contains many highlights, including the aforementioned "Delia's Gone," "Let The Train Whistle Blow," "Drive On," "Why Me," "Oh, Bury Me Not," "Down There by the Train," and "Like a Soldier." Cash and Rubin recorded dozens of songs during these sessions, and ultimately selected thirteen for the album. Rubin's plan was to introduce Cash to a brand-new, younger audience.

Cash's former stepson-in-law, singer-songwriter Nick Lowe, wrote and originally recorded, "The Beast In Me," a scathing and introspective realization that inside the singer, and all of us, lurks a sinful beast, as a metaphor for evil. As such, we must learn to live with pain and restraint. This was Cash's yin and yang, the love and hate that coexisted together within the darkness of his soul. Cash's stark vocal is both menacing and tender at the same time as he warns us about the beast that lives within him. Kris Kristofferson addressed a similar theme in his song "The Silver Tongued Devil and I." We are haunted by Cash's contradictory request for God to kill "the beast in me."

Rubin helped introduce Cash to many recent alternative songs. One such song was the harrowing "Thirteen" by Glenn Danzig, who fronted the heavy metal band Danzig. He wrote this song specifically for Cash, and Cash ably delivers the lyrics about a troubled man who has the number thirteen tattooed on his neck. We are told the man was born in the soul of misery and has no name, just the number thirteen. There's a menacing element to this song and a suggestion that the narrator might just be Satan or evil incarnate.

It's hard to believe that "Bird on a Wire" is the first time Cash had covered a Leonard Cohen song. The critically acclaimed Canadian singer-songwriter and Cash had been labelmates on Columbia for years. Cohen had found great success by writing songs such as "Suzanne," "Hallelujah," and "Sisters of Mercy." Judy Collins originally recorded "Bird on a Wire," and Cohen recorded his own version for his 1969 album *Songs from a Room*. Cohen has described this song as being a simple country song, but the poetic, enigmatic lyrics make it something quite unique. Once you've heard the opening lines of the song detailing the singer's quest for redemption, you can never forget them. "Like a bird on a wire, like a drunk in a midnight choir, I have tried in my way to be free." Cash's performance of this song is nothing less than magnificent, and one only wishes that Cash had somehow recorded a cover of Cohen's "Hallelujah."

"Tennessee Stud" was recorded live at the Viper Room, a Sunset Strip, Los Angeles nightclub owned at the time by actor Johnny Depp. The song was originally a number 5 charting country single for Eddy Arnold in 1959. Songwriter Jimmie Driftwood

("The Battle of New Orleans") wrote the song. Driftwood based the song on two generations of his wife's family. It's an engaging story-song about the narrator leaving Tennessee in 1825 and riding through the Arkansas mud on a Tennessee stud. The narrator drifts down across the Rio Grande and gets in a fight with a gambler, who he ends up shooting and taking his horse. And Cash's ornery side takes over as he describes riding back to Tennessee where he whipped his sweetheart's Pa and outlaw brother, as the young audience in the Viper Room shouts and cheers him on. He rides off with his sweetheart and we learn that they eventually have a baby and the Tennessee stud has a colt with his Tennessee mare, proclaiming, "I loved the girl with the golden hair / And the Tennessee Stud loves the Tennessee Mare." It's that rare happy ending on an otherwise dark album. Cash introduced "Tennessee Stud" to a new audience when it was included on the soundtrack of Quentin Tarantino's 1997 movie *Jackie Brown*, an adaptation of Elmore Leonard's novel *Rum Punch*.

Cash's self-penned "Redemption" addresses salvation through Jesus. The first verse reminds us of the blood Christ shed, "From the hands it came down / From the side it came down / From the feet it came down / And ran to the ground," along with a teardrop from which the Tree of Life grew. And from here we learn about original sin and meet Lucifer who comes along with his associated number, 666. It's a dark, meditative explication of the cost of human life. Cash sounds extra weary here, as if he's fighting to get the words out.

With the Heartbreakers

Two years later Cash released his second American Recordings album, *Unchained*. For this album, Rubin recruited Tom Petty and members of Petty's band the Heartbreakers, Mick Fleetwood and Lindsey Buckingham of Fleetwood Mac, Flea (the bassist for Red Hot Chili Peppers) and Marty Stuart, among others. Despite the plethora of rock and alternative musicians, the album took a decidedly country turn and included songs that spanned the decades from Carter Family folk ballads of the forties, pop and country hits of the fifties, sixties, and seventies, up through more recent alternative rock songs of the eighties and nineties. *Unchained* features three Cash-penned songs: two from the Sun years and a new ballad. Cash wrote extensive liner notes for the album, beginning with the mundane notion of eating a veggie burger, to recalling how he met June Carter in 1956 at the Ryman Auditorium in Nashville (although he had seen her perform before) and how he had said to her "I'm going to marry you someday," to which she replied, "Okay." Cash goes on to say it took seven more years but he knew they were born to be together. Cash writes, "I love songs about horses, railroads, land, judgment day, family hard times, whiskey, courtship, marriage, adultery, separation, murder, war, prison, rambling, damnation, home, salvation, death, pride, humor, piety, rebellion, patriotism, larceny, determination, tragedy, rowdiness, heartbreak and love. And Mother. And God." *Unchained* continued Cash's successful career-resurgence making it up to number 26 on the country album chart and 170 pop. It also won Cash the Grammy Award for Best Country Album in 1998.

Unchained contains fourteen songs, including the previously discussed cover of "Country Boy," "Kneeling Drunkard's Prayer," "Southern Accents," "Memories Are Made of This," "Meet Me in Heaven," "I've Been Everywhere," along with a completely revised cover of "Mean Eyed Cat." Johnny goes back to 1955 to revive "Mean Eyed Cat," another early Sun favorite. With the top-notch lineup of musicians on this album, Cash had a much more dynamic backing band than ever before. And he certainly takes advantage of the musicians on board as he delivers a rousing rendition about the woman who ran off on him after spending all his money on her mean eyed cat. What makes this new version even more interesting is that it has a happy ending. Thanks to a newly written verse we learn that the singer has tracked down his girl in Arkansas, where he finds her working at Trucker's World. He walks in; she leaves with him; they end up back home together curled up on the sofa with her mean-eyed cat. Cash recalled in the liner notes, "'Mean Eyed Cat' took forty years to write. I hadn't finished it in 1955, when, at a session, I sang the first two verses for Sam Phillips. He said, 'That's a keeper. I like that.' I said, 'But, it isn't finished.' He said it was good enough. I was totally surprised when it was released not long afterward. And after all these years, every time I would see the title in print, or hear the song on the radio, I'd cringe. Never once did I do the song on stage, and as the years passed, it bugged me more and more that the song was unfinished. So, about a year ago, I wrote the third verse. When I brought it to the sessions, it was like a new song. Finally, after 41 years, I'm satisfied with 'Mean Eyed Cat.'"

Singer-songwriter Beck, who scored a Top 10 pop single with his song "Loser" in 1994, wrote the ballad "Rowboat," that finds the singer asking the rowboat to take him back to shore after his woman has left him. The singer is hurting badly and reaching for anything to help soothe his pain. There's an angry, destructive underpinning to the song that Cash delivers with subtle menace. Rick Rubin brought this song to Cash, and it was originally recorded by Beck on his 1994 album *Stereopathetic Soulmanure.*

Cash retreats back to more familiar territory with his rendition of the heart-rending ballad "The One Rose (That's Left in My Heart)," which was originally recorded in 1930 by Jimmie Rodgers.

Cash's performance is imbued with pure country devotion to his dear loved one until a black cloud appears out of a blue sky to break his heart in two by taking away the one rose that's left in his heart. This is exactly the type of music Cash wanted to reintroduce to a modern-day audience, and as such is one of the most hauntingly beautiful covers on this album.

Cash's son-in-law and band member Jimmy Tittle brought "Unchained" to him. Nashville songwriter Jude Johnstone wrote the song. She was a friend of Tittle's wife, Kathy Cash, and she had also written Trisha Yearwood's hit "The Woman Before Me." "Unchained" is another song about looking back on one's less than exemplary life and hoping for redemption and freedom from one's worldly chains. The singer prays to "Take this weight from me, let my spirit be unchained." There's a prevailing sense of darkness as the singer confronts his own mortality and yearns to know what lies in store for him.

Also in October 1997, *Cash: The Autobiography* was published. The book was Cash's second autobiography, following *Man in Black*, and was written with journalist Patrick Carr. Shortly after the publication of this book, Cash endured a major health scare on October 25 on stage during a performance in Flint, Michigan. As he reached down to pick up a guitar pick Cash stumbled and nearly fell over. He had trouble standing up and needed assistance. He revealed to the audience that he was suffering from Parkinson's disease. An official press release regarding Cash's condition was issued on October 27, explaining that Cash was canceling his scheduled promotion tour for his new book and that Johnny and June would be postponing their upcoming concert appearances.

A follow-up press release in November revealed that Cash had entered Nashville's Baptist Hospital to treat Shy-Drager syndrome, a Parkinson's-related illness that attacks the nervous system. The original prognosis gave Cash eighteen months to live. Cash was released from the hospital but quickly readmitted suffering from double pneumonia. He was placed on a respirator and put into a medically induced coma. The family had gathered around him, and June asked everyone to pray for him. The prayers seemed to have worked because Cash miraculously emerged from the coma and began the slow recovery process. One year later he was readmitted to Baptist Hospital.

Johnny and June spent January 1999 at their home in Jamaica. Cash's health was in decline. He was feeling tired and needed to get as much rest as he could. In February he was honored with the Lifetime Achievement Award at the Grammy Awards Ceremony. Unfortunately, Cash was unable to attend, so June accepted it on his behalf. In April a who's who of music superstars and legends gathered at New York's Hammerstein Ballroom to salute Cash. *The All-Star Tribute to Johnny Cash* was taped on April 6 and featured live performances by Willie Nelson, Kris Kristofferson, Sheryl Crow, Emmylou Harris, Trisha Yearwood, Chris Isaak, Mary Chapin Carpenter, and Marty Stuart. Bob Dylan, Bruce Springsteen, and U2 offered taped performances to honor Johnny. The biggest surprise of the evening was Cash's unplanned appearance onstage, his first in eighteen months. To the extreme delight of the audience he performed "Folsom Prison Blues" with Bob Wootton, W. S. Holland, Earl Poole Ball, John Carter Cash, and original Tennessee Two member Marshall Grant. This was the first time the Tennessee Three had been together in nineteen years. Cash thanked everyone and closed the show with "I Walk the Line," featuring June and the entire cast joining in. In October 1999, Cash was admitted yet again to Baptist Hospital for stitches after falling and cutting his leg, and later that month he was readmitted to the hospital suffering from pneumonia.

An Eagerly Anticipated Album

Even though Cash's health was in decline at the start of the new century, he was determined to continue recording new material with Rick Rubin. In January, he was in the studio working on new songs for an upcoming album. And in October 2000, Cash's new album *American III: Solitary Man* was released on American Recordings. It contained the aforementioned "Wayfaring Stranger," and the Cash-Haggard duet "I'm Leavin' Now," along with twelve other songs.

It had been four years since his last album, so this new one was eagerly anticipated. John Carter Cash was the Associate Producer and worked closely with his father on the material for this album. John Carter, along with Jimmy Tittle, would be involved in all future American recordings. Cash once again wrote extensive liner notes for this album, discussing the inspiration for various songs and explaining how he recorded the album in a cabin, in the middle of a fifty-acre compound surrounded by cedar trees, deer, goats, and peacocks. The critics responded favorably to another sparsely produced album in the American Recordings series. It made it up to number 11 on the country album chart, Cash's best showing since *One Piece at a Time* hit number 2 in 1976. *Solitary Man* reached number 88 on the pop chart and would also win Cash a Grammy Award for Best Male Country Vocal Performance.

Following his recording of "Southern Accents" from *Unchained*, Cash wisely chose to cover the Tom Petty classic "I Won't Back Down" a scathing song of defiance and resilience. Even with his weakened voice, there is an inordinate amount of power revealed when Cash attests that "you can stand me up at the gates of hell but I won't back down." This is the no-nonsense Cash we've come to expect and admire. Cash asked Tom Petty to sing

with him making this the perfect introduction to a spirited new collection of standards both old and new.

While at first "Solitary Man," an early composition from pop icon Neil Diamond, might seem like an odd choice for Cash, the end result is surprisingly good. With an assist from Tom Petty on guitar and vocals, this song finds the singer listing all the women and pleasures of life he's enjoyed before always ending up alone as a solitary man. Cash certainly may have been frustrated at times during his career, feeling that his audience may have abandoned him at certain points. So the woman he is searching for in the song may be a metaphor for the love and acceptance he felt he might have missed out on during lulls in his career, until now.

"That Lucky Old Sun (Just Rolls Around Heaven All Day)" was one of Johnny's favorite songs as a young man. In fact, he had won a talent contest singing the song as a boy. In the liner notes he says that he can feel lazy just thinking about the lyrics to the song. It was a number 1 pop hit for crooner Frankie Laine in 1949. Louis Armstrong, Frank Sinatra, and Vaughn Monroe also covered the song, with Monroe's version reaching number 9 on the pop chart in 1949. Willie Nelson released his rendition of the standard on his 1976 album *The Sound in Your Mind.*

Cash takes on his second U2 song with "One." It was originally released as a single by U2 from their 1991 album *Achtung Baby.* "One" is a song about unification and banding together in the guise of a love song, explaining, "We're one but we're not the same, we get to carry each other." The lyric warns us that we have but one life and we must do the best we can with it and make it matter. Cash turns U2's rock ballad into an intimate folk song with a grand message.

In the liner notes Cash calls "Nobody" the oldest song on the album and relates how the song's author, Bert Williams, had performed it in vaudeville shows a hundred years before. Cash had first heard the song on a Bing Crosby album, and turns in a theatrical performance of this old warhorse. The singer runs down a list of all the things he's missing, ultimately realizing that he has nobody.

Australian singer-songwriter Nick Cave, leader of the alternative band the Bad Seeds wrote "The Mercy Seat" and released his own version of it in 1988. In this recitation, Cash is the self-professed innocent man who's taken from his home and put on death row with the mercy seat (electric chair) waiting for him. He's at peace believing that he's innocent, and following the example of Christ, knowing that God is never far away as he's prepared to be put to death. The mercy seat also refers to the throne of God the narrator is looking forward to seeing. It's a chilling rundown of the minutes the narrator is counting down before he's strapped into the mercy seat and executed. He's not afraid to die and is almost anxiously awaiting his ultimate freedom from this life.

Cash had previously recorded David Allan Coe's "Cocaine Carolina" on his *John R. Cash* album, and always seemed intrigued by Coe's wild outlaw persona. Coe's irreverent appearance (tattoos, long hair) and contradictory life story (how many years he spent in prison and the nature of his crime) did not obscure the fact that he is a first-rate songwriter. About "Would You Lay with Me (in a Field of Stone)" Cash wrote in the album liner notes, "I realize that generally songs don't say anything that songs weren't saying a hundred years ago; the difference is we are saying it in a different way. Like David Allan Coe's song 'Would You Lay with Me (in a Field of Stone),' a harsh challenge to a lover, coming from his beat vision of possibilities. Good old Coe, there's a man who is different." "Would You Lay with Me" was a number 1 hit for Tanya Tucker in 1974. The song earned its fair share of controversy when some felt it was an inappropriate choice of material for an artist who was then fifteen years old. The song's provocative, sensual lyric recited by a teenage Tanya might have raised a few eyebrows, but it certainly didn't stop the song from topping the country chart.

Cash probably first heard "Mary of the Wild Moor" on the Louvin Brothers' classic 1956 album *Tragic Songs of Life*. Cash claimed that the song never left his mind and he finally had the opportunity to record it. It's a haunting, gothic tale of Mary coming home across the wild moor on a cold winter night, with her child, to her own father's door. She begs her father to let them in before the child perishes from the cold winds of the moor. The father turns her away only to find her dead on his doorstep the next morning, but the child still alive. The father ultimately dies of grief and the child dies too, making this one of the most heartbreaking songs you will ever hear. It's sad, mournful, and as tragic a country song as you will find.

In February 2001, Cash was once again admitted to Baptist Hospital in Nashville, suffering from pneumonia. His poor health kept him from attending the forty-third annual Grammy Awards ceremony to accept his award for *Solitary Man.* Cash kept a low profile during the spring and reemerged only in June to appear at the Carter Family Fold in Maces Spring with June and daughter Rosanne, where he performed a few songs. In July Johnny and June attended Chet Atkins's funeral, and in October he was admitted again to Baptist Hospital suffering from bronchitis.

On February 13, 2002, country music, and the music world in general, suffered a great loss with the passing of Waylon Jennings, after a long battle with diabetes. In April, President George W. Bush presented Cash with the National Medal of Arts at a ceremony at Constitution Hall in Washington, DC. Also receiving an award was actor Kirk Douglas, who costarred with Cash in the 1971 movie *A Gunfight,* Cash's only starring role in a feature film. In September, Cash received the Spirit of Americana Free Speech Award at the first annual Americana Music Awards in Nashville. Also in September, two Cash tribute albums were released: *Kindred Spirits: A Tribute to the songs of Johnny Cash* and *Dressed in Black: A Tribute to Johnny Cash.*

The Last Completed Album

November saw the release of *American IV: The Man Comes Around,* which would ultimately be Johnny's last completed album before his death on September 12, 2003. Cash's health was in steady decline during the recording of this album, but he always found solace in the studio, where he again immersed himself. He recorded two duets with June for her 2002 album *Wildwood Flower* before cutting fourteen new songs for his fourth American Recordings CD. He wrote only one new song for this album, the title song, and revisited two older tracks, one from his early Sun days and the other from the early seventies. The result was one of his most critically acclaimed albums to date and his best ranking on the country album chart, tying *One Piece at a Time,* with both albums reaching number 2. *The Man Comes Around* climbed to number 22 on the pop album chart, his best showing since *A Thing Called Love* in 1972. The album went on to win Cash another Grammy Award for Best Country Male Vocal Performance of 2003 for the song "Give My Love to Rose," which he had first released in 1957. The video for the song "Hurt" won a Grammy for Best Short Form Video at the 2004 Awards. The album also won the Country Music Association's Album of the Year for 2003.

"The Man Comes Around" was one of the last songs Cash wrote before his death and it certainly leaves a lasting impression. It's filled with biblical references, mostly from the Book of Revelation, as Cash ponders his own mortality. Cash claimed that he was inspired to write the song after having a dream in which Queen Elizabeth II of England had told him that he was "like a thorn tree in the whirlwind." Cash used the line from the Book of Job in the song and went from there. The song begins with a frightening spoken introduction with Cash reciting lines from Revelation describing the coming of the Four Horsemen of the Apocalypse. Of course "the Man" refers to the second coming of Christ in Revelations, and the song is filled with vivid imagery taken from the Scriptures. Trumpets and pipers and one hundred angels singing herald the return of the Lord along with the virgins from the Gospel of Matthew, who are trimming their wicks in preparation for His arrival. Cash's breathless vocal makes the lyric even more dramatic as he prophesizes about what's to come. Cash is adamant about what he believes will occur during the final judgment day, when, "Some are born and some are dying, it's Alpha and Omega's kingdom come."

Rick Rubin brought Cash the song "Hurt," a grungy ballad of agony and despair written by Trent Reznor from the perspective of a drug-addled young man who is devastated after losing a lover. The singer sounds self-destructive in the Nine Inch Nails original from the 1994 suicide-themed concept album *The Downward Spiral*. Who would imagine that Cash would turn this song into a self-reflective look backward at this life as it was beginning to slip away from him? All the earthly joys and frustrations were falling away like his "empire of dirt," and something more and better had to be awaiting him in the hereafter. This was Cash's cathartic culmination of his life's journey in song. The award-winning video only added to the impact as we witness a weak and physically deteriorated Cash looking back through the pain on his youth and success and watching it all disintegrate right before his very eyes. This is one of the bravest performances by an artist in any genre of music. To boldly put everything out there for the entire world to see as one's last will and testament in song was unparalleled. Not Hank Williams, nor Jimmie Rodgers, no one had ever undertaken such a breathtaking and vulnerable yet defiant stand in the face of impending death. And no one who listens to this song can come away without feeling his or her own sense of hurt, while marveling at the naked, emotional brilliance of Cash's performance. "Hurt" would win Cash the award for the Country Music Association's Single of the Year 2003, and for Video of the Year. After 137 singles released over forty-seven years, this song would also mark Cash's last appearance on the country chart, making it to number 56.

Cash revisits "Give My Love to Rose," one of his classic early favorites from the Sun years, and the result earned him the 2003 Grammy Award for Best Country Male Vocal Performance. The irony is that country radio had long since given up on Johnny, and this song was hardly played and did not even make the country chart. Radio could ignore Cash, but the Country Music Association could not ignore excellence. Mustering up as much energy as he could, Cash relates the tale as an older, wiser storyteller recounting an age-old story. Bruce Springsteen chose this song to perform for the 2002 album *Kindred Spirits: A Tribute to Johnny Cash.* And it's no wonder, because Springsteen's songs echo back to the plaintive narratives of Cash's early Sun recordings. Springsteen, himself a great storyteller, has recognized Cash as a folk legend and a major inspiration in his songwriting, along with Woody Guthrie. "Give My Love to Rose" is a song that has passed the test of time, as Cash is not afraid to strip away all the intrusive country production and present the song so many years later as the folk ballad it has always been.

Cash takes on the inspirational Simon and Garfunkel classic "Bridge over Troubled Water" and turns it upside down. Art Garfunkel's angelic vocal is replaced with a raw, aching rumination by Cash with Fiona Apple singing harmony. It truly changes the entire scope of Paul Simon's lyric to hear it sung by the ravished Cash who even speaks part of the lyric and struggles to sing his heart out on other parts. Cash manages to bring the song back down to earth and imbue it with a folksy edge that opens the entire song up for reinterpretation. Critics may argue with this choice of song for Cash, but there is no question that he succeeded in reinventing it to fit his own style.

"I Hung My Head" is another haunting tale of atonement written by Gordon Sumner, better known as Sting. The narrator sits on a hill with his brother Jeb's rifle and takes practice aim at a man riding in the distance. The gun accidentally goes off and kills the lone rider. The narrator feels guilt and hangs his head in shame for what he has done. The narrator runs away and is finally caught hiding out by a sheriff who asks him why he did what he did. And the answer he comes up with is that he did what he did for no reason. This notion harks back to the narrator of "Folsom Prison Blues," who shoots a man "just to watch him die." The difference is that in this song the narrator is wracked with guilt and remorse for his actions, all too aware that he's done wrong. In the courthouse the judge asks him to explain his actions to the jury as he feels utter remorse, explaining "I felt the power of death over life, I orphaned his children, I widowed his wife." The reality is that even though he admits his sins and tries to atone, he is still sent to the gallows where he is hanged. But his faith still gives him the strength to pray for God's mercy in the end.

"The First Time Ever I Saw Your Face" was written by British folk singer-songwriter Ewan MacColl, and originally recorded by Gordon Lightfoot. In 1972 Roberta Flack recorded the song as a lovely ballad and took it to number 1 on the pop chart. Cash turns it back into a sparse folk song, as he seems to ruminate back upon a distant lover's countenance. Lightfoot's youthful, courting croon and Flack's lilting, ethereal vocal are replaced by Cash's worn and wearied reading. The song becomes a heartbreaking dirge that finds him affirming his eternal love as if this would be the last breath his tired lungs could muster. This is another song choice critics have questioned. But there is no doubt that Cash succeeded in doing what he set out to do: record a song that would elicit mixed emotions from listeners and leave them feeling stunned and shaken by what they had just heard. When he sings, "I know our joy would fill the earth and last 'til the end of time my love," we sense that the end of time that he speaks of is upon him and approaching sooner rather than later.

English singer-songwriter Martin Gore of the alternative rock group Depeche Mode wrote "Personal Jesus" after reading the book *Elvis and Me* by Priscilla Presley. Just as Elvis was Priscilla's personal savior, the song satirizes the notion that some people turn their lovers into their own form

of deity, relying on them for a sense of self-worth and forgiveness from sin when they do wrong. Cash seems to take on the role of the personal confessor who is able to listen to, and help guide, the individual to find the true faith they are searching for. If one can reach out to his or her own personal Jesus to hear their prayers, then that personal Jesus can lead the individual back to the true faith and help them establish a relationship with God.

Cash selected the oft-recorded Lennon and McCartney classic "In My Life" as his first recorded song by the Beatles. It's yet another questionable song choice for Cash. The nostalgic lament allows Cash to look back on his life and times without regret but the song is sung in a weathered voice that denotes a sense of finality. Gone is the Beatles bright arrangement with lovely harmonies, and its replaced with a thoughtful, somber reading of the thought-provoking and bittersweet lyric.

Cash first recorded the traditional folk ballad "Danny Boy" on his *Orange Blossom Special* album. He told his version of the song's origin and proceeded to render a rich, deep-throated vocal performance. More than thirty-five years later, he turns in an equally evocative rendition, albeit with a more tender and thoughtful reading. Interestingly, this time around Cash sings the song in the first person, changing his original lyric to, "But if you come and all the flowers are dying / And I am dead, as dead I well may be / You'll come and find the place where I am lying / And kneel and say an ave there for me." The older Cash is quite possibly ready to face his own mortality now. His voice begins to break by the end of the song and we can feel the emotional impact the recording has taken on him. But there's a true sense of beauty in its fragility, and the song makes just as strong an impression as ever before.

The Eagles' Don Henley cowrote "Desperado" with bandmate Glenn Frey, and joins Cash on this revelatory reading of a song that seems as if it were written especially for Cash. It feels as if he is conversing with himself about the pitfalls of his own life when he sings, "These things that are pleasing you can hurt you somehow." Cash had certainly ridden his share of fences and if ever a term could best define Johnny Cash, "desperado," would be it.

"Tear Stained Letter" first appeared on the *A Thing Called Love* album. Intended as a single, the song title was boldly highlighted on the album's cover along with "Kate" and "Papa Was a Good Man." Cash never forgot the song, and thirty years later he brings it back with a more fleshed-out and upbeat arrangement than the original. The song is more than worth revisiting; however the new arrangement finds Cash struggling to keep up the pace. But more importantly, Cash adds a few new verses to the song, about how it was the music in their lives that was suddenly gone that made things go wrong between the lovers in the song. It's an interesting new twist that tries to explain why the singer feels compelled to write a tear-stained letter in the first place.

Cash revisits another song from his *Sings the Ballads of the True West* album, this time the western-folk classic "The Streets of Laredo." With minimal production, this song sounds like an old familiar favorite being retold by a master storyteller. Cash revises an integral part of the lyric. In the original recording he beckons that not a word about his death be mentioned to his lover and that in time she'll find another and his name will pass on. In this version it's the name of the man who killed him that he wishes not be mentioned and thus his name will pass on. And in this cover the cowboy is taken and buried in the Green Valley where, we are told, his marker is still standing until this day. Any song revisions Cash made were well thought out and planned, and that's what makes this new recording so essential.

Cash could not have chosen a more fitting finale to this album than the old pop standard "We'll Meet Again." He had first heard the song as performed by the Ink Spots and never forgot it. This would be the last song on a new Cash album before his death nine months later. The 1939 Vera Lynn wartime ballad evokes all the pent-up emotion the listener feels while experiencing this album. It's a fond farewell and a hope that we will meet again some sunny day. There's a sense of optimism behind the sad reality that Cash sensed that it wouldn't be long before he would leave the world singing a song. Of course, the reality is he left us over 1500 songs that we will be singing for years to come.

Johnny and June spent Christmas 2002 in Jamaica. Upon their return, Johnny was admitted to Baptist Hospital in Nashville for surgery to remedy an ulcer on his foot. He was released from the hospital, but readmitted almost immediately after falling at home. He remained in the hospital for three weeks. Upon his release he went back into his home studio to work on a planned gospel album.

In March 2003, Cash was readmitted to Baptist Hospital and placed on a ventilator. And once again he regained his strength and went back home. The CMT TV channel named Cash the most important artist in the history of country music, with Hank Williams coming in at number two. In April, John's sister Louise passed away, but he was too ill to attend the funeral. That same month, June was admitted to the hospital and on May 15, 2003, June died from complications relating to heart-valve replacement surgery. On May 18, June's funeral took place at the First Baptist Church in Hendersonville. Frail and heartbroken, Cash attended the service in a wheelchair.

For the three months following June's death, Johnny threw himself into his work. He found solace in the recording studio and escaped there daily to record with John Carter. His work gave him purpose, and despite his failing health, he arrived at the studio in his wheelchair and recorded until he was too tired to continue.

In June and July, Cash appeared at the Carter Family Fold in Maces Spring, Virginia. On both occasions he summoned enough energy to perform a few songs with attending family and friends. Upon his return to Hendersonville, Johnny's first wife, Vivian, stopped by to visit with him and tell him about a book she was writing about their early years together. He was very supportive and genuinely happy to see her.

On July 30, legendary Sun founder Sam Phillips died after a yearlong illness. And in August, Cash was once again admitted to Baptist Hospital suffering from pancreatitis. He was ultimately released on September 10, and went home to rest before being readmitted on September 11, when he fell ill in his home and had to be rushed to the hospital.

With his family gathered around him, on Friday, September 12 Johnny Cash died at the age of seventy-one, from complications from diabetes that resulted in respiratory failure. Condolences were sent from all over the world. Cash's manager Lou Robin issued a statement: "The family of Johnny Cash in this sad hour is greatly comforted by the outpouring of love and respect for his remarkable life. We take solace in the knowledge that he is again reunited with his dearest companion, June. Our lives, and indeed the entire planet, will forever feel the emptiness of his loss, but his music and the greatness of his spirit will endure."

President George W. Bush issued a statement that read, "Johnny Cash was a music legend and American icon whose career spanned decades and genres. His resonant voice and human compassion reached the hearts and souls of generations, and he will be missed. Laura joins me in sending our thoughts and prayers to his family."

Johnny Cash's funeral took place at the First Baptist Church in Hendersonville, Tennessee on September 15. Among the attendees were Lou Robin, Jack Clement, Kris Kristofferson, Emmylou Harris, and Dr. Franklin Graham. Pallbearers included Larry Gatlin and Marty Stuart. Following the funeral, Cash was buried at the Hendersonville Memory Gardens cemetery.

In October, June's daughter Rosie Nix Adams was found dead on a bus in Clarksville, Tennessee, along with bluegrass fiddle player Jimmy Campbell. Their deaths were attributed to carbon monoxide poisoning. Rosie was forty-five years old. She was buried near her mother and stepfather.

Chapter 17

AIN'T NO GRAVE

THE SONGS LIVE ON

*The songs that Johnny Cash needed to
record near the end of his life*

I n one year and within months of each other, the world had lost both Johnny and June. There's no way to measure the impact their lives had on popular music and pop culture. Their remarkable lives were the subject and inspiration for a critically acclaimed motion picture (*Walk the Line*), a TV movie (*Ring of Fire*), as well as numerous songs celebrating their larger-than-life love story. And there were many more unreleased recordings, compilations and newly discovered masters that would flood the market in the years to come.

On November 25, a little over two months after Cash's death, *Unearthed* was released. The five-CD box set consisted of material that Cash had recorded between 1993 and 2003. The collection was planned before Cash's passing as a celebration of his first decade with American Recordings. The album included new material, outtakes, and alternate versions of previously released songs, a best-of CD of his work on American, and an entire album of inspirational songs taken from Cash's mother's hymn book that would be released six months later as a separate CD. *Unearthed* contains seventy-seven songs along with a book written by music journalist Sylvie Simmons that features the story of the recording sessions and a song-by-song explication by Cash.

The first disc is titled "Who's Gonna Cry" and features all-acoustic performances of songs that Cash had recorded before, or always wanted to record but never did. The first song is "The Long Black Veil," and Cash is in exceptionally fine voice for this cover of the murder ballad he had recorded at various times throughout his career. This time however, he switches the order of the verses, having the woman come to the narrator's grave and cry over his bones before we learn of his fate at the judge's hands. It's an interesting modification that demonstrates how Cash continued to reinvent his catalog of songs right up until the end.

The lovely ballad "Flesh and Blood" benefits greatly from this intimate acoustic performance. It's interesting to note that in the final verse it's a mockingbird that sings for the narrator and not a cardinal as in the earlier hit version. As mentioned earlier, Cash had originally titled the song "You Are What I Need" before changing it to "Flesh and Blood," and the bird in the original lyric was in fact a mockingbird, the state bird of Tennessee. Other songs Cash covers on this disc include "Just the Other Side of Nowhere," "Casey's Last Ride," "If I Give My Soul," and the previously discussed "Understand Your Man," "Banks of the Ohio," "Two Timin' Woman," "Going to Memphis," "No Earthly Good," and "Dark as a Dungeon."

Interestingly, Cash also revisits "The Caretaker," a song that was originally released on Cash's 1959 album *Songs of Our Soil*. Cash was listed as the sole songwriter on the original, but here shares writing credit with Gordon Jenkins, whose song "Crescent City Blues" Cash adapted into "Folsom Prison Blues." In the liner notes Cash recalls writing the song for an album called *Folk Songs* that, according to him, didn't turn out that well. Either he's confusing the title with *Songs of Our Soil*, or it simply slipped his mind that he had recorded it earlier. He goes on to say that he was a young man when he wrote it and admits, "You're right — singing it now — it does seem too much."

In the liner notes Cash says that "Waiting for a Train" is a song that he has been singing all his life, since he was four years old. Rick Rubin had asked him to record Jimmie Rodgers's "T for Texas." Instead Cash offered up this song, a favorite of his that he first recorded for his album *Blood, Sweat and Tears*.

Cash includes a new spoken introduction to "The Fourth Man in the Fire," that first appeared on *The Holy Land* album as "The Fourth Man." That version featured a full-blown arrangement with the Carter Family and the Statler Brothers joining in on the chorus. This performance works well as a stripped-down version, but there's no denying that the original arrangement really brought the song to life.

The first CD ends with "Book Review," a priceless exchange between Cash and Rick Rubin discussing a newly discovered book by Lebanese-American writer Kahlil Gibran, author of *The Prophet*. Rubin had given the book to Cash, who discusses Gibran's disillusionment with the Catholic priesthood and his passionate love for Lebanon. Cash loved the book and expresses his desire to record the audio book. And the disc closes with an alternate take of Tom Waits's "Down There by the Train." It's a more somber reading of a song that first appeared on the *American Recordings* album.

The second disc, titled "Trouble in Mind," contains full arrangements and is similar in feel to *Unchained*. Like that album it also features backup from Tom Petty and the Heartbreakers, and members of the Red Hot Chili Peppers, along with duet performances with June, Carl Perkins, and Willie Nelson. Previously discussed songs on this disc include "Pocahontas," "Heart of Gold," "I'm a Drifter," and "The Running Kind."

Cash explains that Roy Orbison's "Down the Line" was a song that Orbison was performing back during his Sun days, and it's one that Cash always loved. Cash had suggested the song to Rubin but was not happy with the way it turned out, so it was left unreleased until this album. The lighthearted rockabilly rave-up might have felt out of place on Cash's *Unchained* album. But it is a fun song and Heartbreaker Benmont Tench's rockabilly piano carries it along with energy and drive.

Cash included Hank Snow's "I've Been Everywhere" on his *Unchained* album, and here he covers another Snow classic, "I'm Moving On," that fits him just as well. Cash says in the liners that the

song remained at number 1 on the country chart for about forty weeks. Actually it stayed at number 1 for twenty-one weeks in 1950, but that's still quite an accomplishment. Cash's vocal is on the mark, though the arrangement is a bit overpowering.

Cash says that he and June had originally recorded a duet of Peter La Farge's "As Long as the Grass Shall Grow" for *Unchained*. He refers to it as one of his favorite songs. Cash wrote new spoken verses for this cover, turning it into a love song, and sharing writing credits with La Farge. Cash's new verses transform the song into the saga of Johnny and June and how they've weathered many storms together but survived it all through their faith and love for one another. This is the perfect example of Cash's ability to reinvent a song. What was once the story of the survival of the American Indian becomes a story of a couple's undying love.

Cash refers to the session for "Everybody's Trying to Be My Baby," with Carl Perkins and the Heartbreakers, as the highlight of his time at American Recordings. Cash takes lead vocals on this spirited rockabilly barnburner. And "Brown Eyed Handsome Man" is another collaboration with Carl Perkins and the Heartbreakers on Chuck Berry's early rock classic. Waylon Jennings had a number 3 country hit with the song in 1970. In the liner notes Cash says "Those old rock 'n' roll songs are the staff of life to me." There's no question that he comes alive when performing this type of song. This out-and-out duet with Carl Perkins is inspired.

It appears that Rubin finally persuaded Cash to record "T for Texas," also referred to as "Blue Yodel," but the rock arrangement simply does not mesh with the pure country lyric. Rubin may have been influenced by the Lynyrd Skynyrd version from their classic 1976 album *One More from the Road*. A noble effort, but as even Rubin admits in the liners, it does not sound like a Johnny Cash song.

The third CD in the set is called "Redemption Songs" and features more acoustic performances along with a few choice duets. Cash calls the opening track, "A Singer of Songs" a good song but doesn't know where it came from. Rick Rubin clarifies that it was Cash who brought the song to the session. And it certainly is a good song. From the opening lines, "I'm not a savior and I'm not a saint, the man with the answers I certainly ain't," we know that this is a song that Cash could have written about himself. Cash always viewed himself as a singer of songs whose mission was to entertain and enlighten his listeners. This is one of the most honest and genuine songs on this album. Cash's recording engineer David Ferguson clears up the issue of the song's origin, explaining that Nashville songwriter Tim O'Connell wrote the song and John Carter brought it to his father.

The late Joe Strummer, who was the lead singer for the punk rock band the Clash, joins Cash for an outstanding cover of Bob Marley's classic "Redemption Song." Cash had originally recorded this song for *American IV: The Man Comes Around*, but wasn't sure if he had done the song justice. He greatly admired Marley and loved Jamaica, so this song had a special meaning for him. This was another song that John Carter brought to his father, and it was an inspired choice. Joe Strummer adds a jolt of energy as he trades verses with Cash. It's a grand duet and their voices blend perfectly on the chorus. This is a song that one wishes the younger Cash might have attempted, but thanks to Rick Rubin and John Carter, we have a performance like this to enjoy in perpetuity.

Cash first recorded a cover of Cat Stevens's coming-of-age dialogue "Father and Son" as "Father and Daughter," with Rosie Nix in 1974. It was a standout track then and more than twenty-five years later he rerecorded the song with alternative singer Fiona Apple. In the original duet Cash performed the song as a middle-aged father who was "getting old" but happy offering advice to a rebellious young daughter. In this version Cash stays true to Stevens's original and performs the song as "Father and Son," admitting that he is old but happy. Whereas Cash's "Father and Daughter" was a straight duet, this version has Fiona singing harmony to Cash as he sings both parts, the father and son, as Cat Stevens had done on his original version.

Cash takes on George Jones's masterpiece "He Stopped Loving Her Today," considered by many to be the quintessential country song. The song was not originally released because Cash did not feel he had done it justice. And, in fact, no one will ever sing the song with the same degree of pain and heartache as Jones did, but Cash gives the song a different, more folk-like interpretation. He knows not to try to out-sing George Jones, and, as a result, offers his own unique interpretation of a classic song by another country legend.

Cash calls "Hard Times," a Stephen Foster song dating back to 1854, one of the oldest he's recorded. There's something especially sad and poignant listening to Cash's weathered vocal pleading, "Hard times come again no more." He sings, "There's a song that will linger forever in our ears. . . . It's a song, a sigh of the weary," while at the same time revealing a sense of tiredness on the part of the elder Cash as he takes on the weight of all the disenfranchised upon his stooping shoulders. Bob Dylan included his cover of the song on his 1992 album *Good as I Been to You*. Cash's plea resonates so powerfully because he has known hard times himself, as well as good ones. His prayer for us is the dream-wish of better days to come.

Glen Campbell and Johnny Cash both did so much to bring a new audience to country music with their television shows in the late sixties and early seventies. *The Glen Campbell Goodtime Hour* introduced many country stars to a popular audience. "Wichita Lineman" was a number 1 country and number 3 pop hit for Campbell in 1968. Jimmy

Webb is one of popular music's most renowned songwriters. He of course wrote "Highwayman," and dozens of other standards. On this cover of "Wichita Lineman," Campbell's honey-smooth croon is replaced with Cash's more ragged delivery, and as Rick Rubin says, the end result is a lovely new version of a great song.

Cash and Campbell performed duets together on their various television series, and Cash admits that he always loved "Gentle on My Mind," which was recorded by both Campbell and the song's author, the late John Hartford. Cash carries the verses and Campbell joins him in harmony on the chorus. It's a well-intentioned performance, although it certainly is a younger man's song to sing. Regardless, Cash is still able to make us believe that he is that freewheeling rambler who has his sleeping bag rolled up and ready to go.

Regarding "You Are My Sunshine," Cash writes in the liner notes, "If you're looking for a real country classic, 'You Are My Sunshine' is the one you want." The song was written and originally recorded by Jimmie Davis, who went on to become the Governor of Louisiana. Norman Blake and Marty Stuart back Cash up on this traditional slice of pure Americana. Cash slows down the tempo for this cover and bites into every syllable of the lyric. It's a memorable performance that works on many levels, as Cash begs, "Please don't take my sunshine away." The appliance manufacturer Whirlpool used this recording in its 2015 ad campaign.

Cash informs us in the liners that he always wanted to record an entire album in a cathedral. Well, he did get the chance to record two songs in a church in Los Angeles with a pipe organ: "You'll Never Walk Alone" and "Danny Boy," the latter of which was included on the last album released during Cash's lifetime, *The Man Comes Around.* "You'll Never Walk Alone" is from Rodgers and Hammerstein's 1945 musical *Carousel.* It's more an inspirational ballad than a show tune, and Cash delivers it with grand emotion.

An early take of "The Man Comes Around" closes out this CD. This version of the title song from Cash's last album is almost the same melodically and lyrically, but has a sparser feel than the first-released version. It's nice to have the opportunity to hear a song develop in such a way, and we can see how much Rick Rubin's production adds to a song such as this one. The promise is all here but the final version is the revelation.

The previously discussed fourth disc, "My Mother's Hymn Book," is comprised of songs Cash originally learned from his mother. The fifth disc, "Best of Cash on American," features what the producers felt were the strongest songs from the prior American Recordings albums: "Delia's Gone," "Bird on a Wire," "Thirteen," "Rowboat," "The One Rose (That's Left in My Heart)," "Rusty Cage," "Southern Accents," "The Mercy Seat," "Solitary Man," "Wayfaring Stranger," "One," "I Hung My Head," "The Man Comes Around," "We'll Meet Again," and "Hurt."

In November 2005, the movie *Walk the Line* was released nationally and garnered rave reviews. In January 2006, Barry Gibb of the Bee Gees and his wife, Linda, bought Cash's house in Hendersonville with plans to restore it back to its original splendor. Cash had lived in the house on Old Hickory Lake for over forty years. Gibb called the house a "musical inspiration" and hoped to write many songs there. In April 2007, the house burned down. In 2009 Larry Gatlin released "Johnny Cash Is Dead and His House Burned Down" as a single and video.

In May 2006, Legacy opened the Cash vault for the two-CD *Personal File,* a virtual treasure trove of forty-nine previously unreleased tracks featuring only Johnny on guitar and vocal. All the songs were recorded between 1973 and 1982. This was an album Cash always wanted to do, with just himself in a solo acoustic performance. And so this might be regarded as the precursor to the *American Recordings* album. The masters were recovered from a vault of material stored at the House of Cash recording studio. John Carter Cash and Lou Robin served as executive producers on the project, and the songs range from turn-of-the-century folk ballads and Carter Family standards to classic country favorites and Cash originals. Music journalist Greil Marcus, whose work appeared in

Rolling Stone and *Creem* magazines, among other publications, wrote the liner notes. The album made it to number 22 on the country chart and 108 pop.

Hiked a Hundred Highways

In July 2006, three years after Johnny's death, *American V: A Hundred Highways,* the fifth volume of his American Recordings was released and it proved to be the most successful in the series. The album was recorded a few days after the sessions for *American IV: The Man Comes Around* were completed. Cash did not want to take a lengthy break and decided to head right back into the studio to begin work on this project. Rick Rubin produced the album. According to John Carter Cash, in his book *House of Cash*, his father's health was typically not good during the recording of this album: "He was losing his sight, and his diabetes was sapping his strength" (Carter Cash, 139). The album was certified gold by the RIAA and reached number 1 on both the country and pop album charts. This was Johnny's first number 1 pop album since *Johnny Cash at San Quentin* in 1969. The album features two new Cash-penned tracks, along with a few covers of old favorites and some exemplary new material he had recorded for the first time.

The album includes the previously discussed "Like the 309," "If You Could Read My Mind," "Further on (up the Road)," "On the Evening Train," "Four Strong Winds," "Help Me," along with six other tracks.

American V opens with Larry Gatlin's "Help Me," a song Cash had always loved. Cash performs the song solo here, after having recorded it with Gatlin for *The Gospel Road*. It's an aged and weary sounding Cash who is asking the Lord for His help, and the song takes on added significance as the frail singer draws out the word "please" when asking God for help. When the singer asks God to release the chains of darkness so that he can see where he fits into His master plan, we can't help but be moved as we listen to a man coming to terms with his life and very near to meeting his Maker.

Cash offers a defiant last-stand reading of the traditional gospel standard "God's Gonna Cut You Down." Artists including Elvis Presley and folk singer Odetta had previously recorded the song. This was one of the tracks Cash first recorded immediately following June's death. The elder Cash warns us that "you can go on for a long time, but sooner or later God's gotta cut you down." The singer is well resigned to his fate but he is determined to fight the devil until the end and claim his reward in God's heaven. A striking video for this song would win Best Short Form Music Video at the fiftieth annual Grammy Awards ceremony in February 2008.

Cash first performed Rod McKuen's "Love's Been Good to Me" on his television show. In fact, it was used on the commercials promoting the series. Ironically, he never released a recording of the song during his lifetime. It's a lovely reflection on the beauty and joy in one's life. Cash humbly informs us that he has been a rover and a loner who's never found a home. But, ultimately, he's happy with his life because occasionally "love's been good to me." Frank Sinatra originally recorded this ballad in 1969 when he was fifty-four years old. Cash's version is even more sentimental for being sung by man of seventy who had lived a full and rewarding life.

Cash delivers an impressive take on the classic Don Gibson lament "A Legend in My Time." It was a number 1 country hit for Ronnie Milsap in 1975 and has been recorded by numerous singers since. But no one imbues it with the same sense of loss as Cash does on this late-in-life reminiscence of what might have been. Cash's recitation toward the end of the song is priceless as he explains, "If heartaches brought fame in love's crazy game, I'd be a legend in my time / If they gave gold statuettes for tears and regrets, I'd be a legend in my time."

Cash closes out the album with a cover of "I'm Free from the Chain Gang Now," a song he had first recorded back in 1963. The energy and spirit he infused the original with is replaced with a more contemplative sense of acceptance and freedom, albeit freedom from what we can only interpret as the chains of life. No more shackles to bind him, Cash is finally able to soar freely from this life and into the next one.

More Popular Than Ever

Seven years after his death, Cash's popularity was greater than ever. February 2010 saw the release of *American VI: Ain't No Grave,* Cash's sixth American Recordings project (excluding the *Unearthed* box set). It debuted at number 2 on the *Billboard* country album chart and number 3 in pop. His legacy was firmly established and his most recent albums were still anxiously anticipated by music fans the world over. Most of the songs on this album were recorded during the same sessions as *American V: A Hundred Highways.* Along with the previously mentioned "For the Good Times," "I Don't Hurt Anymore," and "Can't Help but Wonder Where I'm Bound," the album contains seven other excellent tracks.

Although the title track is usually credited as "traditional," it was written by Brother Claude Ely, a singer-songwriter and Pentecostal preacher, in 1934. A singer named Bozie Sturdivant was the first to record it in 1941. Then Ely recorded his own version of the song in 1953. Ely's version has a decidedly more spiritual, tent-revival feel to it in contrast to Cash's direct, somber reading. Cash describes the band of angels coming for him as he musters the strength for another classic reinterpretation of an old song. "Ain't No Grave" is Johnny's benediction, as he comes to terms with his life and prepares to meet the Lord, June, and the rest of his departed family, but on his own terms. Of course, the truth is that Cash may be gone, but there simply "ain't no grave" that can ever hold down his incredible body of work. That is his legacy for the ages.

On "Redemption Day," a tired and weary Cash expresses his hurt and compassion for all those less fortunate souls who are awaiting the train to glory and their ultimate redemption day. Even during his final hours, the singer is concerned with the pain and suffering of others and not his own mortality. Singer Sheryl Crow wrote Cash one of his most insightful and impassioned final recordings.

Cash arranges a subtle orchestration as he sings a new song based on and inspired by his reading of 1 Corinthians. The opening lines, "O death, where is thy sting? O grave, where is thy victory? / O life, you are a shining path, and hope springs eternal just over the rise, when I see my redeemer beckoning me," allow Cash to express his faith and hope for redemption upon meeting the Lord, through the very Scriptures he would always turn to and find comfort in.

Porter Wagoner originally recorded the Red Hayes ballad "A Satisfied Mind" in 1955. He took it to number 1 on the country chart. Many other artists have covered the song including Red Foley, Jean Shepard, Roy Drusky, and Bob Luman. But it was the Byrds recording of the song on their landmark album *Turn! Turn! Turn!* that ultimately brought the song to a wider audience. And as narrator of the song, Cash convinces us that there is nothing more important — not wealth or fame — than having a satisfied mind. It's sage advice Cash imparts upon us that even the poorest man is wealthy if he has a satisfied mind, and that all the money in the world cannot buy back our youth when we are old.

For the penultimate song on his last American album release, we find Cash covering "Last Night I Had the Strangest Dream." In his preamble to the 1969 version of this song, Cash discussed his views on the then current Vietnam War. Nearly thirty-five years later, Cash revisits the song as he solemnly continues to dream that the world had agreed to put an end to war. It's a fitting reminder on this last recording from a man who always prided himself on being the voice and the conscience of the people who admired him and his music.

"Aloha Oe," a simple song of farewell, makes the perfect finale for *American VI*. This was a song Cash loved that he and Jack Clement had been singing together for thirty years. Written by Liliuokalani in 1877, recorded by Marty Robbins, and popularized by Elvis Presley on his *Blue Hawaii* soundtrack album, Cash closes out this album with a simple Hawaiian flavored song of parting and goodbye . . . until we meet again.

From the Vaults

Numerous Cash compilations have been released in recent years, including a series of official Bootleg collections from Sony Legacy. On March 25, 2014, Columbia/Legacy released *Out Among the Stars*. John Carter Cash and Columbia Records producer Steve Berkowitz produced this album featuring songs originally produced by Billy Sherrill from sessions in 1981 and 1984. Sherrill had produced *The Baron* for Cash in 1981, and two years later Cash reteamed with Sherrill to record what was to be the album *In Living Color*. Cash was not pleased with these sessions, feeling they were overproduced and not representative of the Cash sound. Both he and Sherrill decided to shelve the project and just move on. Cash chose to work on the *Rainbow* album with Chips Moman, and with the exception of the dismal single "Chicken in Black," and its B-side "Battle of Nashville," these songs remained unreleased for over thirty years. When John Carter discovered the recordings he decided to freshen up the sound with some of the original musicians who played on the original tracks. He substituted five songs from *In Living Color*—"Chicken in Black," "Battle of Nashville," "I Know You Love Me," "My Elusive Dreams," "You Give Me Music"—and replaced them with five different tracks: "She Used to Love Me a Lot," "I'm Movin' On" and "Rock and Roll Shoes" from 1984, along with "Tennessee" and "Don't You Think It's

Come Our Time," which were recorded in 1981 during *The Baron* sessions. The result is a superior new collection of songs that finds Cash in fine voice and top form performing some first-rate songs by some of country music's finest composers.

Canadian singer-songwriter Adam Mitchell wrote the title song in 1979. He went on to cowrite songs with the rock group Kiss, and he also wrote the hit "Dancin' Round and Round" for Olivia Newton-John. Waylon Jennings was the first to record "Out Among the Stars" for his 1979 album *What Goes Around Comes Around*. Merle Haggard covered it seven years later for his album *Out Among the Stars* and the single made it to number 21 on the country chart. The lyric paints a bleak and terrifying picture of life's injustices, as a boy holds up a liquor store in Texas, with the sad commentary that "he can't find a job, but Lord he's found a gun." The boy is relieved to hear the police cruisers coming so they can shoot him and put an end to his sad existence, before we learn that his father's only concern is the shame this will bring that he'll never be able to live down.

Carlene Carter suggested the song "Baby, Ride Easy" to her mother and stepfather. She had originally recorded it as a duet with English rocker Dave Edmunds in 1980, and the single made it to number 76 on the country chart. Texas born songwriter Richard Dobson wrote the song. Artists such as Guy Clark, David Allan Coe, and Nanci Griffith have recorded Dobson's songs. One can't help but sense the feeling of carefree joy and affection as Johnny and June perform this rollicking up-tempo charmer. This is as solid a duet recording as any they had recorded over the years. It's breezy, fast, frisky, and fun.

Songwriters Rhonda "Kye" Fleming and Dennis Morgan collaborated on many hit songs together including Barbara Mandrell's "I Was Country When Country Wasn't Cool" and "Sleeping Single in a Double Bed." For "She Used to Love Me a Lot," they joined forces with songwriter Charles Quillen, who had composed hits for Ronnie Milsap including "Back on My Mind Again." "She Used to Love Me a Lot" is a lovelorn lament about the singer running into the lost love he'd been pining for. He had left her and begs her to rekindle their romance, but the singer ultimately realizes that he'd only been deluding himself, as she refused to take him back again. There's a sense of vulnerability and sadness to Cash's delivery, even as he tries to convince himself that she would still love him so much. When the projected Cash album was shelved, Billy Sherrill had David Allan Coe record "She Used to Love Me a Lot." The single made it to number 11 on the country chart in 1984.

Bobby Braddock and Curly Putman, the duo behind George Jones's maudlin classic "He Stopped Loving Her Today," wrote the offbeat novelty tune "If I Told You Who It Was." It has a melody and delivery reminiscent of "Chattanooga City Limit Sign." The singer has gone out to the Grand Ole Opry and met a famous female country star who propositions him and takes him to a hotel for some non-musical fun. While he chooses to protect her identity, the song has a funny reveal at the end when we learn that mystery woman is not Dolly Parton but Minnie Pearl. It all adds up to another lighthearted ditty that reflects Cash's sense of humor.

Cash wrote "Call Your Mother," one of the strongest songs on this album. The singer implores his lover to please call her mother and tell her that their romance is over. It's a unique perspective and Cash sings it with just the right amount of passion and pathos. It's a fond reminiscence and a tender ballad that proves that Cash could out-write the contemporary songwriters whose songs permeate this album. Cash's second self-penned composition, "I Came to Believe," is another stark ballad of loss and heartache. It's a dramatic, emotional plea for help from God to help the singer survive and endure all the trials and tribulations of this life. It was the first attempt at a song Cash would revive and record years later on *American V: A Hundred Highways.*

Rick Scott, a songwriter who was signed to Cash's House of Cash publishing company, wrote "Tennessee." In the song, the narrator informs his mother that he has settled down and married a blue-eyed girl in Tennessee. The lyric paints a sweet picture of domestic bliss and the rural lifestyle. A children's chorus comes in for the final

In the spotlight. *Courtesy of Sony Music Entertainment.*

verse and chorus, explaining how proud the singer is to be from Tennessee. It's not revelatory by any means, but a nice inclusion on this album.

The great country singer and songwriter Tommy Collins wrote "Don't You Think It's Come Our Time." This duet with June was recorded in 1981 during *The Baron* sessions but left unreleased. Collins had enjoyed a career in music and wrote many classic country standards for artists like Merle Haggard, who immortalized him in his song "Leonard." This is undoubtedly the best song on this album not written by Cash. The devotional, pastoral lyric is lovingly sung by Johnny and June, and why it was hidden away for so long is the biggest mystery of all.

JOHNNY CASH

OUT AMONG THE STARS

Chapter 18

SEPTEMBER WHEN IT COMES

FINAL REFLECTIONS

*Rosanne Cash's profound song
foreshadowing her father's death*

n March 2003, Rosanne Cash released her stunning "September When It Comes," which was recorded as a duet with her father for her album *Rules of Travel*. Rosanne and her husband John Leventhal wrote the song. As much coverage as the song "Hurt" has received for Cash's bravery in facing his own mortality, "September When It Comes" is equally powerful, and sadly prophetic. This is Rosanne's story and her love for her father is clearly revealed, as the song depicts a journey from the cradle to the grave as she tries to come to terms with losing a beloved parent. It was in September, six months after this recording with Rosanne, that Johnny Cash died. The lyrics become so much more than a mere reminiscence; they can be read as an emotionally explosive, yet genuinely tender, cathartic realization. The song is ultimately prescient, as Rosanne's lyrics foreshadow what she and her father knew was inevitable. Rosanne and Johnny become the embodiment of the true "desperados waiting for a train," as they reflect back on their lives together.

The opening lines of "September When It Comes"—"There's a cross above the baby's bed, a savior in her dreams / But she was not delivered then, and the baby became me"—are not about

« Out Among The Stars.
Courtesy of Sony Music Entertainment.

Sony photo shoot. *Courtesy of Sony Music Entertainment.*

Johnny. Rosanne explains, "The cross above the baby's bed is exactly as it was — my mother was Catholic and had hung a crucifix above my crib and I have a picture of me standing in my crib next to the cross. That first verse had nothing to do with my dad — it was setting up the expanse of years by starting with my childhood."

In the second part of the song, the focus shifts to Johnny, who shatters his own carefully created myth by bravely admitting, "I cannot move a mountain now, I can no longer run, I cannot be who I was then, in a way, I never was." Rosanne explains, "'I cannot move a mountain' was written in his voice, as he was weak and frail at that time. I wasn't talking about myself."

The video for the song is both touching and tragic in its depiction of the weakened Cash. Whereas the "Hurt" video portrayed Cash facing his own mortality for all the world to see, "September When It Comes" is more private and personal, and maybe even braver in its emotional nakedness, as Rosanne and Johnny watch the ticking clock, and the sun, as the shadows descend for the final sundown.

Time and distance, years together and years apart, have brought closure to the relationship of father and daughter. The video for "September When It Comes" is a stirring collage of photos taken throughout Cash's life, with his children, June, his parents and his entire family, reminding us, as the lyric states, that when that door forever closes, the memories will always be there. And we know now that September did arrive as Johnny ultimately found the strength to face that day of reckoning, when "they'll fly me like an angel to a place where I can rest."

After all is said and done, the reality is that Johnny Cash's stature has only grown and flourished since his death in 2003. His body of work is more accessible than ever, and he continues to be a relevant force in the music industry. His songs are included in movies and television shows, and his influence is evident in the modern-day superstars of country music. He is an icon for the ages, but more importantly, he is a man who struggled to see his vision realized. And though his life is an inspiration to all, it is his songs that remain the foundation of everything that is Johnny Cash.

Notes

CHAPTER 1

1. Gatlin shared his memories of this song with me. He was extremely proud that Cash had recorded it, and grateful for all the support and encouragement Cash had given him through the years.

CHAPTER 3

1. When Cash and I were discussing politics during our lunch together, he proudly recounted the story of his family's friendship with then–presidential nominee Al Gore. Cash laughingly exclaimed how he had known Gore since he was a little boy, and how happy he was to see him in the race.

CHAPTER 5

1. When I was compiling *Johnny Cash: Timeless Inspiration*, I made it a point to include this song and make it a focal point of the box set. I had the opportunity to explain this to Johnny, who himself seemed to rediscover and embrace this buried gem. He and June would perform it during their last concert appearances together, and Johnny and June would rerecord the song for June's 1999 album *Press On*.

CHAPTER 10

1. Reynolds told me he always liked this song, especially since it's a bit "off-center."

2. Allen Reynolds recalls that Cash and Clement genuinely loved each other and that Clement made Cash laugh and made him play, and generally brought out the best in him. He calls Johnny Cash one of the great friendships of Jack's life.

3. Steve Popovich was a dear friend and I will never forget his excitement and delight when presented with the finished masters for this album, I remember being invited into his office and listening to the album in its entirety. Popovich was enthused and extremely pleased with the final product.

4. Reynolds remembers Cash always being sweet and kind to him, although he admits that he was always shy around Cash. He says Cash was a large guy who was truly larger than life.

CHAPTER 14

1. When I asked Johnny to suggest a list of his favorite recordings for *The Legendary Johnny Cash*, this was the first song on his list and, as such, it always held a special place in his heart.

2. Choosing a favorite Johnny Cash song is almost impossible, however while preparing the CD release of *The Great Seventies Recordings*, Johnny's manager Lou Robin and I both agreed that "Any Old Wind That Blows" is one of them.

Bibliography

REFERENCE

Cantwell, David, and Bill Friskics-Warren. *Heartaches By The Number: Country Music's 500 Greatest Singles.* Nashville: Vanderbilt Press/Country Music Foundation Press, 2003.

Kingsbury, Paul, ed. *The Encyclopedia of Country Music.* New York: Oxford University Press, 1998.

Lewry, Peter. *I've Been Everywhere: A Johnny Cash Chronicle.* London: Helter Skelter, 2001.

Smith, John L. *The Johnny Cash Discography.* Westport, CT: Greenwood Press, 1985.

Smith, John L. *The Johnny Cash Discography, 1984-1993.* Westport, CT: Greenwood Press, 1994.

Smith, John L. *The Johnny Cash Record Catalog.* Westport, CT: Greenwood Press, 1994.

Smith, John L. *Another Song To Sing: The Recorded Repertoire of Johnny Cash.* Lanham, MD: Scarecrow Press, 1999.

Stambler, Irwin, and Grelun Landon. *The Encyclopedia of Folk, Country and Western Music.* New York: St. Martin's Press, 1984.

Whitburn, Joel. *Hot Country Albums, 1964-2007.* Menomonee Falls, WI: Record Research, 2007.

Whitburn, Joel. *Top Country Songs, 1944-2005.* Menomonee Falls, WI: Record Research, 2005.

Whitburn, Joel. *The Billboard Albums, 1956-2005.* Menomonee Falls, WI: Record Research, 2005.

Whitburn, Joel. *Top Pop Singles, 1955-2010.* Menomonee Falls, WI: Record Research, 2010.

GENERAL

Allen, Bob, ed. *The Blackwell Guide to Recorded Country Music.* Cambridge, MA: Blackwell Books, 1994.

Allen, Bob. *George Jones: The Saga of an American Singer.* New York: Dolphin Books, 1984.

Batchelor, Bob, ed. *Literary Cash.* Dallas: Benbella Books, 2006

Bane, Michael. *The Outlaws: Revolution in Country Music.* New York: Country Music Magazine Press, 1978.

Bane, Michael. *White Boy Singin' the Blues.* New York: Penguin, 1982.

Bragg, Rick. *Jerry Lee Lewis: His Own Story.* New York: Harper Collins, 2014.

Bufwack, Mary A., and Robert K. Oermann. *Finding Her Voice: The Saga of Women in Country Music.* New York: Crown, 1993.

Burke, Ken. *Country Music Changed My Life.* Chicago: A Cappella, 2004.

Campbell, Garth. *Johnny Cash: He Walked the Line, 1932–2003.* London: John Blake, 2003.

Carpozi, George Jr. *The Johnny Cash Story.* New York: Pyramid, 1970.

Cash, Cindy. *The Cash Family Scrapbook.* New York: Crown, 1997.

Cash, John Carter. *House of Cash.* San Rafael, CA: Insight Editions, 2011.

Cash, John Carter. *Anchored in Love: An Intimate Portrait of June Carter Cash.* Nashville: Thomas Nelson, 2007.

Cash, Johnny, with Patrick Carr. *Cash: The Autobiography.* New York: Harper Collins, 1997.

Cash, Johnny. *Man in Black.* Grand Rapids, MI: Zondervan, 1975.

Cash, Johnny. *Man in White: A Novel.* New York: Harper and Row, 1986.

Cash, Johnny. *Songs of Johnny Cash.* New York: Dial, 1970.

Cash, June Carter. *From the Heart.* New York: Prentice Hall, 1987.

Cash, June Carter. *Among My Klediments.* Grand Rapids, MI: Zondervan, 1979.

Cash, Rosanne. *Composed: A Memoir.* New York: Viking, 2010.

Cash, Rosanne. ed. *Songs Without Rhyme: Prose by Celebrated Songwriters.* New York: Hyperion, 2001.

Cash, Vivian, with Ann Sharpsteen. *I Walked the Line: My Life with Johnny.* New York: Scribner, 2008.

Clapp, Rodney. *Johnny Cash and the Great American Contradiction.* Louisville, KY: Westminster John Knox Press, 1989.

Collins, Ace. *The Stories Behind Country Music's All-Time Greatest 100 Songs.* New York: Boulevard Books, 1996.

Conn, Charles Paul. *The New Johnny Cash.* Old Tappen, NJ: Fleming H. Revell, 1973.

D'Ambrosio, Antonio. *A Heartbeat And A Guitar: Johnny Cash and the Making of Bitter Tears.* Philadelphia: Nation Books, 2009.

Davis, Clive, with James Willwerth. *Clive: Inside The Record Business.* New York: Ballantine, 1976.

Davis, Clive, with Anthony DeCurtis. *The Soundtrack of My Life.* New York: Simon and Schuster, 2012.

Davis, Don, with Ruth B. White. *Nashville Steeler: My Life in Country Music.* Atglen, PA: Shiffer, 2012.

Dawidoff, Nicholas. *In the Country of Country: A Journey to the Roots of American Music.* New York: Pantheon Books, 1977.

Doggett, Peter. *Are You Ready For the Country?* New York: Penguin, 2001.

Dylan, Bob. *Chronicles: Volume One.* New York: Simon and Schuster, 2004.

Edward, Leigh. *Johnny Cash and the Paradox of American Identity.* Bloomington: Indiana University Press. 2009.

Eng, Steve. *A Satisfied Mind: The Country Music Life of Porter Wagoner.* Nashville: Rutledge Hill Press, 1992.

Escott, Colin, with Martin Hawkins. *Good Rockin' Tonight: Sun Records and the Birth of Rock and Roll.* New York: St. Martin's Press, 1991.

Fine, Jason. *Cash.* New York: Crown, 2004.

Fong-Torres, Ben, ed. *The Rolling Stone Rock 'N' Roll Reader.* New York: Bantam, 1974.

Gatlin, Larry with Jeff Lenburg. *All the Gold In California.* Nashville: Thomas Nelson, 1998.

Govoni, Albert. *A Boy Named Cash.* New York: Lancer Books, 1970

Grant, Marshall. *I Was There When It Happened: My Life with Johnny Cash.* Nashville: Cumberland House, 2006.

Guralnick, Peter. *Careless Love: The Unmaking of Elvis Presley.* Boston: Little, Brown, 1999.

Guralnick, Peter. *Last Train to Memphis: The Rise of Elvis Presley.* Boston: Little, Brown, 1994.

Guralnick, Peter. *Lost Highway: Journeys and Arrivals of American Musicians.* New York: Vintage, 1979.

Haggard, Merle, with Peggy Russell. *Sing Me Back Home: My Life.* New York: Times Books, 1981.

Haggard, Merle, with Tom Carter. *My House of Memories: For the Record.* New York: Harper Collins, 1999.

Hall, B.C., with C.T. Atwood. *The South.* New York: Scribner, 1995.

Hall, Tom T. *The Storyteller's Nashville.* New York: Doubleday, 1979.

Hemphill, Paul. *The Nashville Sound: Bright Lights and Country Music.* New York: Simon and Schuster, 1970.

Hilburn, Robert. *Cornflakes With John Lennon.* New York: Rodale, 2009.

Hilburn, Robert. *Johnny Cash: The Life.* New York: Little, Brown, 2013.

Horstman, Dorothy. *Sing Your Heart Out Country Boy.* Third ed. Nashville: Country Music Foundation, 1996.

Hoye, Jacob. *VH1's 100 Greatest Albums.* New York: Pocket Books, 2003.

Huss, John, and David Werther, eds. *Johnny Cash and Philosophy.* Peru, IL: Carus Publishing, 2008.

Jennings, Dana. *Sing Me Back Home: Love, Death, and Country Music.* New York: Faber and Faber, 2008.

Jennings, Waylon, with Lenny Kaye. *Waylon: An Autobiography.* New York: Warner Books, 1996.

Jones, George, with Tom Carter. *I Lived to Tell it All.* New York: Villard, 1996.

Jones, Margaret. *Patsy: The Life and Times of Patsy Cline.* New York: Harper Collins, 1994.

Kingsbury, Paul, ed. *Country on Compact Disc.* New York: Grove Press, 1993

Kingsbury, Paul. *The Grand Ole Opry History of Country Music.* New York: Villard Books, 1995.

Kleist, Reinhard. *I See a Darkness.* New York: Self Made Hero Press, 2009.

Leimer, Laurence. *Three Chords and the Truth.* New York: Harper Collins, 1997.

Logan, Horace, with Bill Sloan. *Elvis, Hank and Me: Making Musical History on the Louisiana Hayride.* New York: St. Martin's Press, 1998.

Malone, Bill C. *Country Music, U.S.A.* Austin: University Of Texas Press, 1968.

Mansfield, Brian. *Ring of Fire: A Tribute to Johnny Cash.* Nashville: Rutledge Hill Press, 2003.

Marcus, Greil. *The Old, Weird America.* New York: St. Martin's Press, 1997.

Marshall, Jim. *Pocket Cash.* San Francisco: Chronicle Books, 2010.

McCay, Alastair. "Part Two: Texas Country Singer Rodney Crowell." *Uncut,* Jan. 26, 2009.

Millard, Bob. *Country Music: 70 Years of America's Favorite Music.* New York: Harper Collins, 1993.

Miller, Stephen. *Johnny Cash: The Life of an American Icon.* New York: Omnibus Press, 2003.

Morthland, John. *The Best of Country Music.* New York: Doubleday Dolphin Press, 1984.

Neimark, Anne E. *Up Close: Johnny Cash.* New York: Viking, 2007.

Offen, Carol, ed. *Country Music: The Poetry.* New York: Ballantine, 1977.

Patoski, Joe Nick. *An Epic Life: Willie Nelson.* New York: Little, Brown, 2008.

Radcliffe, Mark. *Reelin' in the Years.* New York: Simon and Schuster, 2011.

Reid, Harold, and Don Reid. *The Statler Brothers: Random Memories.* Nashville: Yell, 2007.

Reid, Jan. *The Improbable Rise of Redneck Rock.* New York: Da Capo Press, 1974.

Shelton, Robert. *No Direction Home: The Life and Music of Bob Dylan.* New York: Ballantine, 1987.

Sounes, Howard. *Down the Highway: The Life of Bob Dylan.* New York: Grove Press, 2001.

Streissguth, Michael. *Always Been There: Rosanne Cash, The List, and the Spirit of Southern Music.* New York: Da Capo Press, 2009.

Streissguth, Michael. *Johnny Cash at Folsom Prison: The Making of a Masterpiece.* Cambridge: Da Capo Press, 2004.

Streissguth, Michael. *Johnny Cash: The Biography.* New York: Da Capo Press, 2006.

Streissguth, Michael. *Outlaw: Waylon, Willie, Kris and the Renegades of Nashville.* New York: It Books, 2013.

Streissguth, Michael. *Ring of Fire: The Johnny Cash Reader.* New York: Da Capo Press, 2002.

Stuart, Marty. *Pilgrims: Sinners, Saints, and Prophets.* Nashville: Rutledge Hill Press, 1999.

Thompson, Elizabeth, and David Gutman, eds. *The Dylan Companion.* New York: Da Capo Press, 2001.

Thompson, Graeme. *The Resurrection of Johnny Cash: Hurt, Redemption and American Recordings.* London: Jawbone, 2011.

Tosches, Nick. *Country.* New York: Scribner, 1985.

Tost, Tony. *American Recordings.* New York: Continuum, 2011.

Turner, Steve. *The Man Called Cash: The Life, Love, and Faith of an American Legend.* Nashville: W Publishing Group, 2004.

Unterberger, Richie. *Eight Miles High: Folk-Rock's Flight from Haight-Ashbury to Woodstock.* San Francisco: Backbeat Books, 2005.

Unterberger, Richie. *Turn! Turn! Turn!: The '60s Folk-Rock Revolution.* San Francisco: Backbeat Books, 2002.

Wenner, Jann, and Joe Levy, eds. *The Rolling Stone Interviews.* New York: Little, Brown, 2007.

Wilentz, Sean, and Greil Marcus, eds. *The Rose & The Briar.* New York: W.W. Norton, 2005.

Willman, Chris. *Rednecks & Bluenecks: The Politics of Country Music.* New York: New Press, 2005.

INTERVIEWS

Cash, Rosanne. E-mail interview, November 12, 2015.

Gatlin, Larry. Personal interview in New York, 2012.

Reynolds, Allen. Telephone interview, March 13, 2013.

Index of Names and Songs

LaRousse, Lloyd, xx

"Last Cowboy Song, The," 75

Last Days of Frank and Jesse James, The, 139

Last Gunfighter Ballad, The, 17, 82, 114, 132, 143,

"Last Gunfighter Ballad, The," 74, 147

"Last Night I Had the Strangest Dream," 48, 249

"Last of the Drifters, The," 173

"Last Supper, The," 91

"Last Time, The," 138, 139

Law, Don, 35, 57, 66, 68, 77, 99, 122, 125, 167

"Lay Me Down in Dixie," 17

Lead Belly (Huddie Ledbetter), 8, 27, 33, 106, 160

"Lead Me, Father," 78, 79

Lee, Brenda, 140, 221

Lee, Peggy, 197

Lee, Robert E., 47, 48

"Legend in My Time, A," 248

"Legend of John Henry's Hammer, The," 35, 63, 64, 122

Legendary Johnny Cash, The, xviii, 67, 68, 70, 105, 212, 259

Leiber, Jerry (Gaby Rogers), 106, 159

Lennon, John, 237

"Leonard," 253

Leonard, Elmore, 228

"Let Him Roll," 147, 171

"Let the Lower Lights Be Burning," 95

"Let the Train Whistle Blow," 217, 221, 227

"Letter from Home, A," 71, 175

Leventhal, John, 255

Lewin, Bob, 144

Lewis, Furry, 65

Lewis, Jerry Lee, xviii, 30, 32, 39, 65, 95, 165

Liberto, Vivian. *See* Cash, Vivian Liberto

"Life Goes On," 39

"Life Has Its Little Ups and Downs," 131, 132

"Life of a Prisoner," 114

Lightfoot, Gordon, 137, 150, 151, 237

"Like a Soldier," 49, 227

"Like the 309," 221, 247

Liliuokalani, 249

"Little at a Time, A," 211

"Little Drummer Boy, The," 151

Little Fauss and Big Halsy (Movie), 128

Little Fauss and Big Halsy (Original Soundtrack Recording), 111, 222

"Little Sadie," 103

"Live Forever," 183, 184

"Living Legend," 182

Livingston, Jay, 74

"Loading Coal," 59, 60

Loaf, Meat, 171

Loggins, Dave, 133

Lomax, John A., 27, 60, 63, 64

Lomax, John III, 171

"Londonderry Air," 203

"Lonely Weekends," 131

"Lonesome Valley," 159

"Long Black Veil, The," 9, 104, 105, 109, 189, 242

"Long-Legged Guitar Pickin' Man," 125

Longfellow, Henry Wadsworth, 69

Look, 84

Look at Them Beans, 142, 146, 214

"Look at Them Beans (Papa's Dream)" 13, 207

"Look for Me," 129

Lopez, Trini, 131

"Lord's Prayer, The," 90

"Loser," 230

Loudermilk, John D., 223

Louisiana Hayride, 25, 31

Louvin Brothers, 5, 18, 21, 233

"Love Bug," 197

"Love Has Lost Again," 214

"Love in the Hot Afternoon," 137

"Love Is the Way," 51

Love Lifted Me, 214

Love of the Common People, 127

"Love's Been Good to Me," 247–248

"Love's Ring of Fire," 122

Lovett, Lyle, 52, 146, 185

"Loving Gift, The," 129

Lovin' Spoonful, 110

Lowe, Nick, 171, 227

Lowery, Bill, 35

"Lucille," 16

"Luckenbach, Texas," 181

"Lumberjack," 178

"Luther Played the Boogie ("Luther's Boogie") ("Perkins Boogie")," 28, 41

Lynn, Loretta, 71, 204

Lynn, Vera, 238

Lynyrd, Skynyrd, 173, 244

"MacArthur Park," 181

MacColl, Ewan, 237

Mahr Beverly, 26

"Mama, You've Been on My Mind," 162